Human Rights and Police Administration

About the authors

Kamalaxi G. Tadasad is an Assistant Professor, Department of Political Science, Government First Grade College, Shiggaon Haveri, Karnataka. A keen student of Political Science, her interests lie in Women Empowerment, Human Rights and Social Reconstruction. She has to her credit several research papers and has travelled far and wide to participate in International and National Conferences. She is an active member of Civil Society and a social worker too.

Harish Ramaswamy is a professor of political science teaching in the Karnataka University, Dharwad. A keen student of Political Theory and Public Administation, he along with two other colleagues in the department has authored a book on Karnataka Government and Politics. He is also the author of a concise book on Distance Education, Editor of a commissioned book on Political Science of Kannada University for the PUC-II year, Executive Editor of the Journal of his department "Chanakya". A Bingham Teacher Fellow, a Nippon Fellow of Salzburg and an international visitor in 2007 to USA, he has made a difference in teaching and learning political science in Karnataka by his innvovations. He is an opinion maker and an analyst of Karnataka Politics. He has travelled far and wide and presented his academic papers at international conferences and coordinated them.

Human Rights and Police Administration

Kamalaxi G. Tadsad
Assistant Professor
Government First Grade College
Shiggaon (Haveri)
(Karnataka)

Harish Ramaswamy
Professor of Political Science
Department of Political Science
Karnataka University,
Dharwad (Karnataka)

CONCEPT PUBLISHING COMPANY PVT. LTD.
NEW DELHI-110059

ISBN-13 : 978-81-8069-812-5

First Published 2012

Publishe ' and Printed by

Concept
Since 1974

Concept Publishing Company Pvt. Ltd.
A/15-16, Commercial Block, Mohan Garden
New Delhi-110059 (India)
T: 25351460, 25351794, *F*: 091-11-25357109
E: publishing@conceptpub.com, W: www.conceptpub.com
Editorial Office: H-13, Bali Nagar, New Delhi-110 015, India.

Cataloging in Publication Data--*Courtesy:* D.K. Agencies (P) Ltd. <docinfo@dkagencies.com>

Tadsad, Kamalaxi G.
Human rights and police administration / Kamalaxi G. Tadsad, Harish Ramaswamy.
p. cm.
Includes bibliographical references (p.) and index.
ISBN 9788180698125

1. Human rights—India—Karnataka. 2. Police administration—India—Karnataka. I. Ramaswamy, Harish, 1960-, joint author. II. Title.

DDC 323.095487 23

Dedicated

to

the Suffering Millions
in the World

Preface

Human Rights are often seen as a concept that has lost its shape. General criticism that it is misused and abused both nationally and internationally is not far from truth. Efforts at containing such abuse should be the focus of any right activist or organization/s. This, however, does not happen. Most often it is witnessed that these kinds of abuses right from individuals to powerful states go on without any resistence and even Human Rights Activists watch them as mute spectators. From the brutalities of police to the crisis of Humanity in Daffuer, to the violent rapes in a society that are opting to move backwards and the genocide that takes place in the name of peace, human behaviour exposes its ugliness. Yet, nobody is keen to open their eyes and sensitize their neighbour through a better understanding of Human Rights that envelope the life in the womb to tomb. It is high time that societies and states around the world get sensitive about these noble concept of Human Rights and protect 'life' and its 'dignity', thus bring meaning to the life we live and those of others.

This book *Human Rights and Police Administration* in that sense is a humble attempt made to get my PhD as a student.

We leave this book in the hands of the readers with a hope that it will convert you and sensitize you to work as a Human Rights activist in your locality to reduce the crime against humanity within your vicinity. If that happens any day, we will believe that our effort has seen success and that would be a great sense of satisfaction for us.

We are very grateful to Mr. Ashok Kumar Mittal of Concept Publishing Company Pvt. Ltd. whose encourage-ment and support was responsible to successfully bring out this work to the public domain. As a student of Prof. Harish Ramaswamy by whose efforts this work is seeing the light of day, I take this opportunity to thank him and also to my mother, Madam Mrs. Harish and Master Venkatram H. Belvadi, my brothers and all those who helped me directly and indirectly in releasing this book. Any limitation in the book is solely my responsibility and I shall do the needful after I hear comments on it.

Date: May 10, 2011 **Kamalaxi G. Tadsad**
Place: Hubli

Contents

1

Introduction

In the era of globalization, withdrawal of State is seen as a necessity. While the activities of omnipotent State is taken over by plurality of societal friendly organizations, there is an apprehension, that it would create a uniform society. This, however, has alarmed the developing societies, which are characterized by diversified socio-cultural and ethnic groups, for whom, identity and protection of their rights is of utmost priority. In this process, these groups, having lost their faith in the existing traditional socio-cultural institutions, are increasingly depending on the people friendly and specialized agencies such as Human Rights groups and NGO's for their protection.

Human Rights having its roots firmly established in the discourses of Natural Rights having a wider area of operation, seem to be gaining legitimacy at the societal level by virtue of which people being friendly in their approach. This in fact has put them against the traditional agencies which have statutory powers to protect the rights of citizens. However, these agencies which fall under wide canvas of Criminal Justice System, are today, juxtapositioned to the concept of Human Rights thereby creating a situation of confrontation. Despite many efforts at clarifying these areas of confrontation, there seems to be no demarketed compartmentalization possible to restrict these overlapping in the day-to-day administration of law and order to dispensation of justice.

In India, with the onslaught of globalization several social groups having grievances against the state mostly in the areas pertaining to the Criminal Justice System have only claimed to fight the state with the objective to weaken the state and stake their claim to accede from the main political system.[1] As a result, agencies, which have legitimate concurrence of state to use coercive force against the divisive forces, have become rather activised resulting in the crises of Human Rights situation. From Punjab to North-Eastern States the conflict seems to be between the Human Right organizations and Police which have called for academic attention in the recent past. The State of Karnataka although, quiet and peaceful seems to be slowly experiencing this kind of anti-State activism in the border regions of the State, especially in the border areas close to Andhra Pradesh.[2] This alarming situation which has an effect on the socio-political situation in the State of Karnataka, therefore, has become a major concern for the State. As a result, to counter the activities of these divisive forces, the State of Karnataka is currently thinking in terms of operationalizing the Human Rights Commission in the State, by establishing Human Rights courts at district level[3].

Thus, it is predicted that these Human Rights organizations at the local level would neutralize the situation from further escalation. Although, this attempt of the Government initially is seen only as an expansion of Human Rights Commission's activism, in the years to come, it is likely to contribute to the social emancipation and political correctiveness with increased demand for a civic society. The Andhra Pradesh experience in this regard is worthy of emulation, especially of the role played by activists belonging to Civil Liberties Group, who are acting as buffers between State of Andhra Pradesh and People's War Groups.* Activism of PUCL *vs.* PWG in Andhra Pradesh is an acknowledged fat in this regard In order to support such a progressive step there is also need for an increased attention to be paid to this cause from amongst academic to disseminate more informa-tion about this third generation rights[4].

---

1. Activism of *PUCL vs. PWG* in Andhra Pradesh is an acknowledged fact in this regard.

Keeping these significant aspects of inter-relationship between academics, society and the agencies of the State, the proposed study was undertaken after a thorough study of the literature available in these areas including works of Subramaniam (1992)[5], Chaturvedi, S.K.(1998)[6], Vadackmuchery, J. (1998)[7], Kaul, J.L. (1995)[8], Vadackmuchery, J.(1997)[9], Vadackmuchery, J.(1997)[10], Krishnmurthy (1994)[11], Srivastav (1997)[12], Kalyani, S. (1990)[13], Iyer Krishna (1990)[14], Chaturvedi, S.K. (1996)[15], which are the current studies in this direction. Most of these studies, however, have concentrated on Human Rights in its legal, constitutional and international perspective; while books on Police Administration have thrown light in the managerial, legal and organizational point of view. Thus, one can find an ample number of books, research documents in this direction. But, what distinguishes the present study in its focus covering both Human Rights and Police Administration, is the fact that it subjects to scrutiny, their interrelationship, which of course relatively is a green pasture, hence this study.

Purpose of Study

This being the importance of Human Rights and Police Administration today, it is but tempting and also relevant that this growing area of Human Rights is investigated, keeping in view the current socio-political changes that are occurring worldwide. While the current trend of globalization is hinted at restructuring the state and its various activities, it is also imperative that the various agencies/functionaries working under the supervision of the state are also subjected to change in order to keep themselves abreast with changing time. Despite the fact that the state is subjected to careful scrutiny these days, dependency of the state on the constitutional machinery has often brought to fore the debates about restructuring the constitution and reviewing its contents in the light of the new concepts such as 'Human Rights' and *Hindutva*. These are no doubt gaining primary importance in these debates as can be witnessed. While, it is a fact that such a debate has a hidden political agenda in relation to *Hindutva,* it is with satisfaction that one would agree to the fact that the concept of Human Rights as enshrined in the Constitution also has been consistently performing. However, the global trend towards market economic system has an impact on the traditional society like India. Apart from the political system, this is calling for an increased participation of various societal groups within the society to stake their claim for their share of power, within the powers vested in the state, thus helping to protect the larger interest of the society. Consumerist movement, privatization of civic functions at the local level NGO activism in the locality and at the State level involving rights of displaced peoples, etc., are all thus the necessary results of an expanded market and globalised economy, which have within them the crucial questions pertaining to Human Rights.

Human Rights having its content what is already enshrined in the Constitution, viz., the fundamental rights, etc., constitutes one of the major instrument for an individual to protect his rights, forming an integral part of the components of a vigilant society in a democratic set-up. Similarly, with intrusion of globalization and the varied technology in the socio-political instrumentalities of governance the challenges before traditional agencies of the State such as the Police Administration calls for a sea change among the Police Administration and the Police Organization. The traditional police functions under the umbrella of criminal justice system which was turned to perform its police-thief, police-law and order and police/traffic control kind of roles are fast becoming outdated. Because of the enlarged world and borderless society coupled with changing technology, automation and arms, thus ranging from cyber hacking to corrupting information systems, a new outlook, attitude and reinforcement has become a necessity for these police organizations. Problems of Intellectual Property Rights and such other knowledge based activities of the complex societies of today have demanded a change in the entire Police Administration. As against this requirement of a comprehensive change, the police personnel within the organization seems to have neither the qualification nor the organizational readiness to react to these enormous changes within their society and the world around them. In fact, the Government of India is still to come out with a new bill covering laws and policies connected to various activities related to cyber world, Intellectual property Rights and many such knowledge based regulations that fall under the purview of World Trade Organization agreements. At such crucial juncture when the society is getting activised to enter into a new world of virtual reality in the 21st century leading to sophisticated ways of life — an important agency of State, viz., the police, which is to act as a protector of life, liberty and rights connected with the major task of maintaining law and order no doubt, needs an updating and specialization to ensure that there comes to life a balanced society that is devoid of exploitation in any form. It is in this context that the Police Administration is put under scrutiny keeping in focus and in frame very closely associated concept namely, Human Right, which by versatility of its content has outgrown to such an extent that there are hardly any debates in the intellectual circles that does not encompass this issue today. Therefore the importance of this study.

Problems to be Investigated

Conceptually, rights are those conditions of social life without which man cannot be at his best. State is said to have come into existence to promote man's best interest[16]. Rights therefore, are tools to safeguard the individual from other individuals and also the individual from the state. This ensures protection of Human Rights and permits the individual to maintain his dignity. However, a liberal state may not, despite all prerequisites realize this. Breach of this protection, therefore, results from the state itself. Threat to the interest of the state because of certain acts of an individual may result in loss of rights of an individual. From theft to agitations, the law enforcing agency, namely, the police, acts as a protector of the state instead of working for the protection of the rights of an individual. In the eagerness of maintaining the law and order in the interest of the state, the police often commits excesses. Ignorance on the part of the citizens of their own rights, failure of the police to extend this knowledge to the citizens, need for problem specific investigative modes are thus some of the causes for these excesses, termed as the violation of Human Rights. This act, therefore pushes the citizens and police to opposite banks leading a question of mere problem of maintenance of law and order into situation of crisis involving Human Rights. It is in this context, that this study has been proposed involving the following questions for investigation :

(a) What has been the relation between Human Rights and Police Administration;
(b) How far Human Right as an input can humanize Police Administration;
(c) What is the extent of jurisdiction of Human Rights in matters of Police Administration; and
(d) Are Human Rights a stumbling block in the path of Police Administration, as it is often conceived and many such other issues?

The involvement of non-governmental organizations as active caretakers of Human Rights has in fact further complicated this problem leaving Police Administration in a tight spot. Preliminary survey in this regard has indicated very clearly the existence of mutual respect between Human Right activists/enforcing agencies and Police Administration.

But, certainly there is an uneasy relationship that exists between them as can be evidenced. Hence, the need to investigate this problem.

Objectives

The objectives of the study are as follows :

1. To understand and assess the various dimensions of Human Rights;
2. To assess the strength and weakness of Police Administration ; and
3. To examine the interrelationship between Human Rights activism and Police Administration.

Hypotheses

In order to explore the potential for research in bringing together a conceptual issue with that of an active organization like the Police Administration, a pilot survey was carried out keeping in view the difficulties that may arise in collecting the data from amongst the various strata of Police Administration. In this regard, several rounds of discussions were also held with different levels of officers within the Police hierarchy, with a view to lay hands on the crucial data that may be available. After due analysis of the pros and cons, the study was undertaken with following hypotheses :

1. That the concept of Human Rights may be too complex for specific application in Police Administration :
2. That Police Administration may not be very receptive to the idea of Human Rights ; and
3. That because of above two reasons, Police Administration and Human Rights may not be mutually contributory in their functioning.

Significance of the Study

In an era of Human Rights, any scientific study relating this concept to an institution of a state primarily engaged in dealing with protection of rights as extended by the state would only mutually qualify the subject Human Rights and Police Administration. Being two faces of the same coin, they are expected to jointly promote the progress of the society without causing any hindrance to each other. Unfortunately, there seems to be an impaired relationship between them if one observes closely their functioning. Reasons such as over consciousness and lack of jurisdictional demarcation could be at the outset identified as the cause for such a hindrance which calls for solutions. Since the policy making process cannot ensure these operative necessities for smooth working of these institutions, this kind of research is expected to serve as guideline to create awareness among the organizations concerned while providing them a mirror to observe their own activity. It is in this direction, that this problem assumes significance apart from filling the existing gap in literature and opening new horizons of operational research as shown earlier.

Karnataka State is often referred to as a representative sample of Indian Society and Polity. It has a special status in the India federal structure supported by its enlightened history of having had the experience of a welfare State. This is a State where the rate of crime is comparatively lower, while the consciousness of the people is rated to be much higher and more judicious. From newspapers to literary elites and the enlightened administration to responsible representatives and the benevolent people friendly Police Administration, the State of Karnataka has a good track record. From bride burning to neo-imperialism and from ragging to gender issues, the people's institution in this State have judiciously taken care of punishing the criminals, without leading to any crisis at any point of time.

Being aware of these prime qualities of the State, the other side of the problem is that what concerns the proposed present study. The State of Karnataka is generally identified with two parts, the southern and northern regions. There exists enough reasons to compare them to expose the constrast between them. Be it in matters of development or culture, the basic variables show a clear difference. The fact is that northern Karnataka is generally identified as less forward, less literate, more rustic and crime prone because of its backwardness in terms of development and at far reaching distance from the capital, it is to be investigated that whether these factors are responsible for violation of Human Rights in these areas by those who are in fact expected to protect the very people. Recent cases of Bomb blasting to black magic or earlier cases of custodial deaths, violation of *Dalits* rights, suicide of poor farmers in this region are all referred to as problems stemming out of the backwardness of this region. This being the context of the area chosen for study Human Rights issue though not very popular in the region very well fits in to awaken the masses in the region and to highlight the problems therein. Police being the only hope for people who are victims of such harsh realities of life are also the targeted agencies for politically active society. Under such dilemma, the police is performing its task and this study would only help them to understand their performance and, hence, the significance of this.

References

1. Problem of Punjab originated with the problem of law and order, Bihar has a similar problem today.
2. In the State of Karnataka recently (1990s) in Raichur District there is activism of People's War Groups (PWG), which is noticed by the State. This is stated because of the influence of Andhra Pradesh. Similarly, in the recent past, the ISI Activism has been suspected in some of the places in Northern Karnataka region connected to a series of blasts in Churches, Mandirs Masjids and Indian Institute of Science.
3. Arjun Dev, *et al.* (eds.) *Human Rights : A Source Book,* New

Delhi, National Council for Educational Research and Training, 1996.

Apart from that Social Clubs like the Rotary Clubs have also initiated the establishment of Human Rights groups at their Rotary Districts to work towards bringing about awareness regarding Human Rights through seminars and such other academic and activist endeavours.

4. Arjun Dev *et al.*, *Human Rights : A Source Book*, New Delhi, National Council for Educational Research and Training, 1996.
5. Subramaniam, S., *Human Rights and Police*, Hyderabad, Association for Advancement of Police and Security Sciences, 1992.
6. Chaturvedi, S.K., Police and Emerging Challenges, New Delhi, B.R. Publishing Corporation, 1998.
7. Vadackmuchery; J., Management Thought on Police Administration, New Delhi, APH Publishing Corporation, 1998.
8. Kaul, J.L., (ed.) *Human Rights : Issues and Perspectives*, New Delhi, Regency Publications, 1995.
9. Vadackumchery. J., The Police, The Accused and Criminal Injustice, New Delhi, APH Publishing Corporation, 1997.
10. Vadackumchery, J., *The Police, the Accused and Criminal Injustice*, New Delhi, APH Publishing Corporation, 1997.
11. Krishnamurthy, S., *Human Rights and the Indian Police*, Bangalore, B.R. Publishing Corporation, 1994.
12. Srivastav, V.P. (ed.) *Indian Police : Law and Reality*, New Delhi, Manas Publications, 1997.
13. Kalyani, S., *Police and Development : A Case Study of West Bengal 1951-1971*, Bombay, Popular Prakashan, 1990.
14. Iyer Krishna. V.R., *Human Rights and Inhuman Wrongs*, New Delhi, B.R. Publishing Corporation, 1990.
15. Chaturvedi, S.K., (ed.) *Role of Police in Criminal Justice System*, New Delhi, B.R. Publishing Corporation, 1996.
16. *Ibid.*

2

Concept of Human Rights

A Historical Perspective

Human Rights today is a live issue both at the national and international scenario. Generally, Human Rights are regarded as the Rights, which every human being is entitled to and those which have to be protected by the State[1]. They are also regarded as Human Rights because of their universal nature and application. Human Rights, however, mean different things to different people depending on the context of its use and abuse. But, their perception is often conditioned by the social structure, culture, traditions and needs of the society. Since, there are no constants in human history, all our socio-political concepts, norms and values are in a state of perpetual flux, woven into the wrap and woof of human history. Similarly, the basic fundamentals of Human Rights are also subjected to variation although they are dynamic in nature. Even within the same society, perception of Human Rights may vary from strata to strata, although the fundamental norm governing the concept of Human Right may remain the same, regardless of colour, race, sex, religion or other conditions. Hence, human rights are said to be those fundamental rights to which every man or woman inhabiting in any part of the world is deemed to be entitled merely by virtue of having been born as a human being [2]. Further, Human Rights could also be defined as those rights which are inherent and inalienable to man, simply because being a man[3]. These are Moral Rights, which are derived from the humanness of every human being and they aim at ensuring the dignity of every human being[4]. Human Rights are also defined as a set of legal rights established according to the law and basis of these rights are the consent of governed, that is, the consent of subjects[5].

This being the varied definitions of Human Rights, this concept which encompasses several rights, having the Right to reveal itself at various levels has evolved over the years. Liberalistic tradition is the first in the series as advocated by philosophers like *Locke* and *Bentham*, in which the individual human being was subjected to extreme conditions of suppression by the state. This in other words, is identified as the individualistic approach to Human Rights as seen in American and French Declarations which have resulted in a hierarchy of civil and political rights for individuals. Apart from this, the individualistic approach to rights in the west, is the second level, which covers the economic system, advocating free enterprise and free competition[6]. The legal system advocated within this system is the one that provides a body of predictable and ascertainable standards of behaviour allowing each economic factor to maintain a set of relatively safe exception as to the conduct of other social factors[7].

A further consideration is that, a large section of law in the west being the fruit of political struggles between contending groups have ensured their sustainability by establishing safety passage through Bill of Rights, and constitutions. This kind of placing restraints on the powers of aristocracy and its feudal privileges, have thus helped the evolution of Rights for the benefits of the citizens of a state contributing to their social progress and equilibrium within the society[8].

Gradual secularization of religion, mainly the Christianity, is the third level which has not only helped the gradual erosion of the metaphysical components of religious tenets but also by absorbing its components into daily life and converting them into general moral precepts, the contents of religion has been put into day-to-day use. Which at a later stage of its continued usage took the shape of legal rules acquiring an extra legal dimension enhancing their value. In fact, it was this, which has been instrumental in the evolution of a legal system and law. Its commitment to uphold the dictates of individual rights based on the economic necessities of a *laissez faire* system[9] has since then been vehemently supported and argued in favour. Indeed the states have shown greater resilience towards human enhancement by minimalist interventions in the domain of individual rights, which in fact has greatly contributed to all-round development of the state too.

In juxtaposition to the above school is the *Marxian* concept of Rights which can be considered as the fourth level. This school lays emphasis on group (social) rights rather than individual rights. Dominated by the writings of *Marx* and the *Fabian society*. Most of the writings of this school of thought particularly writings of *Laski* were in full agreement with the fact that full realization of an individual self is possible only within the context of a society[10]. Here the argument is to see and stress the fact that development is as much the concern of a society as of an individual. The society according to them has an interest in facilitating the advancement of individuals since it would ultimately mean social development. The *Marxian* frame, therefore, had placed the agreement that the state has an overwhelming responsibility towards its subject, it is but natural that economic and social rights, should have predominance over the individual[11]. Whereas fifth level or the modern rights theory mentioned above are either a reaction to the earlier theories or the refinements to the existing jurisprudence on Human Rights thereby setting the limits to their contribution. Among them are included the theories of *Rawls, Radberuch, Robert Nozik, Medougal* and *Dworkin*. These theorists in our opinion, display a number of common characteristics including their eclectic character benefiting from each other's insights. It is, therefore, difficult to characterize their theories as simply utilitarian, *natural rights, intuitive or behavioural.*

natural rights, intuitive or behavioural. Secondly, these modern theorists seems to take up certain common means to explain the tension that may exist between the concept of liberty and equality. In doing so, they employ various approaches such as the theories of resolution contending the fact that the goals of these concepts are either reconcilable or irreconcilable. Others evolve refining theories, which accept a relationship between liberty and equality characterized by shifting-readjustments. While most theorists acknowledge the fact that there is a need to reconstruct an entire system of rights[12], keeping in view the popularity of the new dimension of rights — the Human Right groups are of the opinion that there is a need to work towards it.

It is in this context that the last of the levels of liberal traditions can be identified as having taken the shape of moral declarations that are necessarily to be protected by the state and theories of social and political organization summing up in the *Lockean* formula of "life, liberty and property"[13].

As a moral declaration, these rights inflicted the idea of respecting a person by respecting his individual freedom which in other words meant non-interference by others. Thus, rights against arbitrary coercion, physical restraint, freedom of speech and association and right against discrimination have evolved expressing their concern with the protection of the individual 'person' against state/government power. The doctrine of natural rights taking the view of man as a self-determining and self-directing agent living in an environment that provides him ample resources and opportunities to pursue his own goals and choose his own actions free from interference by others also represented the struggle of men against various forms of intrusions and oppressions. They also placed great emphasis on liberty, freedom and independence, however, due to its own inherent in capabilities it became a target for attack. Towards the end of 18th century. *Jermey Bentham* the founder of classical *utilitarianism* and *analytical positivism* mounted an attack on the doctrine of natural rights. In his argument he was in favour of the principle of utility as the only proper basis for determining how people should live and did not agree to the reference made to the existence of natural rights. Thus, in *Bentham's view,* rights were not a matter of moral or political legitimacy but owed exclusively to positive law[14]. Despite this, it is important to know that the doctrine of natural rights had greatly influenced the drafting of *British Bill of Rights (1968),Declaration of Independence (1976) and Declaration of Rights of Man and Citizen (1979)* and formed a part of the US Constitution.[15]

The legal positivists transformed natural rights first by refining the concept of civil liberties and establishing a catalogue of specific rights and then by developing the procedural opportunities to secure these rights. Like natural rights, the traditional individual rights to freedom of speech, assembly, due process and so forth were defined as right to freedom from interference from others. Most of the common legal rights formulated in such concepts as negligence, tort, defamation, liability are (defined) considered as prohibitions against interference with individual freedom. Supporting such an argument in the *Will Theory of Rights* which holds the view that rights make out an area within which a person's moral and political rights are encompassed and can be considered as freedom which require only duties of non-interference. Defining it in other words, it can be framed as, rights make the enforcement of another's duty dependent on one's exercise of will. This theory gives an idea or it pre-supposes the idea that correlating of rights and duties and treating rights as power of waiver over someone else's duty as freedom. *H.L.A. Hart,* contemporary exponent of *Will Theory,* emphasizes the correlatively of rights and duties and place great emphasis on liberty as a fundamental value. He asserts :

> I quote: " *If there are any moral rights at all, it follows that here is at least one natural right, the equal right of all men to be free*"[16].

Thus, all rights are derived from basic right to equal liberty. Rights make sense only in a system where people are left to lead their own lives and be responsible for their own decisions and action. Only when a person's action interferes with the equal liberty of others, then he or she can be restrained by law. Many traditional liberties such as freedom of speech, religion and property can be derived from a basic right to equal liberty. Placing high value to the freedom of action and freedom from interference, therefore, speaks of the idea of rights which involves the right to freedom from interference as well as various rights to welfare or right to assistance of others. What is happening here is that the concept of 'right' is being enlarged to include not only means but also ends. What men are now claiming as rights is not merely that they be left unhindered in their pursuit of values bestowed upon them. The extension of rights in this way has enlarged with obligation to satisfy basic human needs. Hence, origin of Human Rights is quite similar to that of natural rights, each is born of desperation and dedicated to action. But there are also important differences that will have important consequences. Thus, the doctrine of Human Rights appeals chiefly to the feeling of men, while the natural rights speaks more seriously about their minds. The doctrine of Human Rights on the other hand marks the return to that of natural rights but without the metaphysical foundation of the latter.

The modern doctrine of Human Rights, therefore, seeks fresh grounds and content of rights; so that deficiencies of the established theories of rights are exposed and the unmet needs and neglected values are accommodated within the doctrine of rights.[17] Keeping these theoretical perception in mind a brief glance through the historical development of Human Rights is attempted here to facilitate a complete understanding of the blossoming concept of the Human Rights.

Development of Human Rights : A Historical Perspective

The expression "Human Rights" is relatively new, having come into everyday parlance only since World War II. Replacing the phrase "Natural Right", which fell into disfavour in part of the later phrase "the right of man" which was not universally understood to include the rights of women. Human Rights in fact has its origin back in the ancient *Greece* and *Rome*, closely tied up to the pre-modem natural doctrines of *Greek stoicism* and *Hellenistic stoics*[18]. In *Graeco-Roman* and medieval times, natural law doctrines taught mainly the duties, as distinguished from the right, of man. Moreover, as evident in the writing of *Aristotle and St. Thomas Aquinas*. These doctrines recognized the legitimacy of slavery and serfdom and in doing so, excluded perhaps the central most idea of Human Rights as they are understood today.

The teachings of *Aquinas* and *Hugo Grotius* in the European continent and the *Magna Carta* (1215), the *Petition of Right* (1628) and the *English Bill of Rights* (1689) in England, were proofs of this change. All testified to the increasingly popular view that human beings are endowed with eternal and inalienable rights never, renounced when humankind "Contracted" to enter the social from the primitive state never diminished by the claim of *"The Divine Right of Kings"*[19]. For the idea of Human (natural) Rights to take hold as a general social need and reality, it was found necessary that the basic changes in the beliefs and practices of society take place and changes of the sort as evolved from about the 13th century, during the Renaissance and the decline of feudalism be effected. When resistance to religious intolerance and political economic bondage began the long transition of liberal nations talking in terms of freedom and equality, particularly in relation to the use of ownership of property came into force, when the foundations for what are today called truly as Human Rights were laid. During this period reflecting the failure of rulers to meet their obligations of natural law, as well as the unprecedented commitment to individual expression and worldly experience that was characteristic of the *Renaissance*, the shift from natural law as duties to the natural law as right was confirmed.

It was primarily in the 17th and 18th centuries, however, to elaborate upon this modernist conception of natural law as meaning or implying natural rights, that the scientific and intellectual achievements of the 17th century, were to be consolidated. The discoveries of *Galileo* and *Sir Isaac Newton, the Materialism of Thomas Hobbes, the rationalism of Rene Descartes and Gottfried Wilhelm Heibniz, the pantheism of Benedict de Spinoza, the empiricism of Francis Bacon and John Locke,* encouraged the belief that natural law had in the content of universal order. With this impetus, during the 18th century, known as the 'Age of Enlightenment'; a growing confidence in human reason and in the perfectibility of human affairs consolidated its hold and became a more comprehensive expression of this period. Further, during 17th century English philosopher *John Locke* arguably the most important natural law theorist of modern time being in complete agreement mainly with the writings associated with (*Glorious Ren*) the *Revolution of 1688* agreed to the fact that certain rights self-evidently pertain to individuals as human beings and that the chief among them are the rights to life, liberty (freedom from arbitrary rule) and property. Further, he argued that upon entering the civil society (pursuant to a social contract), human kind surrendered to the state only the right to enforce these natural rights and not the rights themselves. However, the state's failure to secure these reserved natural rights (the state itself being under contract to safeguard the interests of its members) gives rise to a right to popular revolution. These philosophers who postulated their theories building their argument on *Locke's* thoughts embracing many and varied currents of thought prevailing them had all agreed to the fact that they all had supreme faith in reason and vigorously attacked religious and scientific dogmatism, targeting even intolerance, censorship and socio-economic restraints. They sought to discover and act upon universally valid principles harmoniously governing nature, humanity and society including the theory of the inalienable "rights ethical and social gospel".

All this liberal intellectual ferment had, not surprisingly, great influence on the western world of the late 18th and early 19th centuries. With practical example of *English Revolution of 1688 and the Bill of Rights*, which provided the rationale for the wave of revolutionary agitation that the then it had swept the west most notably in the North America and France. With these and the idea of Human Rights, playing a key role in the 18th and early 19th century struggles against *political absolutism*. It was indeed, seen as the failure of rules to respect the principles of freedom and equality, which had been central to the philosophy of natural law, which was from the beginning responsible for the overall development of societies. In the words of *Maurice Cranston*, a leading student of Human Rights, absolutism prompted man to claim (human or natural) rights precisely because it denied them.[20] Despite these thoughts the idea Human Rights as natural rights was not without its detractors. Even at this otherwise receptive time, with states frequently associates themselves with religious orthodoxy the doctrine of natural rights became less and less acceptable to philosophical and political liberals. Additionally, because they were conceived in essentially absolutist "inalienable", "unalterable", "eternal" terms, natural rights were found themselves coming to conflict increasingly with one another. Most importantly the doctrine of natural rights came under powerful philosophical and political attack from both the right and the left. In England, for example, conservatives *Edmund Burke* and *David Hume* united with liberal thinker *Jeremy Bentham* in condemning the doctrine, the former out of fear that public affirmation of natural rights would lead to social upheaval, the latter out of concern lest declarations and proclamations of natural rights substitute for effective legislation. *Burke* in his *"Reflections on the Revolutions"* in France (1790) a believer in natural law who nonetheless denied that the "rights of man" could be derived from it, criticized the drafters of the declaration of the Rights of Man and of the citizen for proclaiming the *"Monstrous Fiction"* of human equality, which he argued, serves but to inspire false ideas and vain expectations in men destined travel in the obscure walk of laborious life. *Bentham,* founder of *Utilitarianism* on the other hand, placing his thoughts in this direction submits that "Right" is the child of law, from real law comes real rights: but from imaginary laws, from law of nature, comes imaginary rights. Placing his argument on these lines he regarded natural rights as simple nonsense to quote :

> "Natural and imprescriptible rights, rhetorical nonsense, nonsense upon stilts."

Hume, arguing in his way, in fact, agreed with *Bentham's* view as insisted that natural law and natural rights are unreal metaphysical phenomena.

These assaults upon natural law and natural rights, which began during the late 19th and early 20th centuries once again met their saviour *John Stuart Mill,* who despite his vigorous defence of liberty, proclaimed that rights ultimately are founded on utility. The German Jurist *Friedrich Karl Von Sauigny,* England's *Sir Henry Maine* and other historic lists placing similar arguments emphasized that rights are a function of cultural and environmental variables unique to particular communities. Opposing such a thinking once again it was the Jurist *John Austin* and the philosopher *Ludwig Wittgenstein* respectively who insisted, that the only law is "the command of the sovereign" and that it is the only truth which can be established by verifiable experience. By the time of world war there were scarcely any theorists who would or could defend the 'rights of man' along the lines of natural law. Indeed, under the influence of 19th century German idealism and parallel expressions of rising European nationalism, there were some like *Marxists*, for example who, although not rejecting individual rights altogether, maintained that rights from whatever source derived belong to communities or to the whole of the societies and nations pre-eminently. Yet, despite having its heyday the natural rights proved short to completely strengthen the idea of Human Rights, nonetheless, endured in one form or another. The abolition of slavery, factory legislation, popular education, trade unionism, the universal suffrage movement these and other examples of 19th century reformist impulse afford ample evidence that the idea was not being extinguished even if its transempirical derivation had become a matter of general *skepticism*. But is was not until the rise and fall of *Nazi* Germany that the idea of rights i.e., Human Rights came truly into its own. The laws authorizing the dispossession and extermination of Jews and other minorities, the laws permitting arbitrary police search and seizure, the laws condoning imprisonment, torture and execution without public trial these and similar obscenities brought home the realization that law and morality, if they are to be deserving of the name cannot be grounded in a purely utilitarian, idealist, or other consequentialist doctrine[21]. In post-war period, realizing the atrocities on human beings by the 'state' ventures, reason prevailed upon the actors in the war. German obscenity, Russian conservative time of thought, falling morale of Britain and its weakened double standards, freedom to the newly born nations, emerging Americanism — all lead to the rationale thought of institutionalizing protective mechanism for Human Rights resulting in the establishment of United Nations after they witnessed the failure of the League of Nations.

Human Rights and the United Nations

The Charter of the United Nations (1945) begins by reaffirming as :

> "Faith in fundamental Human Rights, in the dignity and worth of the human person. In the equal rights of Men and Women and nations large and small."

It states that the purposes of United Nations are, among other things, to develop friendly relations among nations bases on respect for the principle of equal rights and self-determination of peoples and to anchor international co-operation in promoting and encouraging respect for Human Rights and for fundamental freedoms for all without distinction as to race, sex, language or religion. In its two articles, all its members "pledge themselves to take joint and separate action in co-operation with the organization", for the achievement of these and related purposes. It is to be noted, however, that a proposal to ensure the protection as well as the promotion of Human Rights was explicitly rejected at the *San Francisco* conference establishing the United Nations[22].

Additionally the charter expressly provides that nothing in it "shall authorize United Nations to intervene in matters which are essentially within the domestic jurisdiction of any state" except upon a Security Council finding of a "threat to the peace, breach of the peace or act of aggression"[23]. Further, although, typical of major constitutive instruments, the charter it is observed inconspicuous in general and vague in its clauses related to Human Rights among others. Thus, not surprisingly, the reconciliation of the charter's Human Rights provisions with the charter's drafting history and its "domestic jurisdiction" clause has given rise not to a little legal and political controversy. Some authorities have argued that, in becoming parties to the charter, states accept no more than a nebulous promotional obligation towards Human Rights safeguards in member-states. Other insists that the charter's Human Rights whatever isolation they may have "enjoyed" in the past, no longer can be considered matters "essentially within the domestic jurisdiction" of states[24].

When all is said and done, however, it is clear from the actual practice of the nations that the problem of resolving these opposing contentions has proved somewhat less formidable than the statements of governments and the opinions of scholars might lead one to assume. Neither the charter's drafting history nor its "domestic jurisdiction" clause or indeed, its generality and vagueness in respect of Human Rights has prevented the United Nations on the basis of individual petitions, statements from witness, state complaints and reports from interested non-governmental organizations from investigating discussion and evaluating specific Human Rights situations. Nor have they prevented it from recommending or prescribing concrete action in relation to them at least not in the case or "a consistent pattern of gross violations" of Human Rights, provided, there has been a majority persuasive enough to force the action desired (as in the imposition by Security Council in 1977 of a mandatory arms embargo against South Africa). Of course, governments usually are protective of their sovereignty or domestic jurisdiction. Also, the United Nations organs responsible for the promotion of Human Rights suffer from most of the same disabilities that afflict the United Nations as a whole, in particular are the absence of supranational authority and the presumption of divine power politics. Hence, it cannot be expected that United Nation's action in defence of Human Rights will be normally either shift or categorically effective. Nevertheless, assuming some political will, the legal obstacles to United Nations enforcement of Human Rights are not insurmountable[25].

Primary responsibility for promotion of Human Rights

under the United Nations charter rests in the General Assembly and under its authority, in the Economic and Social Council and its subsidiary body, the United Nation's central policy organ in the Human Rights field. Much of the commissions activity, initiated by subsidiary working groups, is investigator, evaluative and advisory in character and the commission annually establishes a working group to consider and make recommendations concerning alleged "gross violations" of Human Rights referred it by its sub-commission on prevention of discrimination and protection of minorities (on the basis of communications from individuals and groups, pursuant to resolution 1970 of the United Nations Economic and Social Council and sometimes on the basis of investigations by the sub-commission or one of its working groups). Also, the commission has appointed special representatives and envoys to examine Human Rights situations on an *adhoc* basis, who, in the course of preparing their report findings reliable information submitted in good faith, interview of interested persons or make on site inspections with the co-operation of the government concerned.

In addition, the commission, together with other UN organs such as International Labour Organization (ILO), the UN Educational, Scientific and Cultural Organization (UNESCO) and the UN Commission on the status of women, draft Human Rights standards and has prepared a number of international Human Rights instruments. Among the most important are the Universal Declaration of Human Rights (1948) the international Covenant on Economic, Social and Cultural Rights (1976) and these are collectively known as the International Bill of Rights, these three instruments serve as touchstones for interpreting the Human Rights provisions of the UN Charter[26]. The catalogue of rights set out in the Universal Declaration of Human Rights, which was adopted without dissent by the General Assembly on December 10, 1948 (Appendix-II) is scarcely less than the sum of all the constitutions and legal systems, including equality before law, protection against arbitrary arrest the right to a fair trial, freedom from *ex-post facto* criminal laws; the right to own property; freedom of thought, conscience and cultural rights are the right to work and to choose one's work freely, the right to equal pay for work, the right to form and join trade union, the right to rest and leisure, the right to an adequate standard of living and the right to education[27].

The Universal Declaration, it must be noted here that, is not a treaty. It was meant to proclaim "a common standard of achievement for all people and all nations" rather than enforceable legal obligations. Nevertheless, partly because of an 18 years delay between its adoption and the completion for signature and ratification of the two covenant, the Universal Declaration has acquired a status juridically more important than originally intended. It has been widely used, even by national court, as a means of judging compliance with Human Rights obligations under the UN Charter.

The International Covenant on Civil and Political Rights and the optional protocol : The Civil and Political Rights (Appendix-III) guaranteed by this covenant, which was opened for signature on December 19, 1966, and entered into force on March 23, 1976, incorporate almost all of those proclaimed in the Universal Declaration, including the right to non-discrimination. Pursuant to the covenant, each state party undertakes to respect and to its jurisdiction the rights recognized in the covenant "Without distinction of any kind, such as race, colour, sex, language, religion and political or other opinion, national or social origin, property, birth or other status". Some rights listed in the Universal Declaration, however, such as the right to own property and the right to asylum are not included among the rights recognized in the convenant. Similarly, the covenant designates a number of rights that are not listed in the Universal Declaration, among them the right of all the people to self-determination and the right to ethic, religious, or linguistic minorities to enjoy their own culture, to profess and practice their own religion and to use their own language, to the extent that the Universal Declaration and the covenant overlap, however, the latter is understood to explicate and help interpret the former[28].

In addition, the covenant calls for the establishment of a Human Rights Committee an international organ of the 18 persons elected by the parties to the covenant, serving in their individual expert capacity and charged to study reports submitted by the state parties on the measures they have adopted that effect to the right recognized the competence of the committee in this regard, the committee also may respond to allegations by one state party to another state party is not fulfilling its obligations under the covenant. If the committee is unable to resolve the problem, the matter is referred to an *ad hoc* conciliation commission, which eventually reports its findings on all questions of fact, plus its view on the possibilities of an amicable solution. State party that becomes party to the optional protocol further recognizes the competence of Human Rights committee similar to consider and act upon communications from individuals claiming to be victims of covenant violations[29].

The International Covenant on Economic, Social and Cultural Rights (See Appendix-IV) just as the International Covenant on Civil and Political Rights elaborates upon most of the civil and political rights enumerated in the Universal Declaration of Human Rights, so the International Covenant on Economic, Social and Cultural Rights set forth in the Universal Declaration: the right to work; the right to just and favourable conditions to work; trade union rights: the right to social security; rights relating to culture and science. Unlike its companion international covenant on civil and political rights, however, this covenant is not geared, with modest exception to immediate implementation the state parties having agreed only to take steps towards achieving progressively the full realization of the rights recognized in the covenant and then subjected to the maximum of their available resources. The covenant is essentially a promotional convention, stipulating objection more than standards and requiring implementation over time rather than all at once one obligation is, however, subject to immediate application, the enjoyment of the rights enumerated on grounds of race, colour, sex, language, religion or political or other opinion; national or social origin; property and birth or other status. Also, the international supervisory measures that apply to the covenant oblige the state parties to report to the UN Economic and Social Council on the steps they have made in achieving the realization of the enumerated rights[30].

Other UN Human Rights Conventions

The two above-mentioned conventions are by no means the only the Human Rights treaties drafted and adopted under the auspices of the United Nations. Indeed, because there are far too many to detail even in abbreviated fashion, it must suffice simply to note that they address a broad range of concerns, including the prevention and punishment of the crime of genocide; the inhuman treatment by military and civilian personnel in times of war; the status of refugees; the protection and reduction of stateless persons; the abolition of slavery, forced labour and discrimination in employment and occupation; the elimination of all forms of racial discrimination and the suppression and punishment of the crime of apartheid; the elimination of discrimination in education; the promotion of the political rights of women and elimination of all forms of discrimination against women; and the promotion of equality of opportunity and treatment of migrant workers.

Many of these treaties are the work of the UN specialized agencies. Particularly, the International Labour Organization (ILO) and many also provide for supervisory and enforcement mechanism for example the committee on the elimination of Racial Discrimination established under the

International Convention on the Elimination of All Forms of Racial Discrimination (1965) (See Appendix - V) [31].

Human Rights in the 21st Century

Today, the vast majority of legal scholars, philosophers and moralists agree, that irrespective of culture or civilization that every human being is entitled, at least in theory, to some basic rights. Indeed, except for some essentially isolated 19th century demonstrations of international humanitarian concern to be noted below the last half of the 20th century may fairly be said to mark the birth of international as well as the universal recognition of Human Rights.

In the treaty establishing the United Nations (UN), all members pledged themselves to take joint and separate action, for the achievement of "universal respect for and observance of Human Rights and fundamental freedoms for all without distinction as to race, sex, language or religion in universal declaration of Human Rights (1948) representatives from many diverse cultures endorsed the rights therein set forth "as a common standard of achievement for the people and all nations". And in the International Covenant on Civil and Political Rights (1976), the International Covenant on Economic, Social and Cultural Rights and the each approved by the United Nations General Assembly in 1966 entered into force and effect. However, to say that there is widespread acceptance of the principle of Human Rights on the domestic and international planes is not to say that there is complete agreement about the nature of such rights or their substantive scope which is to say their definition. Some of the basic questions have yet to receive the answers whether Human Rights are to be viewed as divine, moral or legal entitlements, whether they are to be validated by intuition custom, social contract theory, principles of distributive justice, or as pre-requisites for happiness; whether they are understood as irrevocable or partially revocable; whether they are to be broad or limited in number and content.

Despite this, lack of consensus to know about nature of Human Rights is quite essential. However, a number of widely accepted and interrelated postulates may be seen to assist, if not to complete, the task of defining Human Rights.

Regardless of their ultimate origin or justification, Human Rights are understood to represent individual and group demands for the shaping and sharing of power, wealth, enlightenment and other cherished values in community process, most fundamentally the value of respect and its constituent elements of reciprocal tolerance and mutual forbearance in the pursuit of all other values. Consequently, they imply claims against persons and institutions who impede realization and standards for judging the legitimacy of laws and traditions. At bottom, Human Rights limit state power.

Secondly, reflecting on varying environmental circumstances, differing world news and inescapable interdependencies within and between value processes, Human Rights refer to a wide continuum of value claims ranging from the most justifiable to the most inspirational. Human Rights partake of both the legal and the moral orders, sometimes indistinguishably. They are expressive of both the 'is' and 'ought' in human affairs.

Thirdly, if a right is determined to be Human Right it is quintessentially general or universal in character, in other sense equally possessed by all human beings everywhere, including in certain instances even the unborn. In stark contrast to "The Divine Rights of Kings' and other such conceptions of privilege, Human Rights extend in theory to every person on earth without discrimination irrelevant of merit.

Fourthly, most assertions of Human Rights arguably not all qualified by the limitation that the rights of any particular individual or group in any particular instance are restricted as much as is necessary to secure the comparable rights or other and the aggregate of common interest. Given this interdependency, Human Rights are sometimes designated as *prima facie* rights and it makes little or no sense to think or talk of them in absolute terms.

Finally, Human Rights are commonly assumed to refer, "fundamental" as distinct from "non-essential" claims or "goods". In fact, some theorists go so far as to limit Human Rights to a single or two core right for example, the right to life or the right to equal freedom or opportunity. The tendency, in short, is to deemphasize or rule out "mere wants."[32]

Like all normative traditions, the Human Rights tradition is a product of its time. It necessarily reflects the processes of historical continuity and change that at once and as a matter of cumulative experience, help to give it substance and form. Therefore, it is essential to understand the better meaning, content and legitimate scope of Human Rights.

Maurice Cranston defined that "All Human Rights are basic rights, in the fundamental sense that systematic violation of any Human Right Preclude realizing a life of full human dignity"[33].

Alan Grewith viewed Human Rights as "Protective devices, which safeguard the capacities of an individual, a group or the society. Further, he says that they must be respected by every human being and primary justification of governments is that they serve to sever these rights"[34].

Susan Moller Okin defined Human Rights as :

> "Claim to something (whether a freedom a good or a benefit) of crucial importance for human life".

Here Human Rights are viewed, as respect for human being such rights will include right to life, to freedom from arbitrary, coercion and to be respected as human person.[35]

Human Rights, generally defined as the rights which every human being is entitled to enjoy and to have it protected.[36]

The protection of Human Rights Act 1993 defined Human Rights, as:

> "Rights relating to life, liberty, equality and dignity of the individual guaranteed by the Constitution or embodied in the international covenants and enforceable by the courts in India."[37]

Looking at the above definitions, Human Rights in a popular conception requires positive, social, political and judicial action to support the claims said to be rooted in 'humanity' and personal dignity'.[38] If one were to say that or define the meaning of 'Human Right' it would best be said that concept refers to what is considered to be the legitimate entitlement, socially available to the citizens of a state in a given period or state of social development.

Human Rights, therefore, no longer imply merely civil and political liberties for the individual, conceived as some kind of protection or safeguard against state power by the classical as well as contemporary Western Liberal Scholars from *J.S.Mill* to *Rawls*.

The concept of Human Rights today essentially has political, social and economic connections. It is found on the ideal of realization of equality and liberty and most important the social, economic and political justice for all as enshrined in the Constitution of India. If Human Rights are violated under the conditions prescribed for reasons of violation of rights due to neglect, hunger, poverty, the human society can stake its claim for redressal. Thus, the brief through the history of the growth of concept of Human Rights clearly indicates the fact that, this Human Right did not have a bed of roses. From its conceptual level to its empirical realization, one can observe that Human Rights in its conceptual frame is increasingly becomingly institution centred. While in its pragmatic friendly concept. Despite the fact that it has acquired constitutional status in its shortest domination of existence, the paradox is that, it has failed to impress upon those agencies which work parallel with these institutions safeguarding the "individual" and his interest including his rights under the umbrella of criminal justice system of which Police Administration is a prime agency directly incharge of maintenance of law and order in the society. The chapter following this helps us to learn more about Police Administration in particular.

References

1. Kashyap, S.C., *Human Rights and Parliament*, New Delhi, Metropolitan Book Company, 1974.
2. Human Rights, *Question and Answer*, Paris, UNESCO 1981.
3. *Ibid.*
4. *Ibid.*.
5. *Ibid.*.
6. Kaul, J.L., *Human Rights: Issues and Perspectives*, New Delhi, Regency Publications, 1995.
7. Ibid. p. 50
8. *Ibid.*
9. *Ibid.* p. 51
10. *Ibid.* p. 52
11. *Ibid.* p. 52 also Thakur, L.K., *Comparative and International Human Rights*, Delhi, Authors Press, 2000.
12. *Ibid.*
13. *Ibid.*
14. Jermney Waldron, ed., *Theories of Rights*, New York, Oxford University Press, 1994.
15. *Op. cit.*, Kaul, J.L., also Arjun Dev, *et al.*, eds. *Human Rights: A Source Book,* New Delhi, National Council of Educational Research and Training, 1996.
16. Paul, E.F., *et al.*, eds. *Human Rights,* England, Basil Blackwell Publishers, 1984, p.8.
17. *Op. cit.*, Kaul, J.L. (1995).
18. "Human Rights" *The New Encyclopaedia Britannica,* London, 1768.

19. *Ibid.*, Also Vasak Karl, ed., *The International Dimensions of Human Rights*, Paris, UNESCO Press, 1982 also *op. cit.*, *The New Encyclopaedia Britannica.*
20. "Human Rights" *The New Encyclopaedia Britannica*, London, 1768, p. 714 to 715.
21. *Ibid.*, P. 715
22. Chakravarti, R., *Human Rights and the United Nations*, Calcutta, Progressive Publishers, 1958.
23. *Ibid.* p. 50
24. *Ibid.*
25. *Ibid.*
26. *Op. cit.*, *The New Encyclopaedia Britannica* (1768)
27. *Op. cit.*, Chakravarti, R., (1958)
28. *Op. cit.*, Vasak Karl (1982)
29. *Op. cit.,.*, *The New Encyclopaedia Britannica* (1768).
30. *Op. cit.*, Vasak Karl, (1982)
31. *Op. cit.*, Arjun Dev, (1996)
32. *Op. cit.*, *The New Encyclopaedia Britannica*, (1768)
33. Nizami, *et al.* eds., *Human Rights in the Third World Countries*, New Delhi, KIRS Publications, 1994.
34. *Op cit.*, Paul, E.F. (1984)
35. *Ibid,*. P.10.
36. *Op.cit.*, Arjun Dev (1996).
37. Section 2 (d), Protection of Human Rights Act, 1993.
38. *Op. cit.*, Kaul, J.L. (1995), p.3.

3

Police Administration

A Brief Historical Survey

Police have always occupied strategic position in crime prevention. It is not necessary to over emphasise this role of police, since maintenance of law and order from the ancient times has been the primary responsibility of the police. It is in the light of this, that the performance of the police is described as one that "they must repose confidence among the members of the public and that the police as a class is there to protect their lives and properties and safeguard their constitutional rights"[1].

The origin of this 'Bureaucratic Organization of Professional', as termed by Prof. Ram Reddy[2], can be traced back to the time of the early human history, when small roving groups sought the help of the strong and dependable men for watch and ward purposes and to stand guard against the onslaught of animals and the selfish instincts of human beings. These early roving bands with passage of time organized themselves into tribes and settled down in small communities. It is here that they began to evolve rules and regulations for personal and property rights for their own community.

These rules and regulations further developed into customs establishing certain specialized agency with the task of upholding and enforcing these tribal laws. Thus, the earliest law enforcement agency was, perhaps, a kind of police, which functioned at times of peace. There is striking similarity of this kind of evolved police systems even during

Roman period as can be evidenced from *Biblical* times. There were patrols of watchmen which went about the cities during the *Roman* period, it is observed. Indian scriptures also speak of the system of policing. There are references to this in the *Manusmriti* and in the *Ramayana*[3]. Such being the evolution of police in general, this concept today has seen a sea change in its connotations. Today, it is widely accepted view, that the concept and the term *'police'*, derived from the *Greek* words *"polis"*[4] meant *"city"*. The *Greek* tradition defines it "as organized civil force in a town or city meant for preservation of life, property and health of the community and for the enforcement of laws". This, of course, is very much similar to the concept which evolved in the East and West, whereas the *Latin* root of the term police viz. *"Politia"*, literally meaning the condition of a *"polis"* or *"State"*. Its connotation in fact covers under it a class of people who represented the society, while hinting out at a system of administration or regulation.[5] The corresponding *French* word for police is *"policer"* meaning the power of the people, which is rather democratic in its content, highlighting the existence of a civic society where no external regulative force existed to control the social evils, this word in European parlance, meant "a force for the city", which clearly spells out the functioning of this agency despite these facts, it is said that the word "police" was imported from France to England in the early 18th century and that this word carried with it the connotation that was in vogue in France. Further, the term 'police' was officially used first in the famous *police Act of Parliament of England in 1929*[6] it meant efficient paid body of officers. Apart from this, Act became a milestone in the progress of law enforcement. Since then, throughout the world specifically so in case of India and America, this Act of Parliament of England, has executed great influence helping in consolidation of numerous forces of law enforcement agencies that existed in these countries pooling them together into one efficient paid body of officers[7]. As Stuart Bowers,[8] has rightly observed "*Police* force, as regular and recognized part of modern state, is no doubt a modern innovation. As of now, the term 'Police' as described in *Encyclopaedia Britannica* means "the agency that deals with the maintenance of public order and protection of persons and property from the hazards of public accidents and the commission of unlawful acts".[9]

Further, it is interesting to note that the complex structure of modern society and the needs of Governmental Administration have contributed mightily to extend the police activities quite beyond the traditional concept of crime control and pushing the police function into a position that constantly widens its activities, covering uniform patrolling, criminal investigation into various complex contours of crime, traffic regulation, special measures for controlling commercialized vices, dealing with the female offenders, juvenile delinquents, regulation of labour laws and such other types of governmental/semi-governmental/social activities within the recognized domain of state legislation under which the law governs the police.

Police in early India

Police Administration system in India is as old as the Indian civilization itself. As a law enforcing agency ensuring order, the origin of the police in India can be traced back to the earliest period of *Vedic* and *Harappan* civilizations.

> "As noticed in the Harappan seal the figure of a man holding a stick is interpreted by Soviet scholars as portraying *'dhandadhara'* meaning the man holding the *danda* (the stick) which is a symbolic representation of law enforcement agency. This is, perhaps the first pictorial representation of a policeman[10] that can be evidenced when we discuss the origin of police in the early *Vedic* period".

The early *Vedas* eloquently spoke about certain celestial deities too in this regard.[11] *Varuna* is the earliest known prototype of the all powerful 'ubiquitous policeman' who monitored and controlled the lives of the people and ensured their security and general well-being against the insecure living conditions as in the *Vedic* and *Buddhist* times the concept of *danda* as a symbolic representation of Police Administration itself is elaborately dealt in its clear terms, *danda* as "symbol of the coercive power of the state adequately or ruthless"[12] *Kautilya's Arthashastra* treats *danda* as the law of punishment or science of government (*dandniti*).[13] This perhaps is comprehensive definition of a responsible police system that existed during the period of Maurya. *Kautilya,* who put forth an elaborate design of policing system defining several levels of bureaucracy within it, could in fact, be called rightly as the father of the modern Police Administrative System in India.

The concept of *danda* as used by *Kautilya* in his *Arthashastra,* is derived from the root word *'dada'* which means to hold (the primary meaning of *danda* is 'rod or staff". It has been a symbol of command / authority. *Danda* as a term having many connotations also meant an army, a war, a fine judicial sanction besides being an abstract idea symbolising cosmic force. *Danda* in the sense of punishment is found as a necessity of state.[14] The stick is a symbol of the right to punish is *dharma* itself for a king in his function of dispensation of justice. This mention of *danda* is found in the *Arthashastra* where *Kautilya* speaks of physical punishment and also of fines. The early commentators on *Arthashastra* saw *danda* as an important adjunct to the royal office. And in the *Dharmasutras* the king's duty of justly applying *danda* is sought to be supported on the ground that he has the means of ensuring security and welfare of the people.

The concept of *dandniti* on the other hand is associated with the law that regulate human conduct by way of punishment and it conceived *danda* as the essence of government. *Manu* emphasizes the *Arthashastra* ideal of the supreme authority of *danda* by raising it to the level of the foremost political expedient as well as a divine institution. According to him this meaning of *danda* is justified because of its function in ensuring individual security in respect of person and property as well as stability of the social order.[15]

Mahabharat considers the concept of *danda* as the upholder of *dharma* and protector of the people. Metaphorically the king's sceptre was a symbol of his temporal authority which owed its origin to *danda*, i.e., '*stick*' used for punishment and restraining. It was only a matter of time and natural corollary of the concept of coercive factor that *danda* was elevated to a science and ultimately became the art of governance or government itself. Later as a retributive power of state *danda* gradually changed from the power of punishment to the military power. With passage of time it was substituted for '*bala*' or 'armed forces' and became one of the expedients of royalty.[16]

Kautilya's 'Arthashastra', Mahabharata, Manusmriti and *Sukra's Neetisara* have conceived the state as an organic unit which constituted of seven '*angas*'.[17] *Kautilya* and others have graded these elements in order of their relevance to the state and *danda* stands as the sixth element. *Gautamsutra* and *Dharmasutra* of *Sumantu* on the other hand considered *danda* as bodily or pecuniary punishment, which is accorded on the basis of the nature of the offence committed. Hence, *bala*, (force) was substituted for *danda* which came to be known as strength, power or force.[18]

Police as an instrument of *danda* in early societies, with the growth of small states, the king's attribute of *danda* was carried on by the armed forces. Initially security of the people was considered as the preserve of the armed men and consequently the army all along was concerned with the internal security and the maintenance of social order. *Varuna*, the upholder of moral order and who may be considered the prototype of Modern Policemen, has been invariably portrayed as surrounded by a band of reliable all pervasive spies vesting every corner of the earth to cover the evil minded. *Kautilya* in his *Arthashastra* makes a reference of this kind mentioning that, 'king', touches in the nearest approximation the most autocratic police state of medieval and modern times, the only difference being in the objective of the state, i.e., *yogaksema* or well-being of the people. Here *Kautilya's danda* as referred to earlier, represents the coercive power of the state which provides to the king a system of elaborate policing machinery which could be an envy to the developed law and order apparatus of modern government.

Thus, the concept 'Police', had functioned in a rudimentary fashion since *Vedic* period, had its own credits. However, the credit for creating a separate 'police agency', with specific powers of administration, implementation, enforcement of laws, regulations for the prevention of crimes, investigation and prosecution of criminals goes to *Kautilya* because it was at his time that this law. Enforcement agency had developed into a complicated espionage system assigned with more tables such as duties of border control, traffic, control of smuggling, immigration, customs and revenue investigation apart from being an effective vigilance department including political and military intelligence.

The policing system of *Kautilya* was on two distinct lines, i.e., civilian departments entrusted with police powers and a cadre of regular police officers. He conferred police powers on almost all the departments that had public dealings. The cadre of regular police officers comprehended rural and urban branches and functioned on similar lines. Police organization during his times composed of three tier systems constituting *pradeshta* (for rural area), the *nagaraka* (for the urban area) as the officials at the top, who controlled the affairs of the cities and *gramas* keeping watch over the inns, *sarais* and places of entertainment especially to find out the arrival of foreigners and persons with bad character and to detect thieves. The rural and urban *stanikas* in the middle and the urban *gopas* at the bottom and this system functioned efficiently. The subordinate police officers in this hierarchy were referred to as *'Corarajjuka'*, *'Raksinas'* and *'Jivagraha'*.[19] Top police officer, i.e., *Nagarakas* was expected to maintain law and order. They also looked after the administration of jails and made daily check-up of the defence of the city. The duties of the *Nagarakas*, who later came to be known as *'Kotwals'* during the Mauryan period, in fact developed into highly complex system of administration thereby establishing a well organized system of police in a state to maintain all-round welfare of the people.[20] There were court of judges that is *Dharma Sthaniya* and police magistrates known as *Kantaksodhana*. The criminal law was severe and stringent. The defender of the citadel was known as *Kotapala*[21] and protector of city as *Nagarpala*.

Levels of Police Administration in Early India

Police headquarters during this period were located in the capital with representative of police officers in all principal centres including in the important villages. These were stationed in the midst of 800 villages, known as *'Sthaniya'*, 400 villages of this kind was known as *'Dronamukha'*, 200 villages of similar type were known as *'Kharavata'* and 10 villages station was known as *'Sangarahana'*.

Samaharta—A senior officer of the Central Government was variously characterized as the Home Minister under such a set-up. The suppression of crime and the maintenance of law and order as his ultimate responsibility. He would be assisted by a good number of secret agents to report on criminals and anti-social elements. The officer concerned with the maintenance of law and order, investigation of criminal cases and the punishment of criminals also worked under him.[22]

Pradesta—Officials were charged with the executive powers of collection of revenue and police. They normally served in an area covered by 5 to 10 villages having powers to investigate the crimes committed within their jurisdiction and to inflict punishment on those committing the offence.[23]

Kautilya lays down regulations and procedures of investigation for *Pradesta* and *Nagaraka* their staff of the *stanikas* and for *gopas*. Great emphasis was placed on an efficient investigation system in the case of major crimes like theft or murder which comprised of interrogation of the suspect, examination of clues for the stolen property and following the traces of the crime etc. Subordinate police officers at the district and sub-divisional level, including at the village level, viz., *gramabhrataka*, *gramika* and the *gramakuta* are also identified during this period. These officers were invested with executive and police powers within their village jurisdiction. *Jatakas* have similar expression which bears reference to the kind officials referred to above in-charge of police functioning, possession inferior criminal jurisdiction, i.e., maintaining law and order in the village.[24]

Nagaraka incharge of *nagara* or fortified capital had multifarious functions to perform. Almost all facets of town life including the land survey and census operations were looked after by him. Most important duty of his was the maintenance of peace and order in the town. *Nagaraka* was allowed to enforce prohibitory orders during emergency or for a selected period. *Nagaraka* was responsible for the control and arrest of persons who by their demeanour or disguise or for possessing arms on their person gave rise to suspension[25]. As a head of the city police, he was to maintain effective discipline and to ensure that his men do not go haywire and cases of any misdemeanour of policemen in the performance. It was also his responsibility to report to the king on matters of law and order in his jurisdiction.

Purasas—It is the most important category of officers mentioned by *Kautilya*. They have been considered identical with *gudhapurusas*, viz., intelligence officers. They were assigned the duty of watching almost all affairs of the kingdom and making reports secretly to the king.

Vivitadhayaksa— He was to run the administration efficiently, the smallest unit, the village was established which was autonomous. In the intervening areas between the city and the village was *vivitadhayaksa* who exercised police powers. His duties were to protect travellers from thieves, dacoits and wild animals.

Antapala—Kautilya speaks of frontier officers. These officers were incharge of commanding the borders and check posts controlling the entry of men and goods into the country.

Mudradhyaksa— He was to perform police functions and his duty covered issuing passports and visas. None was allowed to enter or leave the state without securing a passport. This job is still being done by authorities all over the world under police control.

Sansthadhyaksa and *Panyadhayksa* were invested with police powers in controlling the markets and traders to ensure that the customers were not cheated by the manipulation of weights and measures or adulteration of goods.

Ganikadhyaksa was an officer of the police department and in cities worked under *Nagaraka* and his duty was to control the prostitution in the state.

Military police was to protect the mobilized troops. Their duty was to look after the army's comfort and security. *Kantaksodhna* courts functioned as police courts for the award of corporal and capital punishment.[26]

Certain changes were made in the organization of police during post-Mauryan period. As a result the role of police also witnessed certain changes. Kusanas who were the link between the Mauryas and Guptas, sought to perfect the administrative system by intermingling the traditions during this period. The terms *Mahadandanayaka* and *Dandanayaka* first time occurred during this period. The contemporary meaning of these terms is interpreted by various scholars as the prefect of police or commissioner of police.

During Gupta poreriod, combined police military and bureaucratic machinery was in existence. The chief police and judicial officers were variously designated as *Dandanayaka, Mahadandanayaka, Sarvadandanayaka* and *Mahasarvadandanayaka*. Apart from these terms other variations in their designations have also been identified. They include *dandadhipa, dandanatha, dandadhinatha, dandapati, dandesa* and *dandesvara*.[27] The judiciary and the police were two most important wings of the state administration during the ancient period too.

The police organization in the ancient period was not very clear. However, the picture becomes somewhat clear during Mauryan and Gupta periods. *Kautilya* and *Megasthenes* have left interesting and detailed pictures of administration of these periods in their work.

Dharmasutra and the *Arthasastra* reveal a fairly well developed criminal justice system with the king at the apex. Since *Arthasastra* not only gives an exhaustive account of administration of ancient Indian society but its validity can be seen in certain respects during the subsequent medieval Indian society. General administration was built around the revenue collection and some continued with slight modifications in the affairs of administration as *Nagarikas* were incharge of administration of city during *Kautilya*'s time in Muslim period and British rule *Nagarikas* were designated as *Kotwals*.

Arthashastra can justly called a treatise on the criminal justice system because it comprises some chapters, which are read like a manual for the police in modern times. Further, in some other chapters detailed instructions are given as to the manner in which an inquest should be held in a case of unnatural death.

The above pattern of criminal justice system continued for five to six hundred years without any major changes. The basic principles of criminal jurisprudence were as follows: (a) the fountain head of justice was the king, who was to be guided by the rules of justice as laid down by the *dharmasastras*; (b) the interpretations of such rules or edicts were guided by customs, traditions and usages of the time; (c) the king or any other functionary designated to discharge the duty of judge was assisted by councils; (d) offences were defined in fairly clear terms and so were punishments; and (e) rules of procedures for conducting the trial were also laid down in meticulous detail. This system of policing continued until 12th century. And to have brief glance at medieval period from 12th to 18th century is worthwhile to switch over to the Muslim period.

Policing in the Medieval Period

With the Muslim incursions on the enforcement of the Muhammadan Law imported from Arabia had not effected a chapter of the traditional Hindu Police system/ organization. Not only that the Muslim rulers were only conversant with the Islamic Law, but also it was their religious duty to follow it. However, neither the Hindu states nor the Muslim states, which were either military or monarchy took serious note of, since it depended on their absolute authority. This system of centralized administration can be traced back to the period of Prophet where institution of police and other administrative organs of Muslim politics were under sources of one law, viz., "*Quran*, i.e., *Law*". As they considered state is only an instrument to serve the creed in the attainment of its objectives or the ideal of Islam as revalued to it through the medium of Prophet Muhammad.

During Mughals rule in India :

> "The police were called *asas* in the beginning and later were called as *shurtah*. They were subordinate to the *quid* and their main function included executing the decrees of the *quid* to bring criminals before him for trial. The duties of

the head of the police, the *Sabib-i- Shurtah* (Police Officer) were performed by an officer known as *Kotwal*. *Kotwal* is a word of Hindu origin, which was adopted by Turks.[28]

It was usual practice of Muslim rulers to establish *thanas* or *chowkies* in different strategic areas for maintenance of internal order in the conquered territory. These *thanas* were more in the nature of military command posts. Mughals being preoccupied with conquest and collection of revenue they were marginally involved in the detailed administration of the countryside. Therefore, maintenance of law and order and administration of justice by and large were left in the hands of the zamindars. Many of them among zamindars in this process also became *faujdars* in the empire. This change of office and status was more formal than real and they continued to function as 'contractors of general administration maintaining a paramilitary police to look after law and order situation under their jurisdictions.[29]

During Akbar's regime elaborate police system was functioning and the police responsibilities were controlled by *Subedars, Faujdars, Kotwal* and *Darogas*. Apart from these higher authorities, Mughals had maintained an expensive system of espionage and informers known as *Waquinavis, Sawanih Nigars, Khufia Navis* and *Harkarahs* who disseminated intelligence information to the *Darogas* orally or in writing.[30]

Kotwal is an urban officer, being the chief of the city police still in India, the down town police station is popularly known as *Kotwal* though his English nomenclature is the Inspector of Police.[31] He supervises the police functions in the city and its suburbs ; and his duties and responsibilities were the basic police functions such as crime prevention, investigation, prosecution and control by following various strategies and adopting measures commonly pursued by urban police departments today.

Thanedar— These were the "men in command of outposts or smaller areas within a *Faujdar* and were appointed by the *Faujdar*. He was working as managerial link in the chain of command of the executive officers who were responsible for maintaining law and order and control crime. *Thanedars* were incharge of police units stationed at various places for guarding communications and maintaining peace. And such units were like small islands in the midst of a vast countryside studded with villages and hamlets. Duties of *Thanedars* seemed to be similar to those of *Faujdars* except in a limited geographical area. *Thanedars* were used to work under the instructions given by *Faujdars*. Even today police stations is designated in local vernacular as "*thana*' in whole of North India and Sub-Inspector of Police is called a "*Thanedar*' as *Daroga*. The institution has defied ups and downs of history.[32]

An important contribution of Mughals is their strong central administrative system and an all India political authority and with it a unity and a single loyalty of Police in India was long modelled after the Mughal fashion. The *Kotwal* was a terror, the evil doers, and sometimes to the innocent as well. The methods of detection of crime continued to be based on the principle that confession, however, obtained is the best solvent of all troubles. Some of the records maintained can trace their origins to the instructions issued by the Mughal emperors. Not only this all the twenty Indian *Subas* of the Mughal empire were governed by means of exactly the same administrative machinery with exactly the same procedure and official titles. Moreover, the significant features could be recounted as :

(a) Almost all the terms concerning the court nomenclatures are the same as those of the Mughal period;
(b) Judicial district administration as well as provincial administration remains almost the same; and
(c) Supreme Court and High Court possess the same

hierarchy as was available during the British days and inherit the powers of "*Sadar Divani Adalat*".

It is often said that the British did not even change the boundaries the geographical administrative divisions fixed by the Mughals.

In police terminology *Daroga, Kotwal, Sipahi* and *Dewan* remained unchanged. Persian continued to be the court language along with English during the time of the British. The Court etiquette, form and formalities of procedure, customs, practices, rituals and ranks remained mostly Mughal and adapted to overall British hierarchy. No wonder that the administrative transition was smooth and continuous. And till the late early sixties, most of the police and court work at lower level was done which was under Mughals. Most of the police during Mughal and then under the British were predominantly Muslim, at the subordinate level. The communal complexion and introduction of martial races into police was an afterthought of the British administration in the beginning of the 19th century when they made "*Divide and Rule*" as an unwritten, but well understood policy of the British imperialism in India.[33]

Police in the British Period

The story of the colonial police begins in Ireland. The colonial model is based on the *Royal Irish Constabulary*. It originated in 1836 and it received its prefix Royal in 1867 and existed till 1922.[34]

Before "Police" system was adopted in India, based on the *Royal Irish Constabulary (RIC)* model, the period was spent as an experiment. Sir Charles Jeffries in his writings observes a three-step development of 'colonial police', in India. In his own words, the first stage was identified as "the phase of improvisation", in which the original policing systems of the country were adopted and amended to suit the conditions of the 19th century. The second style viz., semi-military was introduced in the later part of the 19th and the early part of the 20th century. While the third stage was that of the conversion of this colonial police into civil police forces on the lines that was familiar to Great Britain. The chief characteristics of this system was its central control, rank order stratification, with top officered by governing elite, and lowest and middle ranks, with a carefully graded native mix. According to *Charles Napier*, who (later became the Governor of the Sindh in 1843), this system which was based on two principles (a) that the police must be completely separated from the military, and (b) that they must be an entirely independent body established to assist the collectors in discharging their responsibility for law and order, but under their own officers.[35] In fact, based on this model with slight modification to suit native requirement the police in British India consisted of three classes (1) Mounted Police, (2) Rural Police, and (3) City Police.[36]

Cornwallis introduced the *Daroga* system and made village watchmen responsible to *daroga*. A *daroga* was in-charge of a *thana*, a part of the district, and was answerable to the Judge as well as to the District Magistrate to whom they must deliver a criminal within twenty four hours of arrest. They did not have trained constables.

During this period when Britishers while shaping the East India Company and subsequently as the representations of the Crown, improved the police organization and improved on it measure by measure. In this drawn out effort, the following may rightly be regarded as the important landmarks :

> Introduction of Irish constabulary model in Sindh in 1843. The extension of the above system to the Bombay Police with the appointment of a Superintendent of Police in every district. The appointment of a Police Commission (1860) which recommended the abolition of the Military Police and

> the constitution of a single homogeneous civil force. The promulgation of the Police Act (1861) embodying the above recommendation. The formation of another Police Commission (1902) which recommended major structural changes at all the levels and which hold good even now and the setting up of the Islington (1912) and Lee Commission (1924) whose recommendations led to substantial Indianization of senior ranks in the forces.[37]

However, the uprising of 1857 Mutiny against the British brought the administration altogether to a new focus. Company rule came to an end and the British Crown assumed direct responsibility. A Police Commission was appointed in 1859. On the basis of the Commission's report, a bill was moved in British Parliament and Police Act V came into existence in 1861. Simultaneously, the Code of Criminal Procedure was put into effect. The Police Act of 1861 laid down an elaborate structure of police organization which remains in force till today in India. In every province the police was headed by an Inspector General who was assisted by a Deputy Inspector General. The district police was headed by Superintendent of Police assisted by an Assistant and Deputy Superintendent of Police. The Deputy Superintendent of Police was subordinate to Deputy Inspector General of Police. He was also put under the general control of the District Magistrate police stations or *thanas* and were run by Inspector and Sub-Inspector who were locally called *darogas* or *thanedars*. There were trained constables and head constables under the Sub-Inspectors. Watchmen continued to be responsible to the *darogas*— the officer incharge of a police station.

The Police Act V of 1861 introduced a uniform system of police in British India. It brought organizational changes in police, but failed to change its nature and mode of functioning. The District Magistrate handed over to the Superintendent of

Police some of his old functions. But he remained responsible for everything that happened in his district and yet acquired a colleague who not a subordinate to him in position.[38]

The Indian Police Commission of 1902-03 is a significant landmark in police history. The commission brought some organizational changes envisaging establishment of a criminal investigation department, railway police, enhancement of pay and the provision of armed reserve for at district headquarters. There have been no significant changes in the police cadre or its operational activities thereafter. The same system was left by the British when India became independent.

Police in Post-Imperial Period

The post-independent era starts after 1947. The Constitution of India came into operation on January 26, 1950. Since then additions in police organization at national level with no change in its structures have been taking place. The Central Bureau of Investigation was created in 1963, the Central Reserve Police in 1947, Border Security Force in 1965 and the Central Industrial Security Force in 1964. Except CBI others are para-military, but police organizations. Again, except CBI, others have no investigative or detective functions and, therefore, no public service orientation. They help local police units in emergency situations and are pressed into service for arrangement and other functions which cannot solely be handled by civil police. Later achievement in some of the States was that the office of Superintendent of Police was brought at par with the District Magistrate; and Police Commission system was embraced by the bigger cities. More scientific and technological services were upgraded.[39]

Constitutional Basis

The Constitution of India stipulates that for all legal and

constitutional purposes, the police continue to be a state subject and all policies, plans and procedures pertaining to the administration of security, crime and order fall within the jurisdiction of State governments, subject to certain safeguards and uniformities provided in the Union and Concurrent Lists.

According to the Indian Constitution 'police' is a State subject and the State government has complete control over the State police. The State Legislature has no power to make organizational changes in police. All India Service is the exclusive preserve of Central Government and police budgets are state responsibility. Central Government aids the State for modernization or to increase training facilities, but that is a discretion rather than an obligation. Indian Constitution is said to be federal in form and unitary in spirit, the same can be said about the Indian police. The centralized control of All India Service personnel known as IPS who occupy managerial positions constitute a powerful tool in the hands of the Central Government to manipulate the State police system, through indirect or direct means. It mostly depends on Centre-State relationship and on how powerful the Central Government is. And following are the Constitutional Provisions which permit Central Government to act upon :

(1) The Union Government to condition the framework and working of the Police Administration in the States :
(2) The Union Government to influence policy formulations and their implementation as evolved by Police Administration in the States;
(3) The Union Government to interfere in the functional operations undertaken by the State Police Forces;
(4) The Union Government (if it so desires) to gradually nibble the concept of State autonomy in areas that vitally relate to police tasks; and
(5) The Union Government to override and take over the

State Police Administration as a last resort during emergencies.[40]

The Police Act of 1861 which is still in operation lays down the pattern of organization throughout India both structurally and operationally. It governs most of the internal and external aspects of organizational behaviours of policing. The other substantive acts, central acts, which State Government has no power to legislate, but which govern the legal procedures and Indian Evidence Act. Apart from these there are either Central Acts which extend or restrict or regulate the police powers in the States. In case of conflict between State and Central Legislation, it is the Central Act which would prevail. Realistically, except administrative control, there is very little power remains that State Government can do to resist an interfering powerful Centre. The anomaly of police administration in State and Centre relationship is hardly obvious, much is hidden beneath the surface. Police could be a unifying force, as well as a disrupting factor, depending on the political motives of those who rule.

At the institutional level, the police have constitutional limitations and responsibilities. It cannot violate the fundamental rights enumerated in the Constitution of India. Its power of arrest are limited. It has to observe certain formalities. It has to produce an arrested person before a Magistrate within 24 hours of arrest. It has to observe decency and religious moralities in accordance with the law. The administrative style and the bureaucratic functioning of the new Indian Republic was mere 'carry over' from the past, because once the machinery was adopted as a constitutional mandate, the rest flowed automatically through it, without any change or commitment.

In brief, speaking about the growth and development of Police in India. Historically, police in ancient Hindu India was used as a fort of administrative system which was to be reinforced by State militia or an armed force commanded by the ruling satrap. In fact, it seems that Hindus were more apprehensive of committing social or temporal violations because of unavoidable punishment, invariably sustained due to moral, spiritual and religious beliefs. Life of Hindu was ritually regulated and socially disciplined and was based on an archaic cultural system. Successive waves of foreign invasions and wanton destruction of Muslim crusaders left traces of Hindu administrative system. During Muslim rule, they institutionalized their own criminal justice system and introduced their own language. British, the last to come, did the same by supplanting the western system by replacing existing Muslim institutions and language by their own. Though the British kept the police system, adjusted to the needs of the Empire, but to cope with the administrative local challenges, they shaped police in India on Irish Constabulary model.

The Police Act of 1861 laid down the structures of style of Police in India. Police of today continued to be based on the Police Act 1861 with timely modifications, alterations and expansions but with no substantial structural changes, functional and legal changes were rarely made, but administrative and operational efficiency of police was maintained by making suitable organizational adjustments. In the next chapter an attempt is made to assess and analyze the existing relationship between the two agencies, viz., Human Rights and Police Administration, keeping the context of this study.

References

1. Kapoor, H.L., *Police Administration,* New Delhi, Ess Ess Publications, 1989.
2. Reddy, R., ed. *Developing Society and Police,* Hyderabad, Osmania University, 1972.
3. In *Ramayana* Police considered as the regulative mechanism for peace and order. Ancient law giver *Manu* refers to the police function prevalent in his times for the prevention and detection

of crime. Chatterji, S.K., The Police in Ancient India vide *The Indian Police Journal*, Centenary Issue, Delhi, 1961, p. 11.
4. *'Police' Encyclopaedia Britannica*, Chicago, 1768.
5. *Chambers Twentieth Century Dictionary*. The term has been defined as "the system of regulation for the preservation of order and enforcement of law for the internal government of a state.
6. Laurie Peter, *Scotland Yard*, London, The Bodley Head Ltd., 1970.
7. Coatman, J., *Police*, London, Macmillan, 1966.
8. Bowers, S., *The Police and Civil Liberties*, London, CUP, 1966.
9. Op. cit., *Encylopaedia Britannica*, p. 158.
10. Ghosh, S.K., *et al.*, eds. Encyclopedia of Police in India, New Delhi, Ashish Publishing House, 1993.
11. Crimes and Punishment were known to Ancient India and Vedic Samhitas elaborately illustrate the insecured living conditions of the prevedic community who constantly beseeched to protect them. *Op. cit.*, Reddy Ram, 1972.
12. Ghosh, S.K., *et al.*, eds. *Encyclopedia of Police in India*, New Delhi, Ashish Publishing House, 1993.
13. Shamasastry, R., *Kautilya's Arthasastra*, Mysore, Mysore Printing and Publishing House, 1915.
14. Mishra, K.K., *Police Administration in Ancient India*, Delhi, Mittal Publications, 1987.
15. *Ibid.*, p. 11.
16. *Op. cit.*, Ghosh, S.K. (1993).
17. Viz., King, *Amatya, Kosa, Danda, Mitra, Janapada* and *Pura*.
18. *Op. cit.*, Ghosh, S.K. (1993).
19. *Ibid.*
20. *Op. cit.*, Giriraj, P.17.
21. The present words *Kotwal* and *Kotwali* have been drafted from *Kotpala* of ancient times.
22. *Op. cit.*, Ghosh, S.K., (1993).
23. Dikshitar, *Mauryan Polity*, Madras, Madras University Press, 1951.
24. *Op. cit.*, Ghosh, S.K. (1993).
25. Gautam, D.N., *Police in India: A Study in Fundamentals*, New Delhi, Mittal Publications, 1993.
26. *Op. cit.*, Giriraj, (1993).

27. *Op. cit*. Ghosh, S.K., (1993) P.12
28. Singh, M.P., *Police Problems and Dilemmas in India*, New Delhi, Mittal Publications, 1989, p. 21.
29. *Op. cit.*, Ghosh, S.K. (1993).
30. *Op. cit.*, Singh, M.P. (1989).
31. *Op. cit.*,Ghosh, S.K. (1993).
32. Sarkar, J. *Mughal Administration*, Delhi, Orient Longman, 1972.
33. *Op. cit.*, Singh, M.P. (1989).
34. *Ibid.*, p. 35.
35. *Ibid.*
36. (1) *Mounted Police*: Were the best paid and of superior status. Their duties were partly protective, providing guard and patrol and partly detective; (2) *Rural Police*: Consisted only of infantry and were confined to providing guards for treasuries, gools or headquarters, escorts for prisoners and support for other branches where necessary; and (3) *City Police*: Further were of two classes *mujjeebs* who acted as watchmen, guards and patrols and trackers were distributed throughout the province, one or more at each large *thana*. But all the police of the province had under the command of a captain of police, directly responsible to Chief Commissioner and under him each district had a European Lieutenant of Police and an Adjutant, both army officers. Griffiths : *To Guard my people: History of Indian Police*, London, Ernest and Baru, 1971.
37. Gupta, Anandswarup, *The Police in British India 1861-47*, New Delhi, Concept Publishing Company Pvt. Ltd., 1979.
38. Venugopal Rao, S., ed., *Perspectives in Criminology*, IIA Shimla IIAS, Vikas Publishers Pvt. Ltd., 1988.
39. *Ibid.*
40. *Ibid.*

4

Human Rights and Police Administration

Enemies or Friends ?

In this chapter an analysis of the concept of Human Rights and Police Administration has been detailed facilitating an insight into these important instruments in charge of Protection of Rights. Further, in this chapter an attempt is made to find an interlink between these two operating systems at a theoretical plane, thus trying to prepare a platform on which the chapter following this is worked out.

Human Rights and Police Administration as we see them today, are noticeably different in their functioning. In the Indian context this is rather more apparent given to the familiarity of Police Administration as against the recent entry of Human Rights. In other words, the current status of these in view, of their familiarity to Indian society clearly places Police Administration as an agency in charge of law and order, crime investigation, etc. Thus, identifying it more as an extension or a limb of the state which falls under criminal justice system, much closer to Lenin's argument in his work on *State and Revolution*, while Human Rights is seen more as an agency in charge of protection of Rights of the People because of its much published expressions as a champion and saviour of rights despite the fact that the state itself is a promoter to a full extent and benefactor to a great extent. Further, the complexity of the concept, their institutional structure, their operational area and the agencies involved in operationalising Human Rights activism, having in its composition with people drawn from judiciary thus have given Human Rights an edge over Police Administration which is more an administrative appointment as against that of Human Right which has political nominations. Further, the Human Rights organization headed by retired judge also seem to give them the sanctity desired while placing them above police as an agency scrutinizing and surveillance over the police as an activity. Much to the bitter taste of Police Administration the Human Rights activism is also spreading among NGO's thus increasingly making it difficult for the agencies of state with coercive power to perform. This, however, is not seen in good taste by police and hence this attempt at theorising the relationship between Human Rights and Police Administration.

Between Human Rights and Police Administration there are a large number of areas and wide ranging issues which in fact are overlapping. Observing such areas, their relationship is often interpreted as being interdependent and critical. Police Administration being at the bottom level in the echelons of criminal justice system is rather accessible to positive and negative challenges. While, the Human Right being a larger canvas with universal concern pre-empts respect from amongst the police. This being their relationship at the primary level, interaction between them no doubt presupposes checks and balances while their opposing claims for superiority continues. The word 'Police', as in vogue in India today is indicative of a body of persons selected on the basis of a written and physical examination and who are engaged in the task of prevention and detention of crime and enforcement of laws. It is one of the agencies of stated by means of which state seeks to meet its obligation to protect the Fundamental Human Rights.[1] Any violation of this code of policing, therefore, only causes greater threat to this agency by those specialized bodies of state and NGO's which are constantly monitoring and supervising the activities of this agency. Hence, Police Administration in India is also seen as protector of those rights as enshrined in the Constitution while Human Right, is seen in Indian context as a champion and protector of rights striving to establish legal procedures in common land as constitutional principle that can be evoked whenever, there is an outrage of integrity or personal dignity or violation of rights of human beings. This being the context, within which these two concepts are operating, covering and controlling a wide range of human activity, invariably derives their strength from the basic law and supreme document of the land that is the Constitution.

The Preamble of the Constitution is the key to learn about the objectives and intentions of the Constitution. This being

Graph 4.1 : Have you heard of Human Rights?

	Category I	*Cetegory II*	*Cetegory III*
1	2.52	8.40%	74.79%
2	0.00%	0.00%	7.56%
3	0.00%	0.84.%	5.88%

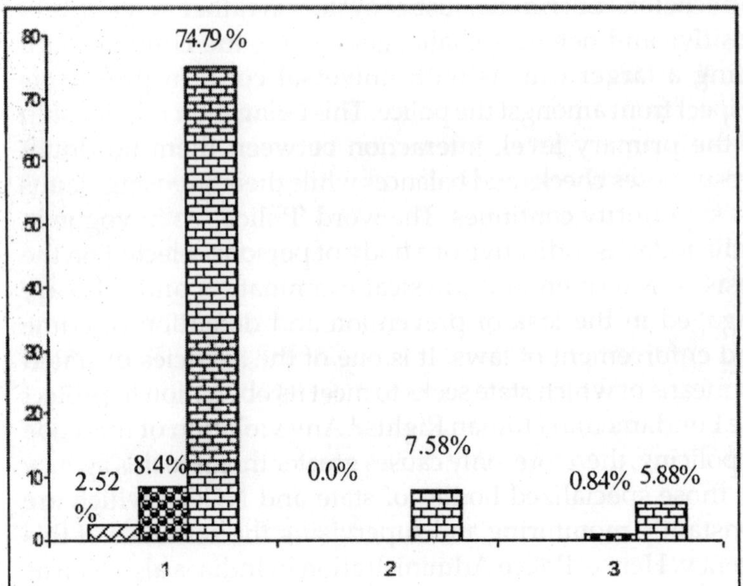

fundamental to the rights enshrined in the Constitution it has provided adequate provisions for its fulfilment under its various articles such as the fundamental rights which have a prime place in the Indian Constitution as in case of the other Democratic Constitutions around the world. Having came into existence in the post-World War era and also being basic document and the law of the land these provisions in the Indian Constitution not only provides to its citizens the positive and negative rights but also speaks of their duties too. While this is a positive contribution to the growth of an individual citizen, nothing under the Constitution prevents the law enforcing agencies to act upon those who misuse or abuse their rights in the society. However, as against this provision of the Constitution, often in the interest of the unity of the nation and integrity of the state, the state itself has reserved the emergency powers that empower them to withdraw all the provisions of rights under its own Constitution. In order to weaken these provisions and strengthen the sovereign power in a democratic state, judiciary and agencies having judicial jurisdiction operate to strengthen the inalienable rights of human beings in a society. Thus, the Constitution of India acts both as a provider and facilitator of Rights. Hence the description of fundamental rights as the very foundation and cornerstone of the democratic way of life. These rights under Indian Constitution have been guaranteed under seven broad categories falling between article 14 to article 32[3] one can clearly see the component of Human Rights enshrined in the equal terms with the Universal Declaration of Human Rights (1948). A comparative table (see Appendix VI)[4] provides an insight into this. Adding on to this our Constitution also has provided to a citizen the right to approach the highest court in the land the Supreme Court directly for any violation of these guaranteed (fundamental) rights within the framework of the provisions of the Constitution subjected to professional and preceding interpretations.[5]

Law and order in fact being the essential prerequisite of civilized society thus falls within the purview of Police Administration. Which in India is designed and designated as an agency incharge maintaining law and order with coercive power sanctioned with restrictions on its use built into the system. While concentrating on their effort at realizing these provisions of providing and facilitating rights enshrined in the Constitution as an immediate goal these agencies also act as protectors of these rights from any misuse or abuse within or from outside the society.

The values of freedom and equality benefiting the dignity of the human individuals thus are made more complete and substantive in India, by adding on to these rights the ideals of economic and social justice in the Constitution which so eloquently is proclaimed in the preamble, elaborated in the fundamental rights and in the directive principles. These objectives of the Constitution, therefore, helps the subsequent governments in power to work on policy alternatives to establish an egalitarian society, free from exploitation of man, guaranteeing liberties not to a few but to all and bringing real freedom to the masses in a positive sense. These extensive provisions dealt at length in the Indian Constitution no doubt in all good sense reflects upon the good intentions of framers of Indian Constitution as their anxious concern to see that the society as a whole and every member of the society within it should get fullest opportunity to participate in the day-to-day affairs of governance having an atmosphere full of liberties and the freedoms made available for the fullest blossoming of one's personality.

Having set out in the Preamble these basic objectives as the national endeavour the fundamental social political ends to be sought by independent India has been elaborated in the ideals of justice, liberty and equality as expressed in the Part III of the Constitution. Having established this relationship between Human Rights and Indian Constitution as also shown in the comparative table (refer Appendix. VI). It would be appropriate to understand the Human Rights in its historical context first and then move further Human Rights being basically a concept enrolling the human being himself, recognizes the dignity of the individual. It starts with the presumption that man is born free and is, therefore, entitled to all the rights and freedoms that exists in his own surrounding without distinction of race, colour, sex, language, religion or other difference of origin. It postulates that everyone has the right of life, liberty and security. In order to ensure that all the citizens avail of these rights equally, certain specific rights are deduced from this for applicability in day-to-day life with the help of certain organizational structures. A specific right deduced from this is the recognition of the concept of 'Rule of law' and the adoption of 'Due Process' and 'Fair Trial' backed by the right to effective remedy. Any breach of these norms, therefore, is to be remedied, which is also provided in the laws of the lands and particularly in the Constitution in the shape of many writs[6] the Constitution being the fundamental law of the land by virtue of its position becomes an obligation on the part to those who live in the land and for those who govern it in equal terms. While citizens who are governed by it enjoy it, as a matter of right those will have to carefully utilize it since the onus of its utility lies in their hands and the delicacy with which they put it into practice. Further, the Constitution, which provides these rights at the same time, has created agencies for protection of these ideals in their practice. Thus, police involving in the process of protection of rights of citizens being one such creation of their Constitution, while ensuring these fundamental rights to their citizens without any hindrance from vested interest also embarks upon certain positive and negative actions to enrich the enjoyment of rights but certainly not violating Human Rights in dealing with public. It is, therefore, a cause for concern for the society and the academics in particular as to see how the performance of these two organizations are to be seen. Police on one court argue which of course is in defence of their performance and their established role as police. Along with this thereby ensuring the protection of Human Rights, does not alone, however, put an end to their efforts at establishing social order in a given society. They, in fact, put forth their case stating that they have two other vital roles to play apart from mere maintenance of law and order, they include :

(a) A Police force has duty under the law to bring law breakers and offenders to book. In other words, to use their initiative where so empowered by law to stop or prevent Human Rights violations occurring in society, try those who are identified as anti-social elements and criminals, etc.
(b) To examine their own methods of actions and behaviour at the time of apprehending a criminal and establishing his interests and alleged activities within the framework of the law established for the purpose in particular and law of the land in general.

Thereby to that protectors of Human Rights are not its major violators.[7] Thus involving the police in the process of protection of these rights of citizens. Since, much of the content of Human Rights as agreed to by nations under UN Charter is seen in the matrix of Fundamental Rights under the Constitution of India. Police Administration incharge of Protection of Rights and maintenance of law and order to facilitate the civil societies to perform, does not wish to see Human Rights as anything above than what is enshrined in the Constitution while discharging their duties. However, the bone of contention between Human Rights and Police Administration is very much hidden in this area of working of police and agencies that are incharge of Human Rights protection. While police believes in the fact that it is performing in handling 'criminal' for violation of the fundamental law of the land, the Human Right activism through its various forms believes in fighting for a fair trial for the 'criminal alleged', facilitating him to have his rights protected by indulging and throwing checks at police functioning. This, therefore, has given way to a feeling among police that Human Right agencies are a nuisance in their functioning.

Police Administration is in fact a sub-system of the larger system, viz., the criminal justice system. It constantly acts as a watchdog of rights including Human Rights in India. Therefore, in order to understand the theoretical perspective of Human Rights in relation to Police Administration it is important to take a look at the larger part of this criminal justice system which envelopes Police Administration. Before we embark upon the Police Administration with focused attention to understand its relationship *vis-à-vis* Human Rights, this familiarity with criminal justice system will help us to appreciate the subject matter better. Conceptually, the criminal justice system may be defined as giving the criminal his due with probable difference to crime in the society. Obviously, its objective is to humanize the process of adjudication, control, arbitrariness and guaranteeing equal status to all citizens as well as translating the motion of liberty in reality.[8] It promotes a sense of security amongst the members of a given society and ensures the rights of victims and the accused. It motivates the public to participate in the process of prevention of crime, facilitating as overall growth of human personality without fear or favour. In other words, it is a mechanism to protect social values which it procedurally ensures for reasons of fair play and justice to all, thereby, supporting to strengthening the philosophy of equality, fairness, due process and functioning as per rule of law. Thus, criminal justice system can be utilized as a barometer of civilization, an indicator of the operational patterns of 'due process 'model' against the 'enforcement model', of the law enforcing agencies that are within a society.

The criminal justice system has before it, the individual

whose protection from the whole system of governance including legislative, executive and the adjudicative agencies of the state itself as its main goal, despite being intricately. related to them. Police Administration being a limb of the executive, judiciary and the adjudicating activity derives its energy from legislative systems. In fact, of all the sub-systems operating under the political system Police Administration is the most significant sub-system, especially within the broad frame of the criminal justice systems as it exists today. Therefore, their role and functions are dealt at length in the pages to follow, keeping view its Constitutional status and the citizen's rights which in its form as Human Right is taken to be the boon of contention here, under this study. Life, Liberty and Property have traditionally been considered as natural rights of the mankind. The foremost duty of the state, therefore, has been to ensure security of its citizens and to provide an atmosphere of safety to support their overall development. Further the state is also expected to protect them from the powerful and dominant sections of the society. People, therefore, have permitted the state to evolve police organization under this garb and to which the state takes care of its obligation. Various Constitutional provisions as enumerated below which are the primary safeguards in this direction. They include :

(a) Right to freedom from unwanted arrest;
(b) Right to reasonable investigation, interrogation, search, seizure, etc.,
(c) Right to legal defence.,
(d) Right to fair pre-trial detention; and
(e) Right to an open (public) and speedy trial.

In the Criminal Justice Administration, police by their restrictive and coercive authority effects arrests, interrogation, search, seizure, detain people prior to trial and all these actions affect individual liberty. Further, these actions when initiated arbitrarily, individuals dignity will be in jeopardy. To prevent this the following provisions incorporated under our Constitution (Diagram 4.1).[9]

DIAGRAM- 4.1

PROVISIONS SPECIFIED IN THE CONSTITUTION

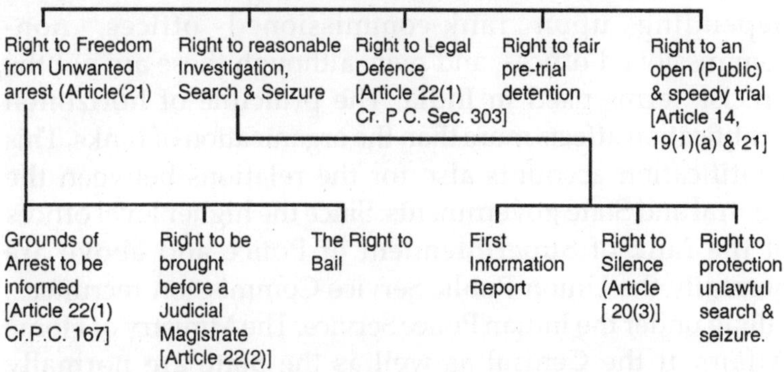

Thus police being an agency of the state has been primarily entrusted with the task of preventive activity and have the duty of maintaining law and order. Prevention of the commissioning of crime and if it has been committed, apprehending the culprit and producing him before the court of law within a stipulated time to get him convicted or punished for the crime committed, however, the functions the police perform today, although it has undergone a considerable change in its style of functioning particularly in a democratic polity.[10]

This argument of the police has in it the strength to support the fact that the police have an indirect obligation to protect and safeguard the constitutional guarantees extended to the citizens. Police organization and its functions since its inception has always played an important role in the prevention of crime. It was and no doubt still is a symbol for many citizens of society, of an imposer and enforcer of laws. The police represent the law in action, the public often sees the organization as the arm of the executive and judicial authorities. In fact, police is the preliminary agency in administration of criminal justice systems in India. It is considered to be first line of defence against crime. In India police has borrowed its structural cadre base, discipline and rigidity from military. Our police system is horizontally stratified like military forces, they are organized into cadres depending upon rank-commissioned offices, non-commissioned offices, and men, although these are not the precise terms used in India. The principle of horizontal stratification affects more than the organization of ranks. This stratification accounts also for the relations between the Central and State governments. Since the higher level offices of the rank of Superintendent of Police and above are normally the Union Public Service Commission recruitees, falling under the Indian Police Service. The Ministry of Home Affairs at the Central as well as the State are normally incharge of Police. These Indian Services Officer Cadre (IPS) which is recruited, organized, trained and disciplined according to national legislation are intermixed with State recruits selected by the State Public Service Commissions whereby a chain relation is established between the Centre and the State. Further in matters of Armed Reserve and Civil Police there exists a vertical divisions. In India, Police is a multi-levelled centralized bureaucracy and, therefore, its territorial as well as functional jurisdiction could be felt at national, provincial, and local level at the same time. But the command structure has hardly changed except that most of the States in India have upgraded the rank of Inspector General to that of the Director General of Police to reduce the bottleneck at the top. Similar upgrading of Senior Police Officers to the rank of Inspector General of Police overseeing Administration, crimes, specialized services followed. The rank structure carries with it the powers, privileges, responsibility and accountability of each rank.

In India police performs mainly the following functions;

- Maintenance of Law and Order: this includes

prevention of criminal activities; to deal with explosive situations created by political mobilization, control of political demonstrations and public meetings organized by political parties; to deal with *'ghearoes'* and *'dharnas'* and student indiscipline. Control of vehicular traffic and to deal with traffic violations and offences, etc.

- Investigations into the offences already committed, arresting the culprit and bringing him before the judiciary with witnesses and evidences collected during investigation.
- The third tasks is implementation of social legislation[11] to identify criminal offenders and criminal activities and wherever appropriate to apprehend offenders and participate in subsequent court proceedings.
- To reduce the opportunities for the commission of some crimes through preventive control and other measures.
- To aid individuals who are in danger of physical harm.
- To protect constitutional guarantees.
- To facilitate the movement of people and vehicles.
- To identify problems which are potentially serious for law enforcement or government problems.
- To create a sense of feeling of security among the communities.
- To promote and preserve civil order and to provide other services on an emergency basis.[12]

Constitutional Position of Police in India

Police is a state subject under the Constitution of India. This falls under the Seventh Schedule under Article 246. The second entry in this State List deals with Police.[13]

Apart from this, Articles 309, 310 and 311 govern the service conditions of Police officers like any

> other government official, but the fundamental rights of police personnel are on different levels. Police officers occupy a peculiar position under the Constitution. They are treated as holders of civil posts within the meaning of Article 311 while at the same time they are brought under disciplinary rules like Defence Forces Personnel.

A Police officer is governed not only by the Police Regulations framed under the Police Act, but also by the rules made under Section 241 of the Government of India Act, in sofar as they are not repealed or not inconsistent with the Constitution. Government has the option to proceed against a Police Officer under any of these rules, provided that there is no substantial difference to the prejudice of the delinquent officer between the procedures under the two sets of rules.

The awful amount of power with the government at the centre as opposed to the State government which maintains the Police, indicates how anomalous, ambiguous and tenuous the situation would be for members of the police force who had to serve competing interests of politicians not only at two different levels (State and Federal) but at various polarities co-exists to cater the needs of ruling individuals. However, despite of all these, the constitutional status of police provides continuity for them right from the colonial period. The Constitution has neither changed the organizational form nor the police powers or the functional formulations, style and modalities of role models. Virtually, nothing has been changed and has left everything that was in practice or in philosophy; and Police, public and politicians were left alone to adjust themselves to the changed realities of the times. Despite these safeguards, one can trace the lack of effective Constitutional safeguard to police officials which in fact have reduced them to the level of servility and humility. A new Police Act is yet to be drafted to redefine the role of Police under the change circumstances. Under the existing Police Act, the Police are working as a colonial instrument. The Constitution of India neither purified nor sanctified the colonial police model but left it to get congealed. The apparatus was made pliable by politicians by applying unmindful of any long term or short term consequences.[14] The current structure of Police was organized in 1950 when the Constitution of India came into operation.[15] The most important Ministry that runs internal administration of Police Administration is known as Ministry of Home Affairs. The Ministry of Home Affairs consists of a Secretariat, and eleven subordinate officers. The Ministry has exclusive direct control over the offices like Central Intelligence Bureau, Central Bureau of Investigations, Central Reserve Police, Central Vigilance Commission, etc.[16]

In spite of all these differences Police department at the State and National levels have identical pattern of organizational structure, mode of functioning, the style and problems. Structurally, State Police in India is a four entry-level system; Constable level, Sub-Inspector level, Assistant Superintendent level and Deputy Superintendent level. This being the organizational structure of Police in India and in Karnataka (See Diagram 4.2) are currently performing at minimum satisfactory level. On the other hand Human Rights Commission is formulated on the following lines.

DIAGRAM NO. - 4.2

Indian Police System

- Inspector General of Police
- Deputy Inspector General
- Superintendent
- Assistant Superintendent

State Police Service

- Deputy Superintendent
- Inspector
- Sub-Inspector
- Assistant Sub-Inspector
- Head Constable
- Constable

National Human Rights Commission

The National Human Rights Commission was constituted in October 1993 under the Human Rights Ordinance or 28th September, 1993, which was soon after enacted as the protection of Human Rights Act, 1993.[17] It is fully an autonomous body. Its autonomy is derived out of the method of the appointment of members, their fixed tenure and statutory guarantees. The status they have been accorded the manner in which the staff is expected to be responsible to the Commission, their conduct and its financial powers also ensures its autonomy.

Composition of the Commission

The Act envisages that the Commission shall consist of :

(a) Chairperson who has been a Chief Justice of the Supreme Court;
(b) One Member who is or has been, a Judge of the Supreme Court;
(c) One Member who is, or has been the Chief Justice of a High Court; and
(d) Two Members to be appointed from amongst persons having knowledge or practical experience in matters relating to Human Rights.

The Chairperson of the National Commission for Minorities, the National Commission for the Scheduled Castes and Scheduled Tribes and the National Commission for Women shall be deemed to be Members of the Commission for the discharge of certain functions. There shall be a Secretary General of the rank of the Secretary to Government of India who shall function as the Chief Executive Officer of the Commission. The Headquarters of the Commission shall be at Delhi and there is an enabling provision in the Act to establish offices at other places in India with the previous approval of the Central Government.

Functions of the Commission

The following functions devolve on the Commission under the Act :

(a) Inquire, in its own initiative or a petition presented to it by a victim or any person on his behalf, into complaints ;

- Violation of Human Rights or abetment thereof: or
- Negligence in the prevention of such violation, by public servants.

(b) Intervene in any proceeding involving any allegation of violation of Human Rights pending before a court with the approval of such court;

(c) Visit, under intimation to the State Government, any jail or any other institution under the control of the State Government, where persons are lodged for purposes of treatment, reformation or protection to study the living conditions of the inmates and make recommendations thereon;

(d) Review the safeguards provided by or under the Constitution or any law for the time being in force for the protection of Human Rights and recommend measures for their effective implementation;

(e) Review the factors, including acts of terrorism that inhibit the enjoyment of Human Rights and recommend appropriate remedial measures;

(f) Study treaties and other international instruments on Human Rights and make recommendations for their effective implementation;

(g) Undertake and promote research in the field of Human Rights;

(h) Spread Human Rights literacy among various sections of society and promote awareness of the safeguards available for the protection of these rights through publications, the media, seminars and other available means :

(i) Encourage the effort on non-governmental organizations and institution working in the field of Human Rights; and

(j) Such other functions it may consider necessary for the promotion of Human Rights.

State Human Rights Commissions

There is an enabling provision in the Act for State Human Rights Commissions to be constituted by the respective State Government.

The State Commission shall consist of :

(a) A Chairperson who has been a Chief Justice of a High Court;

(b) One member who is, or has been, a Judge of a High Court;

(c) One Member who is, or has been a District Judge in that State;

(d) Two members to be appointed from amongst persons having knowledge of practical experience in, matters relating to Human Rights.

Functions of the State Commission

A State Commission may inquire into violations of Human Rights only in respect of matters relating to any of the entries enumerated in List II (State List) and List III(Concurrent List) is the Seventh Schedule of the Constitution. However, if any such matter is already being inquired into by the National Commission or any other Statutory Commission, the State Commission shall not inquire into the said matter. Subject to this, the powers, the procedure of investigation, inquiry and steps to be taken thereafter are comparable to those of the National Commission.

Annual or Specific Report of the Commission

The State Commission shall submit Annual Report to the respective State Governments and may, at any time, submit Special Reports on any matter which in their opinion is of urgency or importance. It is enjoined on the State Government to cause to lay on the Table of the respective State Legislature the Annual and Special Reports of the State Human Rights Commission.

Human Rights Courts

The Act envisages that for the purpose of providing speedy trial of offences arising out of violations of Human Rights, State Government may with the concurrence of the Chief Justice of the concerned High Court specify for each District Court of Sessions to be a Human Rights Court to try such offences. For every Human Rights Court, the State Government shall specify a Public Prosecutor for the purpose of conducting case in the Court.

Thus, Police Administration and Human Rights seem to overlap each other's powers and functions depending on certain issues while, they seem to present a consensus picture other times. If this is so in terms of these theoretical frame in the field level the reality seems to be quite different despite the fact that they are complimentary to each other. The Chapter Five, which is purely analytical in this regard, speaks of it much more clearly with evidences.

References

1. Lenin, *The State and Revolution*, Moscow, Progress Publishers, 1969.

2. *Viz.*, Right to Life, Liberty and Security of Persons, Right to Fair Trial and Equal Protection of Law.
3. Basu, D.D. *Introduction to the Constitution of India*, New Delhi, Prentice Hall, India, 1997.
4. Subramaniam, S., *Human Rights and Police*, Hyderabad, Association for Advancement of Police Security Science, 1992, p. 11-15
5. Kashyap, S.C., *Human Rights and Parliament*, New Delhi, Metropolitan Book Company, 1978.
6. Prerogative writs are *viz., Habeas Corpus, Mandamus*, Prohibition, *Certiorari* and *Quo Warranto., op cit.*, D.D. Basu. 1997.
7. Ghosh, S.K. *et al.*, eds. *Encyclopedia of Police in India*, New Delhi, Ashish Publishing House, 1943.
8. Chaturvedi, S.K., ed. *Role of Police in Criminal Justice System*, Delhi, B.R. Publishing Corporation, 1996.
9. *Op. cit.*, Subramaniam, S., 1992.
10. Srivastav, V.P., *Indian Police: Law and Reality*, New Delhi, Manas Publications, 1997.
11. Singh, M.P., *Police Problems and Dilemmas in India*, New Delhi, Mittal Publications, 1989.
12. Sen Shankar, *Indian Police Today*, New Delhi, Ashish Publishing House, 1986, p. 57.
13. Wilson, O.W., *Police Administration*, New York, McGraw Hill, 1950.
14. Police (including Railway and Village Police' subject to the provision of entry 2A of List I, Entry 8 in list I (i.e., Union) pertains to Central Bureau of Intelligence and Investigation. Police Officers belonging to State and Union cadre are posted to these Bureaus. Entry 9, List I (Union) deals with preventive detention for reasons connected with Defence, Foreign Affairs or the Security of India. Entry 80 of List I deals with extension of the powers and jurisdiction of members of Police Force belonging to any State or to any area outside that state. For detail see *op. cit.*, Singh, M.P. (1989).
15. *Ibid.*
16. *Ibid.*
17. (No. 10 of 1994) hereinafter referred to as 'the Act' Arjun Dev *et al.*, eds, *Human Rights : A Source Book*, New Delhi, National Council for Educational Research and Training, 1996. Changes if any by way of amendments to these commissions are not included uptil 2011. This is for information.

5

Human Rights and Police Administration

An Empirical Analysis of their Interrelationship

In a democratic society, every organ of the state is expected to be accountable to the people. This applies more appropriately to the police than others. As per *Encyclopaedia Britannica* :

> " Police is the executive civil force of a state, which is entrusted with the duty of maintaining public order and of enforcing regulations for the prevention and detention of crime"[1].

The police should not, therefore, take amiss any wholesome criticism of their conduct in this regard. Any criticism with a view to improving the image of the police should, therefore, ensure better "Police-Public Relations"[2] police in today's society is empowered to use legitimate and situationally justified force against law breakers and offenders. This mandate of the police to use violence to curb or prevent violence raises the key issue that the people themselves should not indulge in unnecessary or excessive use of force, although there are laws, rules and number of instructions, which lay down norms for the use of force by the police. This, however, acts as a check on the use of their powers. Yet, at times, the police in situations of grave emergency may override their prescribed limitations, whereby, the excesses are committed. Treading the liberty of those whom they protect under law even under these grave situations is an unpardonable offence. Therefore, in order to keep police under constant surveillance the maxim "Safety of the people is the highest law" is highlighted.[3]

However, in a democratic society protests and right to strike are (enshrined) a part of the implied meaning in the discourses on fundamental rights. It is expected that the society takes these instruments to fight the exigencies of a state or other institutions for the purposes of seeking justice in a way as prescribed by *Rousseau*.[4] While doing so, it is possible that the state uses its coercive force to repress and suppress these reactive movements often leading to an impression that the forces initiated by state like police performs in the interest of the state as observed by *Lenin*.[5] However, no amount of rights enshrined in the Constitution permits any movement or protest in an organized society beyond certain limitations prescribed for reasons of maintaining peace and order. If liberals argue that they have a right to protest against any harmful act of the state, it is not without certain prerequisites and limitations. Keeping in view these arguments among liberals and the left leaning reactive groups the present study is designed to have a balanced view on the issue and, therefore, an attempt was made here with a purpose to understand the limitations of both the police, as representing the coercive power of state and the Human Rights as representing the organized liberal state. Further, an attempt is also made here to establish any relationship that may exist between Human Rights and Police Administration in order to understand whether these two agencies of the state are mutually supportive or mutually repressive. More so, in a globalized world where the need for a civic society is seen as a necessity.

Studies conducted in the areas of Human Rights and Police Administration, however, have confirmed the much discussed subject matter that the lack of awareness about Human Rights among Police is clearly an indicator of the fact that there is need to make deeper study of the Human Rights concept not only as an independent concept but also, as an important component in the police organization.

Thus, this study of Human Rights and Police Administration in Hubli-Dharwad Commissionerate in Karnataka based on the hypotheses drawn earlier, is an original empirical work which is in conformity with the sample size given in Chapter One.

In order to collect the data and to know about the position of the concept of Human Right as a factor in the Police Administration this field work was undertaken by using stratified sampling method keeping in view the necessities of doctoral dissertation. A schedule was used to elicit the opinions of police personnel on the issues related to Human Rights in their day-to-day functioning and while stress was laid on informal discussions with *Human Rights activists* to collect their opinion about Police Administration. Altogether out of 123 selected Police Personnel, about 119 respondents have responded; starting from the Commissioner of Police down to constabulary level police personnel have shown their concern for this study by responding to our requests. These respondents were in the age group falling between 20 to 30 years which is about 23 per cent. 24 per cent of them were in the age group of 30 to 40 and a good number of respondents which is about 53 per cent were in the age group of 40 and above. In matters of education, which was taken as another important variable, 3 per cent of the respondents had post-graduation, 20 per cent had graduation, 22 per cent had completed Pre-University College (PUC) and majority of them up to 55 per cent had passed out SSLC,[6] which is the minimum qualification required to enter into this service at the cadre of a constable. The total number of respondents consisted of 87 per cent men and 13 per cent of women.

In this study, Police Administration has been taken under the close scrutiny. An attempt has also been made to unveil the relationship between Human Rights and Police

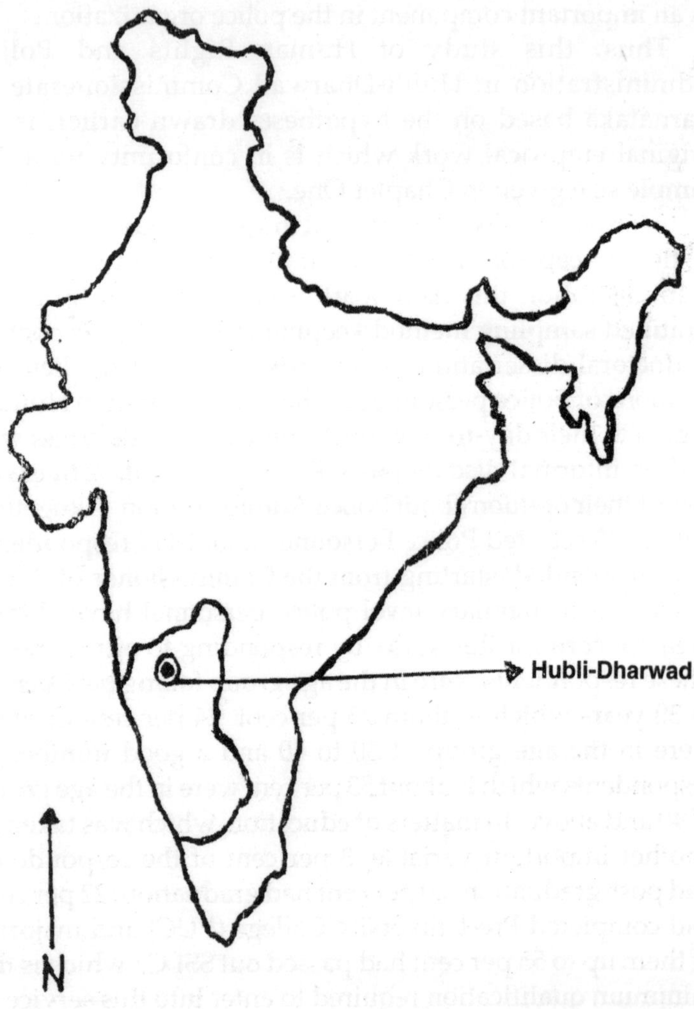

Map 5.1. Map Indicating Area of Study within Karnataka

Administration. Emphasis is laid on informal discussion held while administering the schedules apart from formal discussions held with police personnel and Human Rights activist groups.

To begin with, the schedule was designed to start with the basic question of awareness about Human Rights, especially amongst the controlled stratified group of police personnel. We asked them whether they had heard of the concept of Human Rights, nearly 85.71 per cent of them responded to the question positively, while about 7.56 per cent of them responded negatively and another 6.72 per cent of them replied as "do not know". By any yardstick this response is quite impressive and strengthened the initial attempts at understanding the level of basic information of this group about the muchpublicized Human Rights. 'Awareness' of one's own field of working has been in Indian context greatly referred to as a reliable indicator of the commitment of those who are in the field concerned. This total percentage of response though impressive, in this respect does not represent a clear picture of the respondents level of commitment, which is rather very important in the stratified sample studies (see Graph. 5.1)

Testing hypothesis determines the validity of one of the two assumptions, technically described as null hypothesis H_0 and alternative hypothesis H_1 with a view to choose between two conflicting hypotheses about the value of a population parameter. Testing hypothesis helps to decide whether a hypothesis about population parameter is likely to be true or false on the basis of the sample observations taken from the population under the study. For this purpose statisticians have developed several methods to test hypothesis and these have been broadly classified into two categories :

(a) Parametric Tests of Hypothesis; and
(b) Non-Parametric or Distribution Free Test of

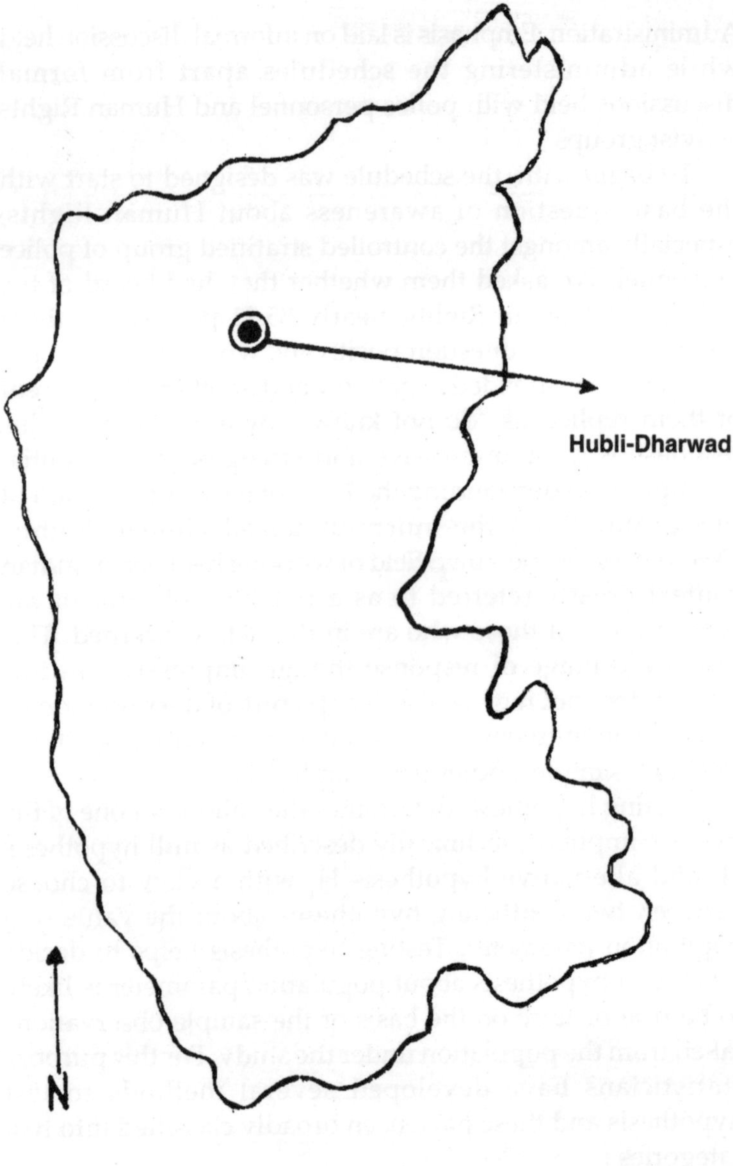

Map 5.2. Map Indicating Karnataka State and the Area of Study

Graph 5.1 : Have you heard of Human Rights?

1.	Yes	85. 71%
2.	No	7.56%
3.	Don't know	6.72%

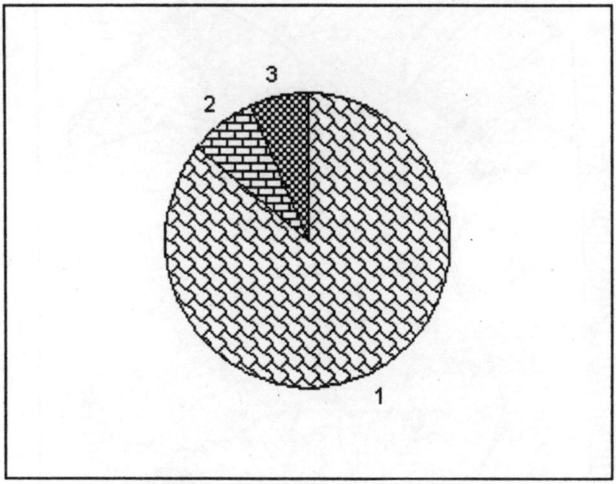

Hypothesis.

Here in the present study, we use Z-test statistic to test two contradictory hypotheses which fall in the category (a) as described. Z-test normally applies when the assumption of normality holds true and generally it holds true whenever the sample size is large. Let us call the hypothesis to be tested as null hypothesis H_0 and the conflicting hypothesis as alternative hypothesis H_1.

The Z-Test statistic for testing hypothesis such as :

H_o : Yes against H_1 : is given by :

$$Z= \frac{P-p}{\sqrt{PQ/n}}$$

where p = proportion of the sample says 'Yes'.

p = Proportion of the sample says 'Yes' or 'No'

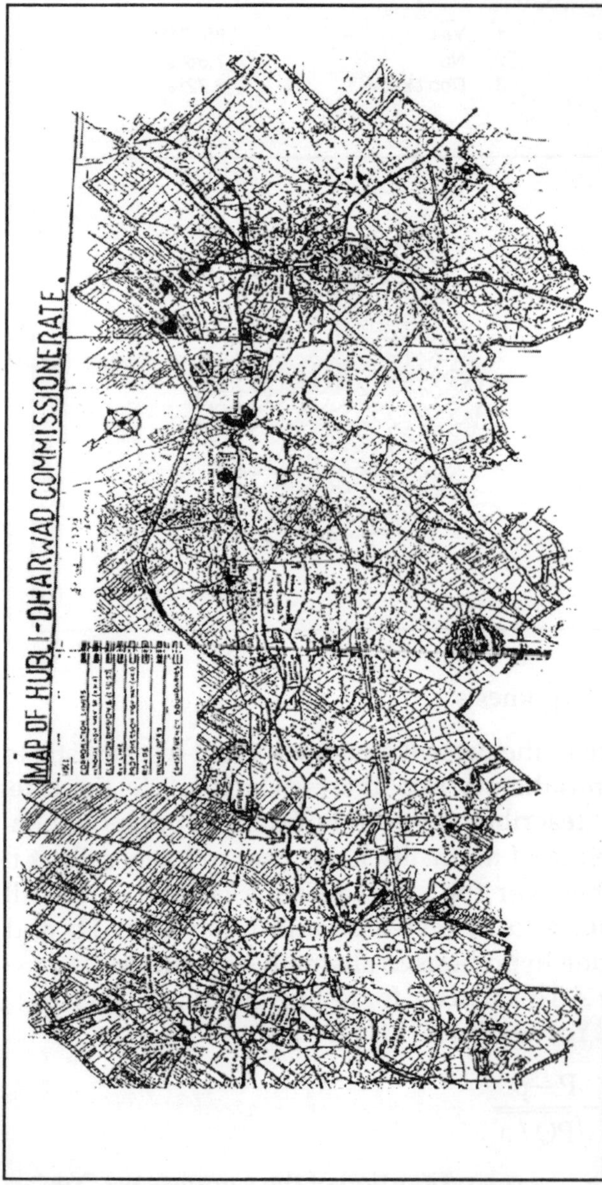

Map 5.3. Map of Hubli-Dharwad Commissionerate

Note : Hubli-Dharwad has its own website also.

are qual to 0.5.

Since $P + Q = 1, Q = 1 - P = 0.5$

n = size of the sample

By comparing the value of Z (i.e. calculated Z), with table value of Z (observed from normal table) at 5% (1%) level of significance a decision regarding accepting H_0 or (H_1) is arrived. For most of the problems to be tested in the study of Z - statistic suits well and we prefer this to test various hypotheses under study and are given below :

Considering the question : Have you heard of Human Rights?

In the present study, sample about 92 per cent have said 'Yes' and remaining 8 per cent have said 'No'. To know the sizeable people in the sample heard about Human Rights or not.

Let, H_0 : Proportion of Police heard of Human Rights are equal.

Against, the alternative hypothesis is :

H_1 - Significant number of police personnel have heard of Human Rights.

To test H_0 *Vs* H_1, first we shall compute population of police who heard Human Rights from the sample, that is,

$$p = \frac{\text{Number of police heard of Human Rights}}{\text{Total number of persons in the sample}}$$

$$= \frac{102}{111} = 0.9189$$

Since the sample size n=111 is large, we use Z-test, defined as,

$$Z = \frac{p-P}{\sqrt{PQ/n}} \quad .... \quad (1)$$

where the value of P under H_0 =½, therefore Q=1-P=0.5 Substituting all known values in equation (1) we found that the calculated value of Z=8.8183.

Now the table value of Z, denoted by Z_1 at 1 per cent level of significance is 2.58. Since calculated Z= 8.8183 > Z_1

=2.58, the null hypothesis H_0 is rejected. Hence, the alternative hypothesis H_1 is accepted, *viz.*, significant number of police personnel have heard of Human Rights.

However, a break-up of these responses was further attempted to locate and to see how the stratified groups namely higher level officers,[7] middle level officers[8] and lower level officers[9] responded to this question. Of the small number of higher officers who constituted about 2.52 per cent of the total respondents, nearly all of them were aware of Human Rights. While of the 8.40 per cent of middle level officers, all of them had shown their awareness about Human Rights and of the 88.24 per cent of lower level officers who actually deal with public and interact only 74.79 per cent of them had heard about Human Rights. Yet, there was almost 7.56 per cent of this group who responded as having 'not heard' about Human Rights. While nearly 5.88 per cent from among the lower level officers have responded as 'do not know', to this question. This is represented in Sub-Graph 5.1.1.

Although not much of work on Human Rights and Police Administration in particular have been made so far, any judgment on this result can be taken as an indicator of the growing socialization of the concept of Human Right in developing society. Many of the socializing agents like political parties, media, both electronic as well as print, activist groups and other needs can be held as taking active part in this process. As noticed many of them are consistently holding a number of discussions in this area of Human Rights on a regular basis. However, in case of the current study, the controlled groups as the respondents were expected to know and hear it from within the organization either through the literature supplied or during their training period. Since Police Administration is a formidable part of the criminal justice system anything related to their operational jurisdiction is considered to be an integral part of their pre-service or in-service training curriculum apart from them being the contents of circulars and codes for the organization.

In order to ascertain this, out of the total 119 respondents, 85.71 per cent of the respondents consisting 2.52 per cent of higher officers, 8.40 per cent of middle level officers and 74.79 per cent of lower level officers were asked to identify their sources through which they had heard about this concept. Not surprisingly, 2.52 per cent of them had heard about Human Rights from police manuals, 24.37 per cent of them from police academy training centres and more than half of the total respondents, i.e., 51.26 per cent had heard about it from mass media/newspapers. Only 7.56 per cent of them had heard of Human Rights either during their formal education or on their own specific interest (See Graph. 5.1.1). The break-up of this response however, threw a surprise in

Graph 5.1.1 : If 'Yes' from where have you heard about it?

1.	From Police Manuals	2.52%
2.	From Police Academy/Training Centre	24.37%
3.	From Media/Newspapers	51.26%
4.	Any other	7.56%

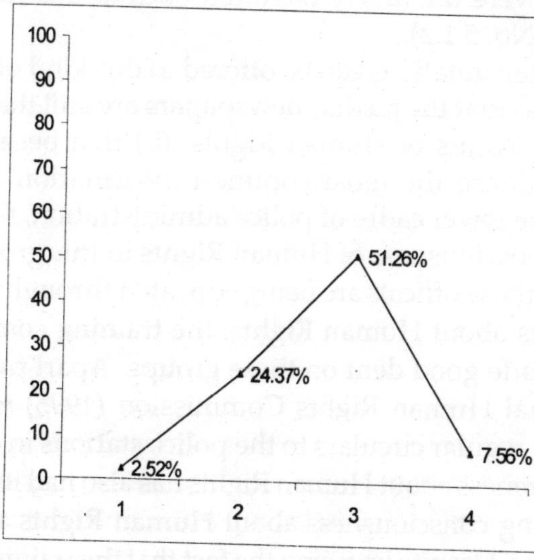

the sense, that 2.52 per cent top officials had heard about Human Rights during their recruitment period, that is from the academy/training centres where they received pre-service training. Since most of these officers are recruited from the Indian Police Service and State Police Services, they had a definite mode of training and they had heard about Human Rights during their training. In case of middle level officers, nearly 5.04 per cent of them had heard about Human Rights at the time of their recruitment and training period, while 2.52 per cent of these officers had heard about it from the media. In case of the 74.79 per cent of respondents belonging to third category, about 2.52 per cent of them had learnt from police manuals such as "Manuals on Human Rights Training for Police Personnel" and "Training Programme on Human Rights for Police." Nearly 16.81 per cent had heard about it during in-service training and 47.90 per cent of them had heard it from mass media/newspapers. About 7.56 per cent of them had this information right from their school education itself and most of these police personnel were the newly recruited ones to this field (See sub-graph No. 5.1.2).

Two interpretations can be offered to this kind of data at this stage (a) that the media/newspapers are still the largest socializing agents of Human Rights; (b) that because the newspapers are the most common information sources amongst the lower cadre of police administration, there is a growing consciousness of Human Rights in this group.

While, these officals are being educated through media/newspapers about Human Rights, the training component also has made good dent on these groups. Apart from this, the National Human Rights Commission (1993) which is circulating regular circulars to the police stations in order to create awareness about Human Rights has also had its impact on spreading consciousness about Human Rights amongst these groups. Despite knowing the fact that the training input

Sub-Graph 5.1.2 : If 'Yes' from where have you heard about it?

	Category I	*Cetegory II*	*Cetegory III*
1.	0.00%	0.00%	2.52%
2.	2.52%	5.04%	16.81%
3.	0.00%	3.36%	47.90%
4.	0.00%	0.00%	7.56%

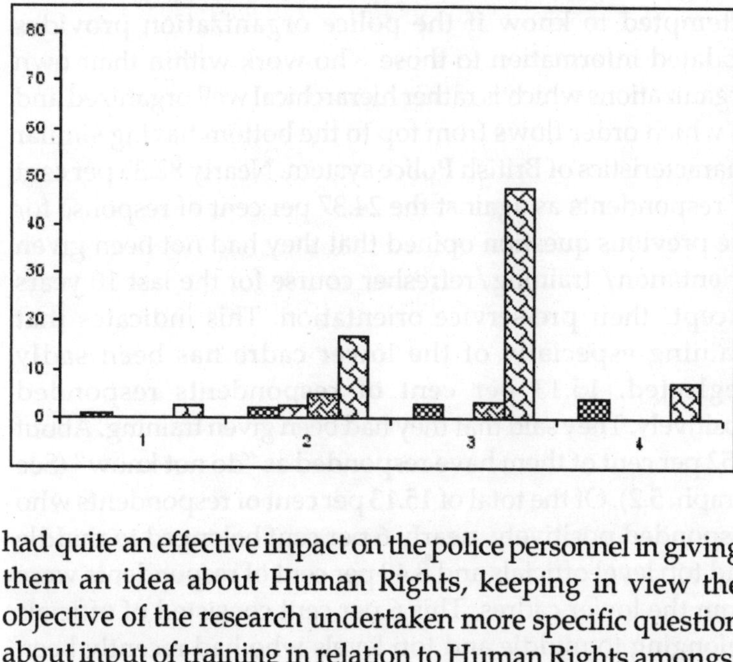

had quite an effective impact on the police personnel in giving them an idea about Human Rights, keeping in view the objective of the research undertaken more specific question about input of training in relation to Human Rights amongst the police personnel was taken up. A question pertaining to this was, whether police personnel were given training/ orientation/refresher courses in Human Rights. Such a question was specifically designed to learn from the respondent whether there was a trend amongst the police to ignore the prescriptions of Human Rights knowingly or unknowingly or whether there was any weakness in the process of investigation itself that did not allow the police personnel to be conscious of Human Rights. These hypothetical notions were thought to react on the mode of training imparted to these police officers. A possible explanation for these kinds of attitude amongst the Police was also thought of to throw light on one time training, i.e., pre-service training imparted to the police for all the cadres which is not followed by an in-service or on-the-job training at regular intervals. Apart from that, the question also attempted to know if the police organization provides updated information to those who work within their own organizations which is rather hierarchical well organized and in which order flows from top to the bottom having similar characteristics of British Police system. Nearly 82.35 per cent of respondents as against the 24.37 per cent of response for the previous question opined that they had not been given orientation/ training/refresher course for the last 10 years except their pre-service orientation. This indicates that training especially of the lower cadre has been sadly neglected. 15.13 per cent of respondents responded positively. They said that they had been given training. About 2.52 per cent of them have responded as "do not know" (See Graph. 5.2). Of the total of 15.13 per cent of respondents who responded positively, nearly 6 per cent belonged to middle and top level officials and 8.40 per cent of respondents were from the lower cadres. This 6 per cent consisted of officials belonging to middle and top levels who had recently been given refresher course on Human Rights. The 9.24 per cent of respondents belonging to the lower cadre were probationary constables (see sub-graph 5.2.1).

Talking about the training aspects in any organization, they constitute two types of training, viz., (a) pre-service training; and (b) in-service training. Pre-service training is generally defined as a preparation for entrance into the public service, while in-service training is defined as the training imparted to a person after his appointment to the Government service. The terms like orientation and refresher course falls under the respective training periods. As such, orientation course is supposed to be the training imparted during the in-service training period only and the refresher courses are supposed to be conducted during the intensive field training period.[10]

Graph 5.2 : Have you been given Orientation/Training/Refresher Course in Human Rights?

1.	Yes	15.13%
2.	No	82.35%
3.	Don't know	2.52%

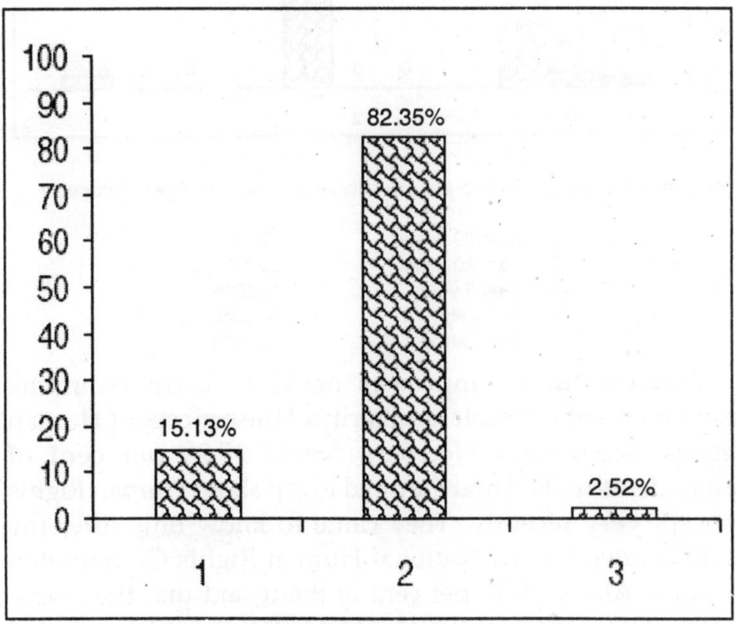

Sub-Graph 5.2.1 : Have you been given Orientation/Training/Refresher Course in Human Rights?

	Category I	*Cetegory II*	*Cetegory III*
1.	2.52%	3.36%	9.24%
2.	0.00%	0.00%	76.47%
3.	0.00%	0.00%	2.52%

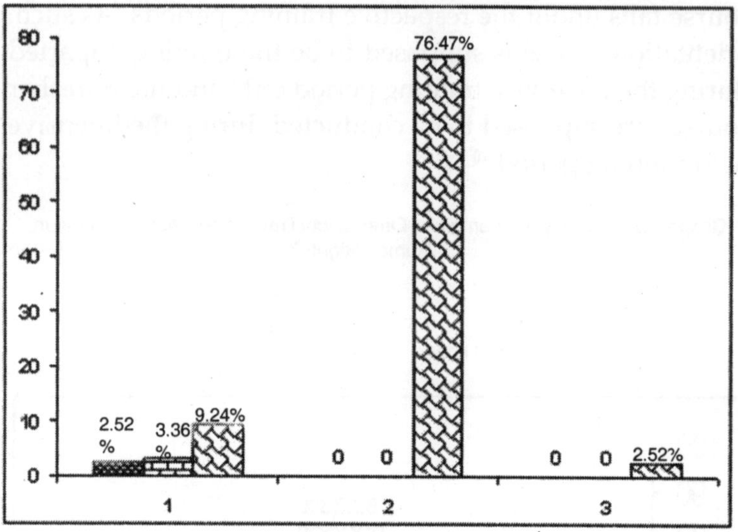

Graph 5.3 : Since how long are you familiar with Human Rights Concept?

1.	Last 20 years	13.45%
2.	Last 10 years	20.17%
3.	Last 5 years	15.97%
4.	Recently	35.29%
5.	Don't know	15.13%

Further, an attempt was made to learn from the respondents about their familiarity of the concept of Human Rights (see Graph No. 5.3). Nealy 35.29 per cent of respondents replied that they had learnt about Human Rights concept very recently. They came to know only after the establishment of the National Human Rights Commission in India. About 20.17 per cent of them said that they were aware of it for the past 10 years and 15.97 per cent responded as having known about Human Rights in the past 5 years, 15.13 per cent replied as 'do not know' and 13.05 per cent of respondents responded as having known of this concept for the past 20 years. Category-wise responses to this question revealed the fact that 3.52 per cent of higher officers are aware of Human Rights from a longer duration. While in case of middle level officers, 8.40 per cent of them were familiar with

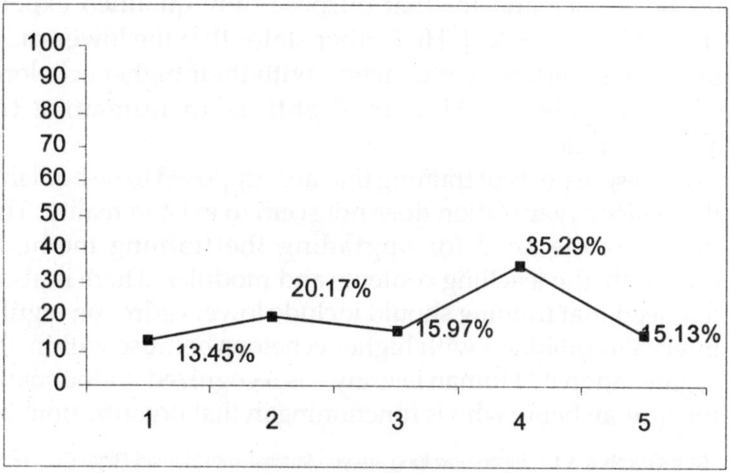

Human Rights concept from a reasonable period ranging between 10 to 15 years. While a meagre of 0.84 per cent of them said that they came to know about it 'recently' and as 'do not know' respectively. In case of lower level officers, about 34.45 per cent agreed that they were familiar with this concept only recently and most of them expressed that their entry into service was the point of their learning about Human Rights.[11] 16.81 per cent were familiar with it for the past 10 years, 14.29 per cent responded as do not know, 11.76 per cent were familiar with it for the past 5 years and 10.92 per cent for the past 20 years. These responses in fact helped us to measure further the in-depth knowledge of Human Rights, these respondents may have had *vis-à-vis* the length of service they had put in. It was only at the bottom level that could give us a clear picture about the correlation between the length of service and depth of knowledge about Human Rights, which of course was not as anticipated (see Sub-Graph. 5.3.1). Relating to this James Vadakumchery explains in his book on *Indian Police — 2001: What Went Wrong Here? (1998)*"[12], observed that it is the duty of the organization concerned to give information on the subject to tall members in the service and for that purpose only qualified experts should be appointed. He further states that the lower cadre need a very effective interaction with their higher echelons, since the idea of Human Rights is to humanize the administration.

These aspects of training that are supposed to be built into the police organization does not seem to exist in reality. This indicates the need for upgrading the training methods, especially the teaching contents and modules. There is also a felt need that training should include lower cadres on regular intervals combined with higher echelons because within the organization if "Human Dignity", is recognized undoubtedly, the human being who is functioning in that organization will

Sub-Graph 5.3.1 : Since how long are you familiar with Human Right Concept?

	Category I	*Cetegory II*	*Cetegory III*
1.	0.84%	1.68%	10.92%
2.	0.84%	2.52%	16.81%
3.	0.84%	3.36%	11.76%
4.	0.00%	0.84%	34.45%
5.	0.00%	0.84%	14.29%

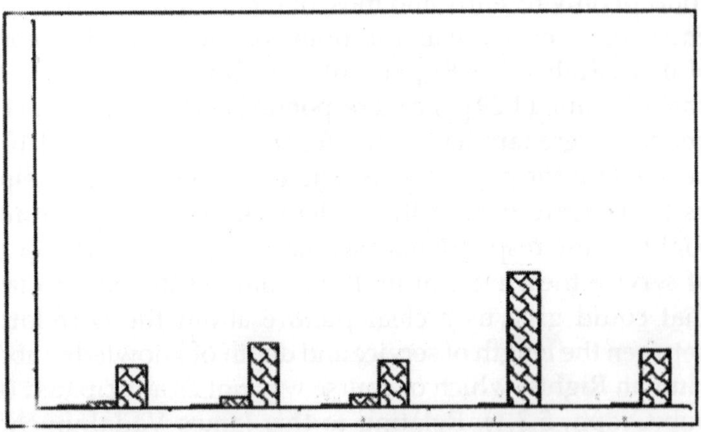

definitely carry the same attitude or approach towards the people whoever comes to seek assistance from them.[13]

To a question about what according to the respondents

was the concept of Human Rights, substituted with the following options : (a) Universal Concept of Human Right; (b) Protection of Human Rights Act 1993,[14] and (c) Textual definition of Human Rights as ensured in Universal Declaration of Human Rights.[15] Nearly 68.91 per cent of them opted for definition of Human Rights Act (1993) as enshrined in the Fundamental Rights under Articles 14 to 32 in the Indian Constitution which are enforceable in Courts of India. Since this is the most routine activity that the organization of police comes across in their day-to-day activity, this seems to be their most favourite choice. 23.53 per cent of them preferred what is enshrined in basic document of Universal Declaration of Human Rights, although in our discussions with them the respondents failed to identify the basic documents connected to this. About 2.52 per cent of them responded to the concept of Human Rights as universally understood, while the same

Graph 5.4 : What according to you is the Concept of Human Right?

1.	Human Rights are those that belong to an individual as a consequence of him being human	2.52%
2.	Human Rights are those related to life, liberty, equality and dignity of an individual, guaranteed by the Constitution or embodied in the international covenants and enforceable by the Courts in India	68.91%
3.	Human Rights are those, which every human being is entitled to enjoy and to have it protected	23.53%
4.	All the above	2.52%
5.	Don't know	2.52%

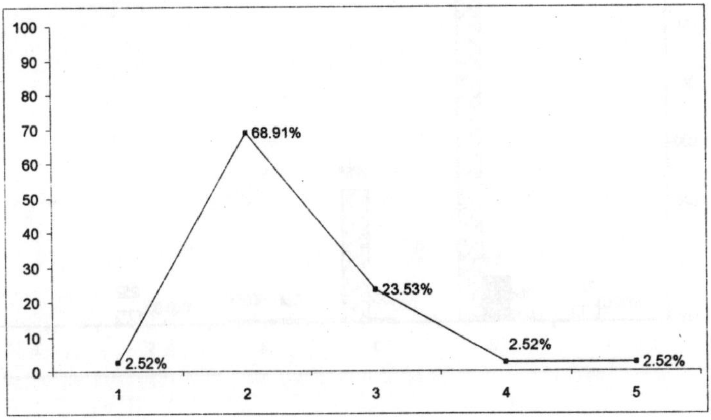

percentage preferred all the above as an answer and 'do not know', respectively (see Graph. 5.4). What is the most interesting is the break-up of these answers. Amongst the top officials, 1.68 per cent of them preferred constitutional context of Human Rights and 0.84 per cent of them referred to the response all the above. Among the middle level officers, nearly 7.56 per cent of them preferred constitutional aspect of the Protection of Human Rights Act 1993. 0.84 per cent each agreed to the context of basic document which is in the Universal Declaration of Human Rights and all the above responses. Variation came up with the lower level officials, nearly 59.66 per cent preferred Protection of Human Rights Act (1993), i.e., constitutional aspect, 22.69 per cent preferred basic document of Universal Declaration of Human Rights, 2.52 per cent preferred the Universal Context of Human

Sub-Graph 5.4.1 : What according to you is the Concept of Human Rights?

	Category I	*Cetegory II*	*Cetegory III*
1.	0.00%	0.00%	2.52%
2.	1.68%	7.56%	59.66%
3.	0.00%	0.84%	22.69%
4.	0.84%	0.84%	0.84%
5.	0.00%	0.00%	2.52%

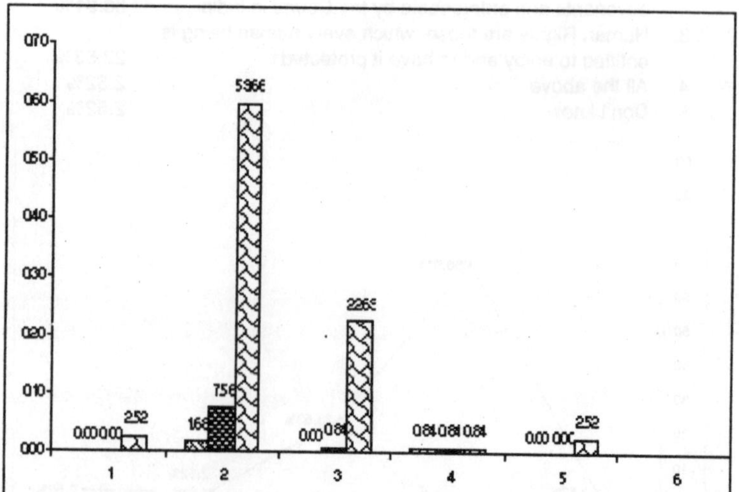

Rights as well as 'do not know' and 0.84 per cent preferred 'all the above' (See Sub-Graph. 5.4.1).

However, an analysis of this clearly indicates that Human Rights content coming under all the three aspects is only understood by a very few respondents in all the levels. Protecting an individual as consequence of him being human and his rights being a citizen of a country and to have it protected by the organization incharge is only understood by the respondents because they are familiar with this in day-to-day media. As noticed earlier, familiarity and day-to-day interaction of their administration seems to be dominating in minds of most of the respondents as against the other choice, clearly brings to the fore the issue that Human Rights is a comprehensive concept understood by the police in only limited context, that too in the context that affects them in their day-to-day affairs. It is possible that either these officers have not attempted to learn about this or simply does not believe in attempting to know more about it as they feel that it is of no consequence to them, unless they are on the wrong side of the law.

To penetrate further, a question that was posed to respondents to elicit from them the depth of their knowledge and familiarity about the basic documents that govern the matter connected to Human Rights in India and its status in the international scenario. The respondents were asked to name the Acts/Declarations that govern Human Rights in India and three options were given to them. Primarily, India being signatory to the decisions of the United Nations Organization and had given its consent to Universal Declaration of Human Rights in the year 1948. As a consequence of this, the Indian Constitution had enshrined under its Fundamental Rights these components. With the beginning of globalization and growing concern for Human Rights around the world, India too had initiated recently the Protection of Human Rights Act 1993. For an agency like police all these options are of consequence and it was anticipated that they would lead all of them together. The response, however, not surprisingly was an overwhelming 84.87 per cent of 'do not know'. While 10.92 per cent preferred fundamental rights as governing Human Rights in India, 1.68 per cent each preferred Protection of Human Rights Act 1993 and all the above responses and only 0.84 per cent believed Universal Declaration of Human Rights as governing Human Rights matters in India (see Graph. 5.5.). Although it is true that fundamental rights as a consequence of day-to-day administration as said earlier is the most popular answer amongst police, only 10.92 per cent of the total respondents had preferred this. If read together the responses to questions posed earlier (5.4 and 5.5), there is a clear gap that a researcher can notice between the understanding of the

Graph 5.5 : Can you name the Acts/Declarations that govern Human Rights in India?

1.	Universal Declaration of Human Rights (1984)	0.84%
2.	Fundamental Rights (1950)	10.92%
3.	Human Rights Act in India (1993)	1.68%
4.	All the above	1.68%
5.	Don't know	84.87%

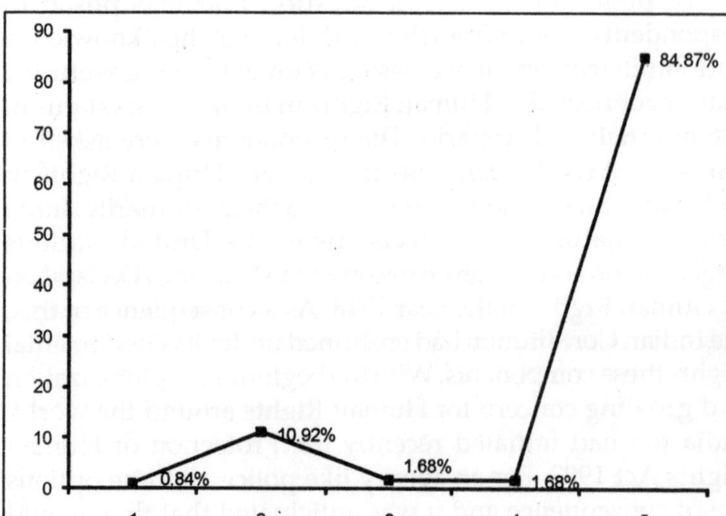

'concept' of Human Rights by police and its operational aspects. Although there are about 2.52 per cent of higher officers, as respondents their responses are also divided in this case between Universal Declaration of Human Rights and Fundamental Rights as governing Human Rights matters in India. While a meagre 0.84 per cent have responded correctly as all the above. In case of 8.40 percent of middle level officers who are otherwise seen as active participants in maintaining law and order in society and who often are accused as violating the limits of Human Rights including issues like custodial death, etc., nearly 6.72 per cent of respondents responded as 'do not know' while mere 2.52 per cent saw fundamental rights as governing Human Rights in India. Similarly, those who are active at the field level, i.e., the constabulary category of police organization which is the lowest rank among the organization had not surprisingly responded as 'do not know' amounting to 78.15 per cent. Only about 7.56 per cent of respondents in this category believed that fundamental rights governing Human Rights matters in India; and while 1.68 per cent responded Protection of Human Rights Act 1993 as governing Human Rights matters in India. Only 0.84 per cent have responded in this case also as all the above. This is indeed quite a fearing response, because this explicitly speaks of the input of Human Rights in police organization. In fact, as mentioned earlier, the expectations of response for this question and the responses of the officers at all levels, not only is indicative of the dearth of knowledge of Human Rights but also speaks of the needed socialization of Human Rights and orientation required. If 84.87 per cent of the respondents including the top brass officers can say that they are not aware of what governs Human Rights matters in India than this would leave us gaping at the violations of Human Rights without any surprise (See Sub-Graph. 5.5.1).

In order to strengthen this kind of belief a further penetrating question was asked about some of the Acts/ Declarations which cover the Human Rights content that are

Sub-Graph 5.5.1 : Can you name tha Acts/Declarations that govern Human Rights in India?

	Category I	*Cetegory II*	*Cetegory III*
1.	0.84%	0.00%	0.00%
2.	0.84%	2.52%	7.56%
3.	0.00%	0.00%	1.68%
4.	0.84%	0.00%	00.84%
5.	0.00%	6.72%	78.15%

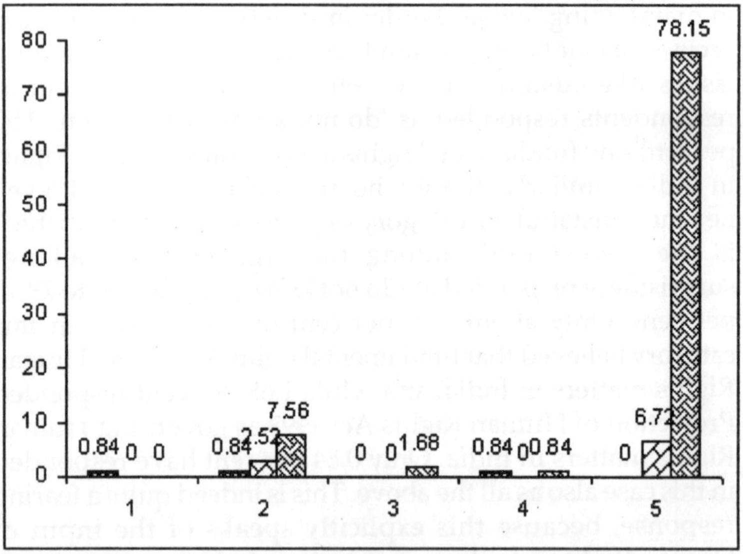

specific to Police Administration with a view to find out how close these issues are to 'police'. As can be seen in the graphical presentation (see Graph. 5.6) about 0.84 per cent of the total respondents did speak of United Nations Declaration of Rights of Offenders (1955) and same per cent have knowledge about Convention Against Torture and Other Cruel, Inhuman, Degrading Treatment or Punishment (1984). 1.68 per cent of policemen are aware of Standard Minimum Rules for the Treatment of Prisoners (1977). 2.52 per cent of respondents are aware of the Code of Conduct for Police in India (1985). An analysis of this response reveals that the responses for this question has mainly come from

Graph 5.6 : Can you name some of the Acts/Declarations, which cover Human Rights content but are specific to Police Administration?

1.	United Nations Declaration on Rights of Offenders (1655)	0.84%
2.	Standard Minimum Rules for the Treatment of Prisoners (1977)	1.68%
3.	United Nations Code of Conduct for Law Enforcement Officials (1979)	0.00%
4.	Convention against Torture and other Cruel, Inhuman or Degrading treatment or punishment (1984)	0.84%
5.	Declaration of Basic Principles of Justice for Victims of Crime and Abuse of Power (1985)	0.00%
6.	United Nations Standard Rules for the Administration of Juvenile Justice (1985)	0.00%
7.	Code of Conduct for Police in India (1985)	2.52%
8.	Don't know.	94.12%

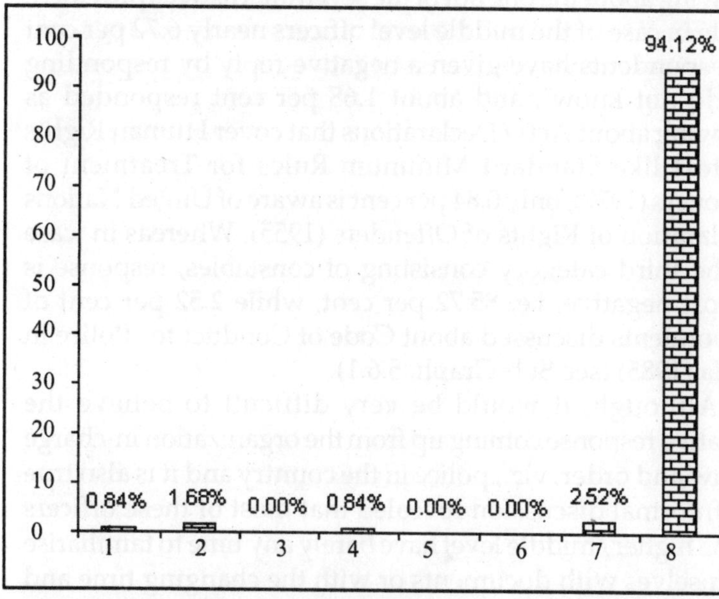

higher officers and the middle level officers belonging to Sub-Inspector and above cadres. Although one could consider this as a positive sign, what is regrettable is the fact that the 'police,' which is most significant sub-system within the criminal justice system does not seem to be up to the expectations of an elite organization. Any functionary performing in an organization is expected to know the laws that govern their activity. Ignorance on their part in these matters can only be considered as a negative point, while stress will have to be laid on the necessities of orienting the functionaries about the laws that govern them. However, in this focused research it is noted that this is an overwhelming per cent of 94.12 respondents have responded as 'do not know'. A break up of this response indicate that every higher level officer who constitute nearly 2.52 per cent of respondents also have little knowledge of these Acts/ Declarations which are specific to Police. Because 1.68 per cent of respondents from this cadre responded as 'do not know' and only one (0.84) per cent have responded as knowing about the one out of the seven alternatives provided, while in case of the middle level officers nearly 6.72 per cent of respondents have given a negative reply by responding as 'do not know', and about 1.68 per cent responded as knowing about Acts/Declarations that cover Human Rights context like Standard Minimum Rules for Treatment of Prisoners (1977), only 0.84 per cent is aware of United Nations Declaration of Rights of Offenders (1955). Whereas in case of the third category consisting of constables, response is almost negative, i.e. 85.72 per cent, while 2.52 per cent of respondents discussed about Code of Conduct for Police in India (1985) (see Sub-Graph. 5.6.1).

Although, it would be very difficult to believe the negative response coming up from the organization in-charge of law and order, viz., police in the country and it is also true as ifnformal discussion revealed that most of these officers at the higher/middle level have barely any time to familiarise themselves with documents or with the changing time and affairs that are occurring at the global level. As a result of this, those men who are functioning under this organization have very little time to update themselves. Engrossed in their mundane activity of day-to-day administration like writing beat book, adhering to regular attendance and concentrating on routine offenders or attending to higher officers at lower levels, while at middle level their preoccupation with their

Sub-Graph 5.6 : Can you name the Acts/Declarations, which cover Human Rights content but are specific to Police Administration?

	Category I	*Cetegory II*	*Cetegory III*
1.	0.00%	0.84%	0.00%
2.	0.00%	1.68%	0.00%
3.	0.00%	0.00%	0.00%
4.	0.84%	0.00%	0.00%
5.	0.00%	0.00%	0.00%
6.	0.00%	0.00%	0.00%
7.	0.00%	0.00%	2.52%
8.	1.68%	6.72%	85.72%

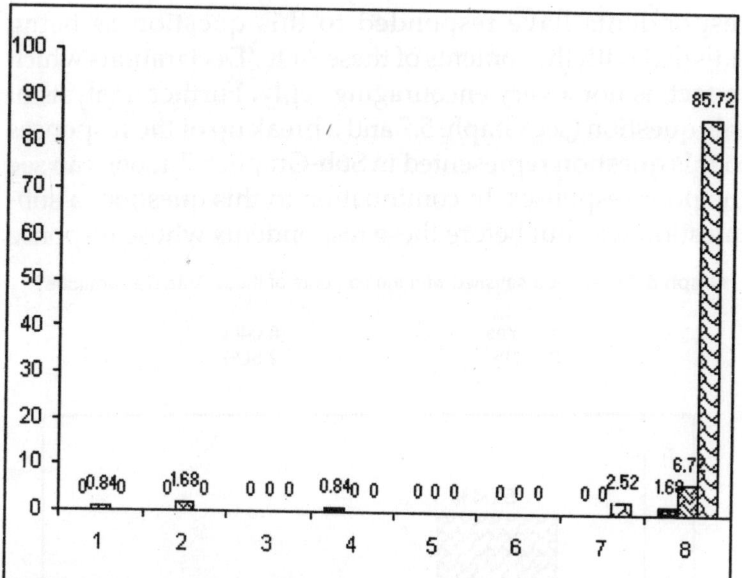

routine round up beats and monitoring activities seems to hinder their understanding, although many of them in these cadres showed their keen interest in knowing about these acts. Higher officers, who actually have more or better opportunity to spare time to learn and impart, are engaged in social functions or other obligatory activities both personal or otherwise. Their preoccupation with administration rather than concentrating on upgradation of their knowledge and imparting the same to the lower level officers or to juniors does not seem to interest them more. Although, the respondents were not very clear about the acts that govern them, being conscious of the fact that experience is a great teacher, a further question to this was asked to know from the respondents by virtue of their experience if they were satisfied with the contents of above Acts/Declarations. The responses to this question was also quite shocking in the sense that the respondents were not at all in a position to offer their opinions on this. A very meagre 5.04 per cent of respondents have responded to this question as being satisfied with the contents of these Acts/Declarations which in fact, is not a very encouraging reply. Further analysis of this question (see Graph. 5.7 and a break up of the responses to this question represented in Sub-Graph. 5.7.1, one can see the poor responses. In continuation to this question, a sub-question was put before these respondents whose response

Graph 5.7 : Are you satisfied with the contents of those Acts/Declarations?

1.	Yes	5.04%
2.	No	2.52%

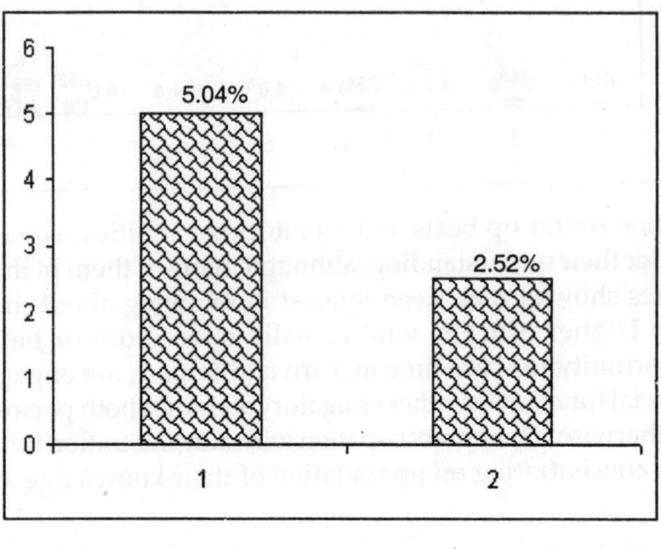

Sub-Graph 5.7.1 : Are you satisfied with the contents of those Acts/Declarations?

	Category I	*Category II*	*Category III*
1.	1.68%	1.68%	1.68%
2.	0.84%	0.84%	0.84%

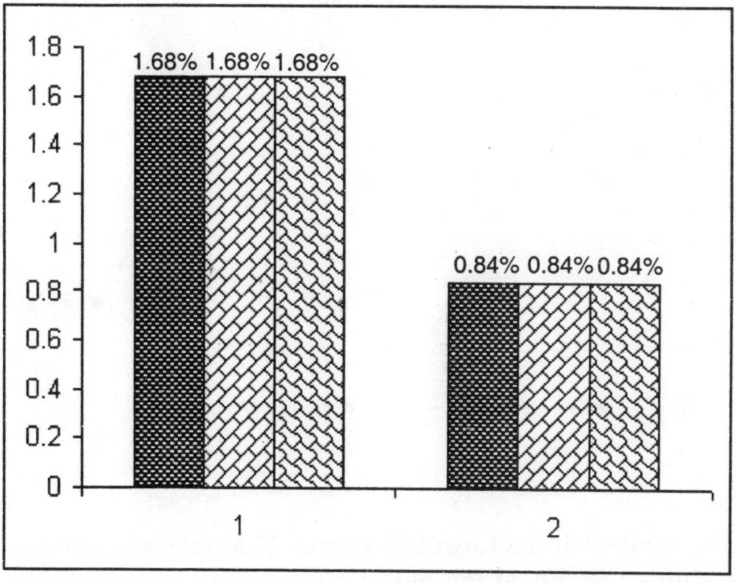

was also not very encouraging. 2.52 per cent of them expressed the reason for 'not satisfactory is that these Acts/ Declarations are unsuitable for Indian conditions (see graph. 5.7A) and category-wise responses also can be seen in sub-graph. 5.7A.

After ascertaining from the respondents their level of understanding of the various documents connected to Human Rights, a further attempt was made to know about the matrix the possible relationship that may have existed between Human Rights and Police Administration. Human Rights today has outgrown in proportions encompassing a large operational area, involving nations beyond the border, covering the national/local interests and also the rights of

Graph 5.7A : If 'No' give reasons?

1.	They are elite in content	0.00%
2.	Formulated under ideal conditions	0.00%
3.	There is need to change in the content of these Acts/ Declarations to realize them in full	0.00%
4.	Not suitable for Indian conditions	2.52%
5.	Don't know	0.84%

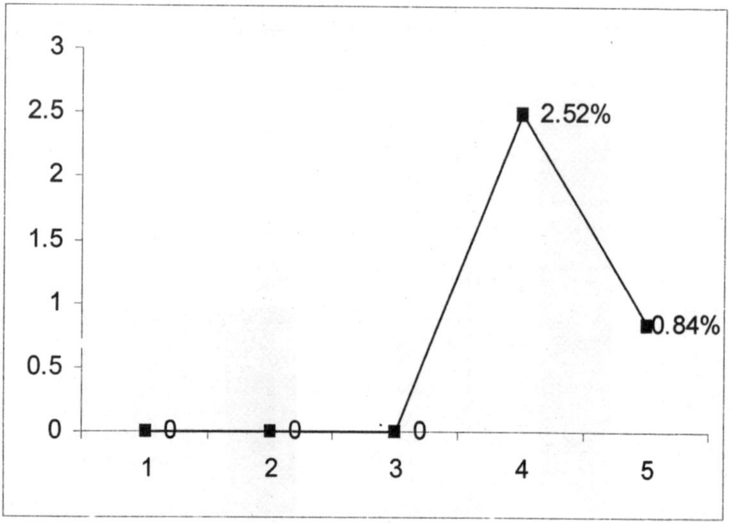

communities down to an individual. This enlarged version of Human Rights at the outset gives an impression that it also covers the rights of the citizens, may have and also those interest groups that are fighting against the state to restore the rights. Such juxtapositional counter view often confuses any researcher pursuing Human Rights *per se* and also its interrelationship with various other agencies that is operating within the society.[16] This being the crux of the problem, Human Rights and Police Administration from the angle of rights gives and impression that they are two sides of the same coin. However, if the rights are deleted then the operational area of Human Rights will demand a redefined position. This being the relationship between Human Rights and Police Administration, it is important to study how each

Sub-Graph 5.7B : If 'No' give reasons

	Category I	*Category II*	*Category III*
1.	0.00%	0.00%	0.00%
2.	0.00%	0.00%	0.00%
3.	0.00%	0.00%	0.00%
4.	0.84%	0.84%	0.84%
5.	0.00%	0.00%	0.84%

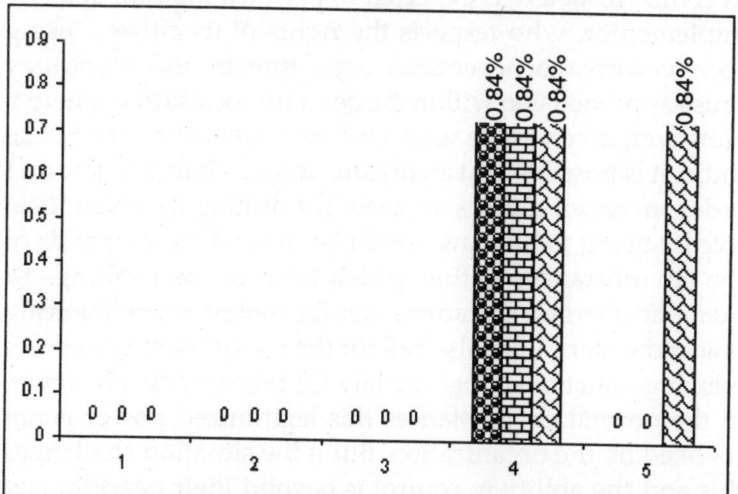

of them behave towards the other in the context that demands differential functioning of police. Having said this, let us discuss a bit about the rights as defined earlier. In fact, it is an accepted fact that rights are those privileges of every human being in a given social system to facilitate blossoming of his complete personality. The primary job of any organization within and under the jurisdiction of the state, therefore, is to work positively towards this and protect this right of an individual from being harmed by any of the existing relationships within the society. Administration being one of the more specifically established agencies with their jurisdiction falling within the broad criminal justice system is expected to work towards this goal with greater commitment. To facilitate such a committed performance, police also like any other organization under the state is established as a clearly defined organization attributed with various characteristics of an organization like hierarchy, accountability, span of control, etc., controlled by the in-built discipline, imparted social values and an operational methodology. With these attributes, Police Administration in civilized society is expected to perform the role of a law implementor, who respects the rights of its citizens using coercive force whenever necessary to threaten those who may cause apprehension within the peaceful social atmosphere.[17] However, given to the socio-cultural milieu of a society like India, it is possible that an organization incharge of law and order may not always succeed in fulfilling its given ideal role by being totally law bound because of the demands of the circumstances within which they are performing. To exemplify this fact, we can examine the context where enforcing law and order might also call for the use of coercive powers which is sanctioned legitimately for this agency. However, in the normal circumstances this legitimized power is not revoked by the organization. But if the situation challenges this and the ability to control is beyond their peaceful law implementation, then the police will in order of ascendancy use its coercive force to quell the problem confronted by them thus, involving actions beyond the stipulated jurisdiction of operation. Here, the action of police as an agency of the state will be subjected to scrutiny leading to the questions involving rights and for justice compensation, etc., in order to establish the fact that the individual in a society has the sovereign right to protect himself as per the fundamental law of the land and so these actions will have to be evoked by those agencies that in are charged with the task of bringing about justice. It in such a context that Human Rights often gets involved with police breaking with it even the minimal relation it has with Police Administration consensus in these matters, therefore, it will be the need under such circumstances to avoid any feeling amongst these agencies that one is overlapping over other's jurisdiction. The ideal relationship between Human Rights and Police Administration, therefore, is expected to be as represented in this diagram given below, an equal one and possibly, mutually contributory.

(a) *Matter of Responsibility* :

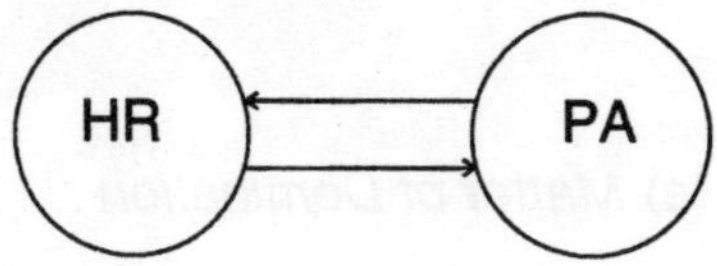

Since various constitutional rights similar to Human Rights come under the direct supervision of Police, from law and order to arrest of the criminal, etc., in a country like India, protection of these rights becomes a major concern of Human Rights activism. In spite of all these ideal conditions, due to various reasons beginning from education to constabulary level to that of the orientation and regular training intervals, there is always the likelihood of abuse of powers by the Police. Therefore, a realistic approach should be thought of to reconcile the individual rights, liberties and privileges with individual duties, obligations and responsibilities keeping the collective interest as utmost.[18] The diagram below represents this kind of an interest.

(b) *Matter of Consensus* :

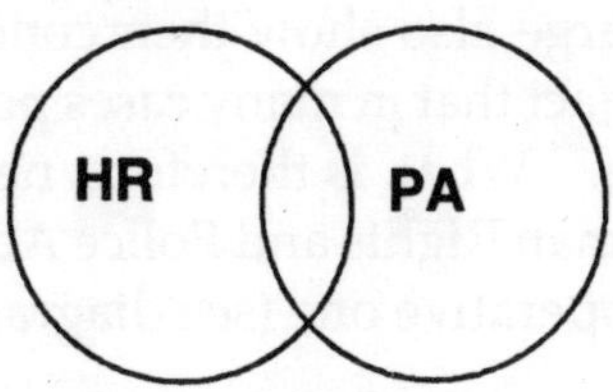

Human Rights Groups and Police Administration, therefore, are expected to work together understanding each other towards one purpose in a democratic set-up. If police on one hand is expected to uphold the Constitutional Rights and Civil Rights, Human Rights on the other, should ensure that the police as an agency does not overstep their powers and if done so, must help the citizens to restore their faith in the state and their rights that are bestowed upon them not allowing domination of anyone over the other which often happens. Diagram below represents this.

(c) *Matter of Domination :*

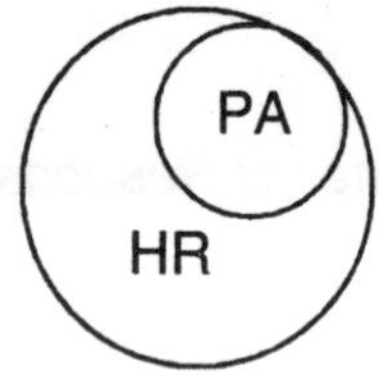

As a result of such circumstance, Police often do think that Human Rights is dominating over their administration. And this fact is revealed in our research too. A police officer with a sense of discipline, respect to his self, decorum to his role in society, morality in his profession, honour to human beings is expected to show respect and honour to Human Rights. However, this in not always the case. Often, one finds that there is some resistance from police officers to show due respect to Human Rights. They often express themselves saying that police work will become ineffective if Human Rights are fully honoured. Many a time the police always found themselves at the point of getting blames. The people at large also show their concern for Human Rights despite the fact that in many cases police are found to be on the right side.[19] What, is therefore, needed is a relationship between Human Rights and Police Administration that defines it as a co-operative one (see diagram).

(d) *Matter of Co-operational/Ideal :*

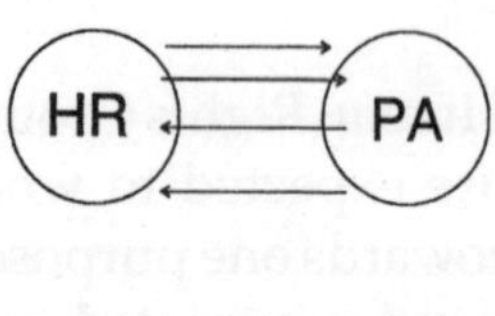

Misconceptions about each other between these two agencies are the primary reason for this. This is evidenced in our study too. Of course one cannot anticipate these things to happen overnight, but definitely can hope to find a synthesis in due course when everything will be balanced. As days pass by, the police will become more receptive to the Modern Concepts of Human Rights and Human Rights will soon reciprocate.

Having this preconceptions, a question was posed to the respondents who are functioning within the organization of police to find out if there exists any relationship between Human Rights and Police Administration. This of course, was the content of formal discussions with Human Right Groups in the study area. To this question majority of the respondents, i.e., nearly 75.63 per cent of them favoured the positive reply and they said that they believed that there exists a relationship between Human Rights and Police Administration. About 16.81 per cent of respondents gave a negative reply for this and 7.58 per cent of respondents replied as 'do not know'. Apparently, since respondents had agreed to the fact that there exists an undefined relationship between Human Right and Police Administration (see Graph. 5.8). As described in the analysis of statistics in previous question, we have tested other questions also applying the test Z-statistic and are described as below :

Considering the question :

> Do you see any relationship between the concept of Human Rights and Police Administration.
> Number of individuals said 'Yes'—82% and 'No'—18%

Based on this the hypotheses to be tested are:

H_0 : There will be one to one relationship between the concept of Human Rights and Police Administration.

H_1 : There is no such relationship.

The computed test statistic Z value (procedure as described in previous test) is 0.3182, which is greater than

Graph 5.8 : Do you see any relationship between Concept of Human Rights and Police Administration?

1. Yes 75.63%
2. No 16.81%
3. Don't know 7.58%

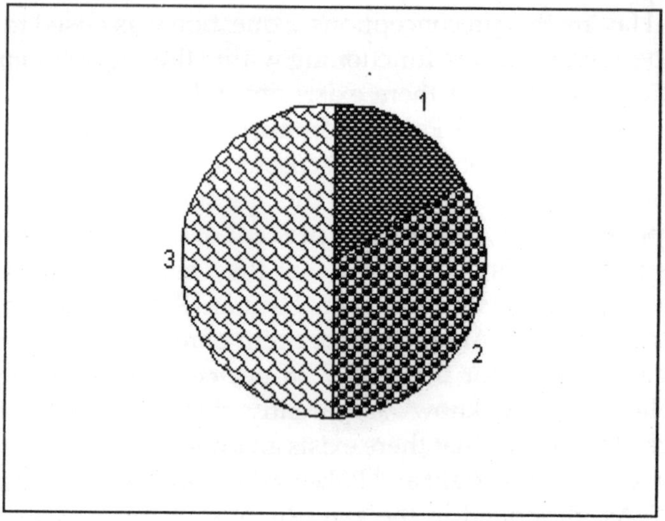

table value of Z=2.58 at 1% level of significance. Hence, the null hypothesis H_0 is accepted, implying that, significant number of police personnel have accepted that there is one to one relationship between Human Rights and Police Administration.

All the 2.52 per cent of top officials, 7.56 per cent of the middle level officers and about 65.55 per cent of lower level officers believed that there exists a relationship between the Police Administration and Human Rights. Perhaps, this is the reason why irrespective of what Human Rights actually means, that nearly 85.71 per cent of respondents had said that they had heard about Human Rights. The high profile propaganda given to introduce Human Rights in India might have induced these to believe that there exists a relationship between Human Rights and Police Administration. Only 1.68

per cent of middle level officers and nearly 15.13 per cent of the bottom level category responded negatively to this. About 7.56 per cent of constabulary category replied as 'do not know' (See Sub-Graph. 5.8.1) to this question.

Sub-Graph 5.8.1 : Do you see any relationship between Concept of Human Rights and Police Administration?

	Category I	*Category II*	*Category III*
1.	2.52%	7.56%	65.55%
2.	0.00%	1.68%	15.13%
3.	0.00%	0.00%	7.56%

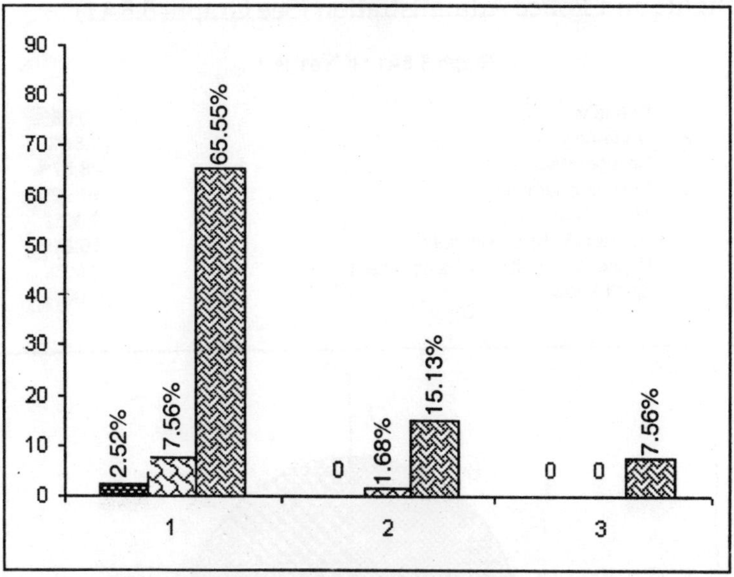

In order to get an answer and ascertain from the functionaries who have responded positively to the question about the relationship between Human Rights and Police Administration, a further rider was added to learn from them the nature of such a relationship that exists between Human Rights and Police Administration. As many as seven options were given to choose their responses that included friendly relation, co-operative relation, mutually influencing or dominant relationship and so on. Interestingly, 28,57 per cent of respondents believe that the nature of this relationship is co-operative, while 10.08 per cent have identified it as friendly. About 8.40 per cent of respondents agreed to the fact that relationship is mutually influencing and 0.84 per cent believed that relationship was unfriendly. 10.92 per cent said that it is a non-co-operative relationship and nearly 16.81 per cent believed that Human Right is dominant. This mosaic of responses clearly indicates that there is a need to give a definitive framework to this relationship between Human Rights and Police Administration (See Graph. 5.8A1).

Graph 5.8A1 : If 'Yes' is it....

1.	Friendly	10.08%
2.	Unfriendly	0.84%
3.	Co-operative	28.57%
4.	Non-co-operative	10.92%
5.	Mutually influencing	8.40%
6.	Human Right is dominant	16.81%
7.	Police Administration is dominant	0.00%
8.	Don't know	0.00%

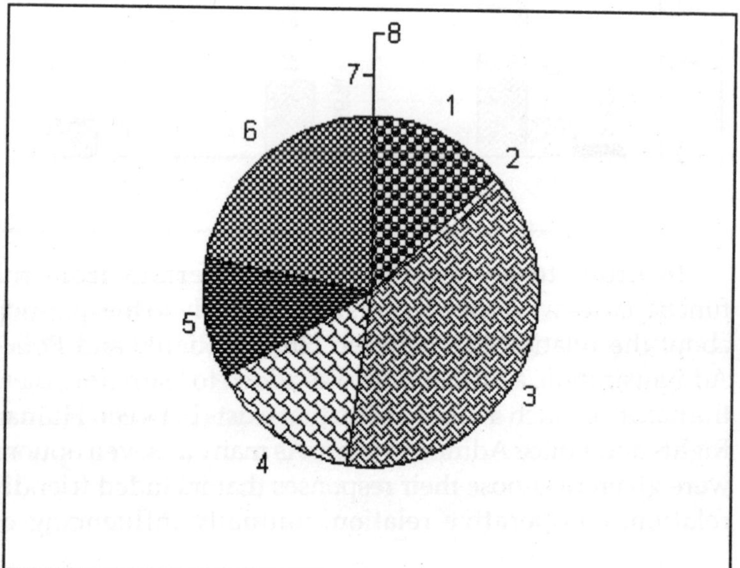

Further, if one observes the variation in the above responses closely it also gives an impression that the respondents are not clear about the kind of relationship that exists between Human Rights and Police Administration. The respondents belonging to the top officials category seem to suggest that this relationship is a kind of one sided dominance, apart from this in our informal discussions these respondents outrightly argued that Human Right is a dominating force over Police. In case of middle level officers nearly 2.52 per cent each believed that between Human Rights and Police Administration, there exists friendly and co-operative relationship. While 1.68 per cent of them joined their top officials and agreed to the fact that Human Right is dominant over Police Administration, mere 0.84 per cent of them believe that relationship between these two as mutually influencing. Among the lower level officials consisting of constables gave a surprise, since they have a totally different shade of opinion about the relations between Human Rights and Police Administration. To them this relationship is rather co-operative and 26.05 per cent of them have opted for this response, while quite a sizeable majority, i.e., 12.61 per cent believed that Human Right are dominant over Police Administration. Nearly, 10.92 per cent opined that the relationship between Human Rights and Police Administration as non-co-operative, 7.56 per cent of them each believed that it is friendly as well as mutually influencing relationship that existed between Human Rights and Police Administration. The response of top officials who are actually expected to have a complete knowledge of Human Rights and related matters somehow give a feeling that it was a calculated response that they gave to sort publicize of their allergy to Human Rights which often seeks to play a major role in the jurisdiction of Police Administration (See Sub-Graph. 5.8A2).

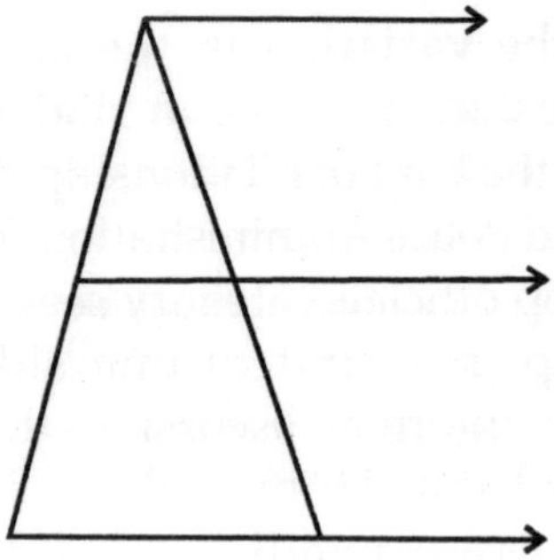

Sub-Graph 5.8A2 : If 'Yes' is it....

	Category I	*Category II*	*Category III*
1.	0.00%	2.52%	7.56%
2.	0.00%	0.00%	0.84%
3.	0.00%	2.52%	26.05%
4.	0.00%	0.00%	10.92%
5.	0.00%	0.84%	7.56%
6.	2.52%	1.68%	12.61%
7.	0.00%	0.00%	0.00%
8.	0.00%	0.00%	0.00%

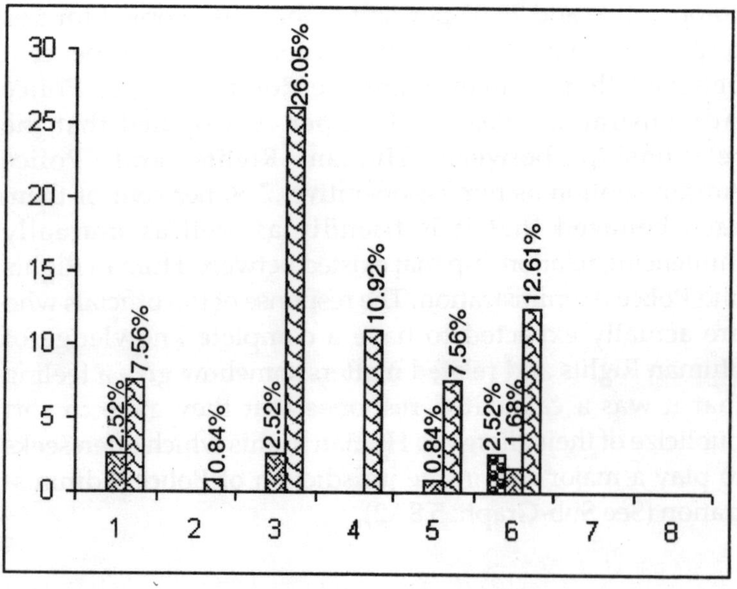

Since, Police Administration like most governmental organizations is also hierarchy ridden in structure, where towards the apex the concentration of power is high, this response (see above, i.e., Sub-Graph 5.8.A2) that Human Rights an dominating the police seems to be a conscious attempt of these higher officers to avoid Human Rights participating and intruding in their power of jurisdiction and thereby diluting this power. In the current study, it was noticed that the police were aversive to the excessive exposure given to Human Rights. In our formal discussions it was revealed that they were finding it uneasy to accept the fact that Human Rights was slowly but surely enlarging its operational jurisdiction by assuming and usurping powers of those agencies which were incharge of law and order, viz., Police.

Added to this the number of cases against police officers including the latest issues of "lawyers" strike at Delhi or the case of "Idgah Maidan" in Hubli where higher officers were targeted by activists for their decisions, also came up in the course of the discussions held with them.[20] Apart from this, these officers also brought to the centre of discussions the lacuna that exists in Indian Civil Service even to this day, where an officer holding the authority of a revenue district or taluka will have more powers over an officer of almost the equal rank merely because he carried with him the Magisterial powers to dispense justice. Citing this as an example, they voiced their disgruntleness about Human Rights in a similar fashion because Human Rights with it also carried an image of an authority that can dispense with 'justice, while police is seen merely an authority incapable of dispensing 'justice', despite the fact that Police Administration in India is operating under the umbrella of Criminal Justice System.[21] The respondents further said that perhaps it is this edge over dispensing justice that gives the feeling that Human Rights is better than Police that helps the Human Rights to dominate over Police Administration, were rather critical of this and were very vocal about it.

However, this did not seem to be the case with the middle level officers. Although, in reality it is these officers in the hierarchy of Police Administration who are responsible to implement the law and if need be to initiate necessary action at the field level. The possible disposition of these middle level officers in having a role to receiving orders from above and executing them and if needed to use coercive powers may have prompted them to locate the relation between Human Rights and Police Administration as being friendly and co-operative. Their presence at the field level and their interactions with the Human Rights group as suggested by a leader of the Human Rights Group may have been the cause for such a response. It was evident from their response that the middle level officers were aware that it would be difficult for them to perform in a society, where Human Right is given a higher value and greater degree of acceptance combined with much wider understanding publicity as compared with Police Administration, which by their own actions over a period has earned a disrepute. The middle level officers agreed to the fact that Human Right Groups have an advantage to identify themselves as an agency flowering at the people's level itself and that this legitimacy out beats the traditional position of Police Administration.which is likely to change according to them if a civic society surfaces in the future with a third power called the NGO's can grow between state and the society, they said that in the debate of globalization where rolling back of the state becomes the agenda and also more particularly the composition of the state will slowly reduce the importance of state, the majority of middle level officers were sure that they will have to accept the domination of Human Right over Police Administration. What is really hurting at this level of discussion is the fact that a very meagre per cent of respondents at this state believed that relationship between Human Rights and Police Administration is mutually influencing. While it should by any yardstick have been the correct response. Further, if one observes the responses of the third category (See Sub-Graph. 5.8.A2) which in fact in reality has direct access to public, by working on the areas such as keeping the track records of habitual offenders or criminals of all sorts and defining the relationship between Human Rights and Police Administration as being co-operative. Thus, if one observes the overall responses to this question it is very clear that a majority of them believed that the concept of Human Right has a very close co-operative and friendly kind of relationship with Police Administration and there are no hassles between these two. While there is a second opinion that Human Rights are dominant over Police. A negligible per cent of respondents, however, believed that there is non co-operative relationship between the two to a greater level. This is a satisfactory reply so far as our research is concerned, since it strengthens our hypotheses.

However, to support this observation, a question was posed to learn from the respondents as to how the concept of Human Rights mattered in their day-to-day administration. This question was designed to see whether Human Right was a cognizable part of Police Administration to establish the kind of interface that may exist between Human Rights and Police Administration. It is needless to say that Human Rights interest despite any amount of barriers has the ability to sneak into the arena of Police Administration especially at the operational level to lay check and balance, while the use of coercive powers vested in Police Administration is put to use. Out of the total 119 Police personnel, 84.03 per cent of respondents have agreed that Human Rights matter in day-to-day Police Administration. This is a very crucial response which helps us to notice the established control mechanism on use of force in Police activity. Although, it is difficult to substantiate this argument with necessary statistical input since nobody is worthy to share the fact revealed in our informal discussion is that there exists amongst the rank and file of police officials a consciousness regarding the activism of Human Rights. As against this many of the Human Rights activists believe that they involved in the issue connected with the Police only when they are sure they are playing safe. Most of the Human Rights activists interviewed here have the 'law' background. Some of them are also practising lawyers. They, like any other ordinary citizen also share the apprehension that dealing with police is not easy. They are as agreed by most of them influenced mostly by the success stories of Human Rights activism elsewhere, but on their own would think twice to get involved unless they are assured of a good support base to fight. This timidness is of course not revealed completely before the police by them. Their background of 'law' as they opined often comes to their rescue rather than their activism was of course a revelation. In this regard, they also pleaded for Human Right education at the University level too. This being the story behind Human Right activism, the response of police relating to Human Right as a matter of concern for police can be seen from another angle too. Only 7.56 per cent of respondents replied as 'no' and 8.41 per cent responded as 'do not know' also (See Graph. 5.9) the break-up of these top/middle/constabulary levels reveal the fact that 2.52 per cent of top officials have agreed to this fact and substantial percentage (i.e. 8.40%) of middle level officials also accepted that Human Right matters in their mundane administration. Approximately, 73.11 per cent from constabulary group also accepted the view expressed by their higher officers and only 0.84 per cent from middle level and 6.72 per cent from the constabulary level have responded 'no' and while 8.40 per cent from constabulary have responded as 'do not know' (see Sub-Graph. 5.9.1), these respondents although agreed to the fact Human Right matters in day-to-day administration but they did not reveal the nature of this kind of relationship. In order to understand the delicacy of this statement about the interface of Human Rights with Police Administration and also to countercheck their response to earlier question about

Graph 5.9 : Does Human Right Concept matter in day-to-day Administration of Police?

1.	Yes	84.03%
2.	No	7.56%
3.	Don't know	8.41%

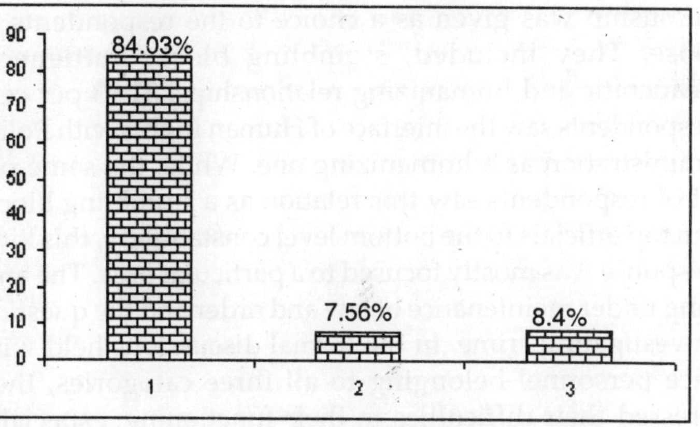

Sub-Graph 5.9.1 : Does Human Right Concept matter in day-to-day Administration of Police?

	Category I	*Category II*	*Category III*
1.	2.52%	8.40%	73.11%
2.	0.00%	0.84%	6.72%
3.	0.00%	0.00%	8.40%

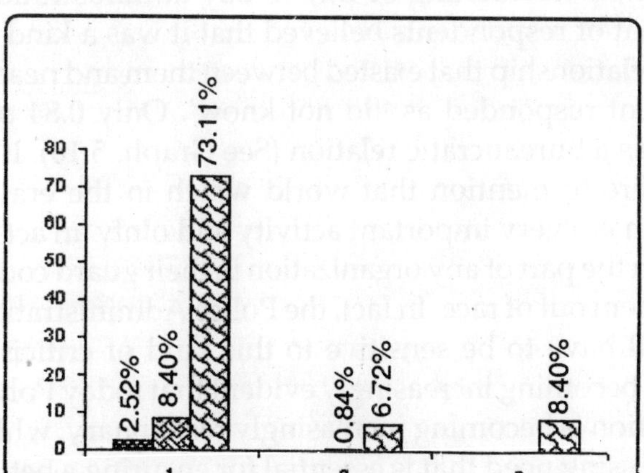

the nature of relationship that exists between Human Rights and Police Administration much more straight question was asked to learn about the possible kind of interface that Human Rights and Police Administration may have and the nature of such a relationship. Four options of such relationship was given as a choice to the respondents to choose. They included, stumbling block, bottleneck, bureaucratic and humanizing relationships. 31.93 per cent of respondents saw the interface of Human Rights with Police Administration as a humanizing one. While, the same per cent of respondents saw this relation as a stumbling block. From top officials to the bottom level constabulary, this kind of response was mostly focused to a particular area. The area falling under maintenance of law and order and the question of investigating crime. In the formal discussions held with police personnel belonging to all three categories, they expressed their difficulties in their functioning, especially while handling the allegedly accused/criminal, because of the instructions given by the Supreme Court of India in case of *D.K. Basu* Vs. *West Bengal* (instructions to protect the Human Rights of accused (see Appendix.VII). Courts imposition of a lot of responsibilities on them in these matters they felt was hampering their activity and making them feel uneasy in their functioning of day-to-day administration. 22.69 per cent of respondents believed that it was a kind of bottleneck relationship that existed between them and nearly 12.61 per cent responded as 'do not know'. Only 0.84 per cent saw it as a bureaucratic relation (See Graph. 5.10). It is pertinent here to mention that world watch in the era of globalization is a very important activity and olnly an act of ignorance on the part of any organization in their guard could only push them out of race. In fact, the Police Administration in India will have to be sensitive to this kind of criticism because it is becoming increasingly evident that today Police Administration is becoming increasingly reactionary, while the most pressing need that is essential for ensuring a better

Graph 5.10 : Do you consider that Human Rights and Police Administration as having....?

1. A stumbling block relations 31.93%
2. A bottleneck relations 22.69%
3. A bureaucratic relation 0.84%
4. A humanising relation 31.93%
5. Don't know 12.61%

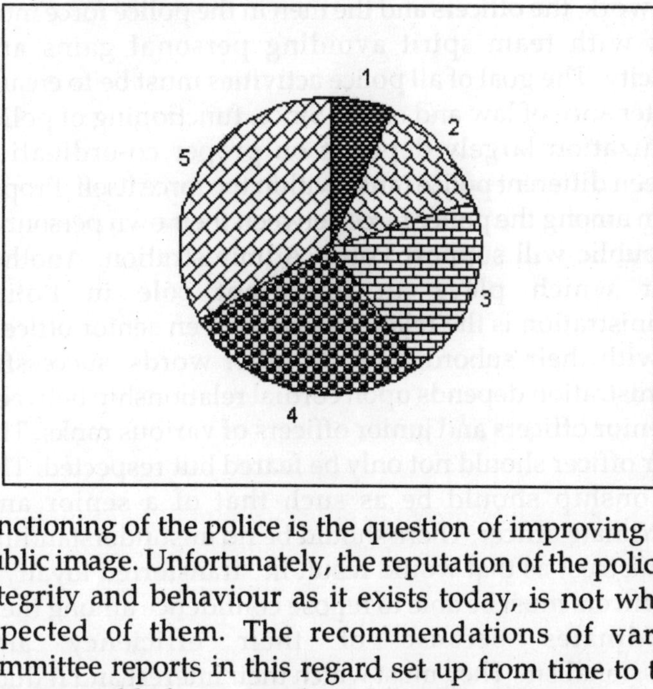

functioning of the police is the question of improving their public image. Unfortunately, the reputation of the police for integrity and behaviour as it exists today, is not what is expected of them. The recommendations of various committee reports in this regard set up from time to time, has not yielded any result or brought about any radical change. Certain prerequisites required for efficient police administration needs to be effected. They include; proper leadership, team work among various police ranks, honesty, discipline, high moral standards, etc. Referring to the recommendations made in the *Sixth Report of the National Police Commission*[22] which in fact focused upon the strong police leadership in administration calls for greater public co-operation also, which of course, is another important factor for its successful functioning. Since without public assistance it will be difficult for the police to perform. Leadership being of paramount importance helps the subordinate officers to follow the directions of their superiors if the superiors cut a niche above the rest as leaders. It is, therefore, imperative that the higher echelons of the police force are not only expected to be efficient but also are expected to be capable to provide leadership of a very high order. Similarly, the team work, the officers and the men in the police force must work with team spirit avoiding personal gains and publicity. The goal of all police activities must be to ensure maintenance of law and order. Since, functioning of police organization largely depends on proper co-ordination between different police ranks within the force itself. Proper liaison among the police force between their own personnel and public will support Police Administration. Another factor which plays an important role in Police Administration is the relationship between senior officers and with their subordinates. In other words, successful administration depends upon cordial relationship between the senior officers and junior officers of various ranks. The senior officer should not only be feared but respected. The relationship should be as such that of a senior and subordinate officer. There should be no misunderstanding and mistrust as that would result in "transferred loyalty". The officers must be able to repose confidence among their subordinates because of their efficiency and professionalism. They must watch their interest and reduce heavy load work and initiate steps to improve their service conditions.

Proper Liaison with Magistracy

It is pertinent to mention that there should be close co-operation between the District Superintendent of Police and the District Magistrate. The former is responsible for maintenance of law and order and the latter is considered to be his director in the matter of wide policies, powers that be, must ensure that District Magistrate does not overrule the District Superintendent of Police and browbeat him in the matter of transfer of subordinate officers as dual control would not be workable.

Scientific Methods

Police should not resort to third degree method as the same do not play and usually land the investigating officers in trouble. In order to bring reforms in administration, the mechanism of investigation should shift from the traditional methods (such as beating, concoction, framing of charges, framing of false cases) to new scientific methods. To work out the cases and look for finger prints, blood stains, in-depth inquiries, studying of *modus operandi* adopted by the criminals, sustained questioning of suspects, collection of criminals intelligence, watch on the activities of the criminals, surveillance on bad character, etc., would certainly pay dividends. To meet these new methods it is necessary that the forensic science laboratories are well equipped for examination of certain materials like blood stains, inks, remnants of explosions, firearms, blood, earth bullets, etc. Even latest equipments for the force will be an absolute necessity, but also the force would need to be adequately manned. In case the force is not well equipped, it would not be able to face the hostile groups and challenging situations.[23]

In order to attract good and qualified men in the police force, the service conditions need to be improved. The police, as is known have to perform long hours of duty which affects their efficiency. They, being on duty for all the 24 hours, remain under constant tension, anxiety and mental strain. It is, therefore, necessary to improve service conditions and are to be given more benefits. In this regard, the National Police Commission in its second report has been dealt with this in detail about improving service conditions, i.e., welfare measures in two categories.[24] This effort not only brings the good and qualified persons but minimize chances of corruption also. Apart from these, other factors like extensive training for policemen, periodical courses may be arranged which should include training in handling of explosives, lifting of finger prints, foot prints and scientific methods of investigation. Resistance to political pressures and supervision are the other important factors which are essential for Police Administration to function effectively.

Since Human Right has recently picked up the conscious of an average individual, Police Administration will have to be sensitive to this and act upon. About 22.69 per cent officers even to this day believe that Human Right has a bottleneck relationship with the Police Administration as referred to earlier. There is a need for working towards changing this kind of a relationship between Human Rights and Police organization who tend to presume that any agency that performs to safeguard rights of an individual seems to be having an opposing stand in relation to Police Administration. In this connection, it is pertinent to bring out the feelings expressed by the officers. They feel that unlike their organization Human Rights beyond its statutory status also has its existence in the form of NGOs and this has not only restricted their free atmosphere but also have dwindled their horizon of operation and police activism by shrinking their arena. They opined that Human Rights in fact has allowed little breathing space for them thereby choking their activity. When discussed further and asked to illustrate, they exemplified their experience with a number of cases. In today's context, having known the suspect with whom the police have been interacting, it is making extremely difficult for them to push him into police custody beyond 24 hours, during which time various degrees of investigations take place to extract the needed information from him. Even if they are permitted to retain the alleged/criminal they are apprehensive about employing any harsh methods to extract information, consequences of this the police believes in enlargement of criminal nexus and activity. They pose two reasons to strengthen their argument in this regard. (a) Human Rights activism is trying to empower the criminals by treating them as gentlemen, which according to police will not solve the problem and (b) police do their duty of tracking the alleged anti-socials within the society and producing them in person in the court. But, now-a-days in the name of Human Rights, police are not in a position to do this because of their apprehension of being made to face the trials of law by Human Right Groups. In fact, the police feel that they should be left to operate with their own experience and any reform introduced within a society should also find an exception and also act as a safety valve for performing the functions of police all by themselves. The police also were concerned when they said that they were a part of the same society and treating them as people without heart is wrong. About 0.84 per cent of them said that it was a bureaucratic relation that existed between Human Rights and Police Administration. These officers expressed their concern about the lengthy procedures that they have to follow starting from the case of registration up to finalizing and get approval of judiciary and clear the case. What is important here is not the procedure as such but there is need to maintain them in order to safeguard the interest of police themselves at times when Human Rights activists in any form would put the 'police' themselves to hardships. This over-consciousness according to the respondents, had led them to believe in the bureaucratic relation and they felt that too much bureaucratic procedures cannot help in maintaining law and order. There is need for more number of police force, specialization in terms of office maintenance, higher degree of qualification, etc., which in other words would call for a total overhaul of their organization. In the category of middle level officers nearly 4.20 per cent of each believed that there was bottleneck and humanizing relation with Police Administration, some of the officers amongst them having had their training recently from 'the Human Rights Centre of National Law School of India University, Bangalore. Since this was the training imparted to the younger officers, those who had not had this training were of the opinion that there exists bottleneck relations. One could find a distinct difference in the response of those who trained and those who did not at this stage. Most of them who felt that there existed bottleneck relation supported the arguments of their superiors. While they were excessively conscious about recent cases of Hubli-Dharwad.[25] about 0.84 per cent of the middle level officers believed that there existed a stumbling block relationship between Human Rights and Police Administration. But the total number of respondents among third category, viz., constabulary level nearly 31.09 per cent of them were of the view that it was stumbling block relation that existed between Human Rights and Police Administration. Most of them were conversant about recent incidents about Human Rights activism not only in Karnataka but also outside Karnataka and were clear about their expression that Human Rights interfered too much in their procedural ways of investigation of a crime as adopted by them.

Certain pertinent questions raised by this category like need for upgradation of arms and ammunitions, need for use of gadgets, need for training in the newest forms of investigation, in-service training, etc., related mostly to organizational efficiency, modernization and improvement needed in Police Administration. In fact, all these are legitimate demands of police and state or society seemed to have done little to answer their requirements. They in fact put forth the basic questions like their welfare, their equipments, the impetus they received as awards and rewards and wanted the state and society to contemplate on these issues before expecting too much from them. While they expressed sense of satisfaction over the concept of Human Rights outside the question of their jurisdiction, they wanted the society to react to their needs positively. Starting from their uniforms, their pay scale, training modes, recruitment procedures, service conditions, knowledge exchange, interface with international standards and organizational capabilities, renewal of laws made and procedures followed, physical fitness, service protections, support after superannuation period, utility for their expertise and many such other technical and non-technical service matters, etc., were brought by them for discussion pleading for a review. They in fact felt that these were at times the reasons for diminished police image since they were not satisfied with present organization. They reminded the fact that the police whether in media or in day-to-day activities were used/abused/belittled by way of comic expressions. By being represented as completely corrupt which could not be generalized according to them, they said, and had hampered their performance. As a researcher, it was noticed that most of these were facts and needed a thorough review.

Although, a number of reform reports have suggested these things, hardly any of these recommendations have been implemented. Therefore, one sided boost for Human Rights as against the people who deal with grim situation everyday have demoralized and, therefore, police largely are of the opinion that Human Rights and Police Administration are having a kind of stumbling block, bottleneck and bureaucratic relationship. While it is expected that they should see humanizing relation also which is mutually beneficial. About 16.81 per cent of them have expressed that there existed a bottleneck relation as against 27.73 per cent response supporting the humanizing relation and 12.61 per cent as 'do not know' (See Sub-Graph. 5.10.1) here again it is identifiable that the majority of respondents are between the age group of 30 to 40 years who are quite sensitive to this day-to-day changes in the society who have accepted the humanizing effect as a fitting reply. The fact, that there is a psychology which clearly is dominating the minds of police-

Sub-Graph 5.10 : Do you consider that Human Rights and Police Administration as having....?

	Slumbling Block Category I	*Bottleneck Category II*	*Bureaucratic relationship Category III*
1.	0.00%	0.84%	31.09%
2.	1.68%	4.20%	16.81%
3.	0.84%	0.00%	0.00%
4.	0.00%	4.20%	27.73%
5.	0.00%	0.00%	12.61%

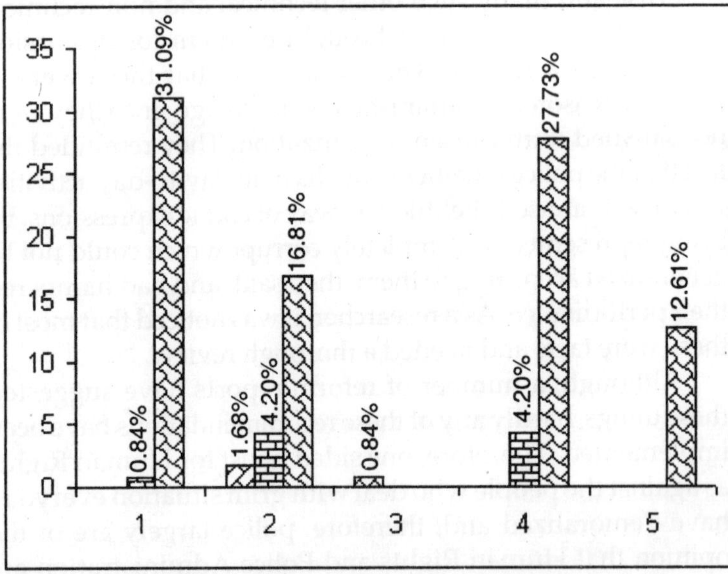

that Human Right is a superior agency and it has a boundary to operate beyond any jurisdiction and that it would question the activity of police and support the cause of criminals. Some of the interviewees openly made a remark that why these Human Rights are functioning for the benefit of criminals, although such an expression depicts their misconceptions about Human Rights activism. It was rather not easy to clear these deep impressions amongst police personnel. Despite our attempts when asked whether Human Rights interfere in Police Administration out of 119 respondents about 61.34 per cent said that Human Rights interfere in Police

Administration and 26.05 per cent opined as 'no' and 12.61 per cent replied as 'do not know' (See Graph. 5.11). Response to this question clearly indicates that significant number of police accepted that there is interference of Human Rights. Let us see this through Z-test.

Graph 5.11 : Do you think the concept of Human Rights interfere in Police Administration?

1.	Yes	61.34%
2.	No	26.05%
3.	Don't know	12.61%

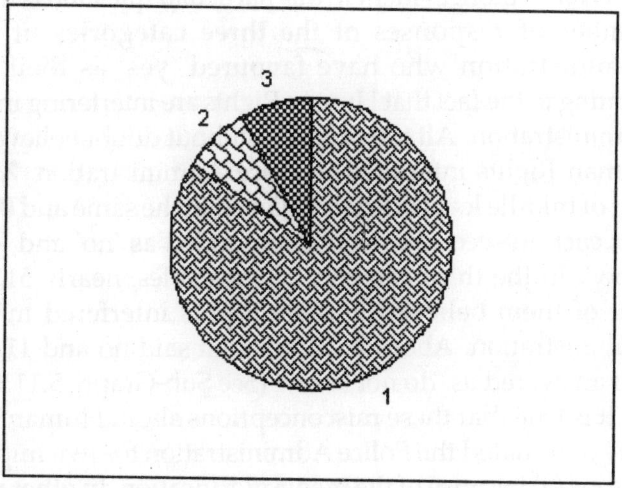

Considering the question :

Do you think the concept of Human Rights interfere in Police Administration :

Nearly 70 per cent of police personnel said 'Yes' and 30 per cent 'No'. Based on this the hypotheses to be tested are :

H_0: A proportion of Police says 'Yes'; and a proportion of Police says 'No'.

As against the following :

H_1: Significant proportion of police says 'Yes'.

The computed test statistic-Z (Procedure as described in previous test) value is 4.118, which > table value of Z which is 2.58. Hence, null hypothesis H_0 is rejected at 1 per cent level of significance and H_1 alternative hypothesis is accepted, that means significant number of police have accepted that Human Rights interferes in Police Administration.

What is more evident in this particular question is the total number of responses of the three categories of Police Administration who have favoured 'yes' as their reply, pointing to the fact that Human Rights are interfering in Police Administration. All top officials without doubt believed that Human Rights interfered in Poice Administration. 7.56 per cent of middle level officials believed in the same and 0.84 per cent each in second category responded as 'no' and 'do not know'. In the third category of constables, nearly 51.26 per cent of them believed Human Rights interfered in Police Administration. About 25.21 per cent said no and 11.76 per cent answered as 'do not know' (See Sub-Graph. 5.11.1)

It is true that these misconceptions about Human Rights have dominated the Police Administration for two important reasons (a) because of the media glorification. In other words, the glorification of media regarding Human Rights activism as against the police for no fault of theirs have made Police Administration to strongly believe Human Rights as an interference. As it happens in any developing society, since there are no civic society and that most often the other agencies like bureaucracy, military, political executives are beyond the jurisdiction of common citizens and that it is uncommon to find a case based on gender the focus of attention of media always happens to police, who are open to scrutiny. The media and Human Rights activists without looking into the complex nature of the whole issue will ony hold police

Sub-Graph 5.11.1 : Do you think the concept of Human Rights interfere in Police Administration?

	Category I	*Category II*	*Category III*
1.	2.52%	7.56%	51.26%
2.	0.00%	0.84%	25.21%
3.	0.00%	0.84%	11.76%

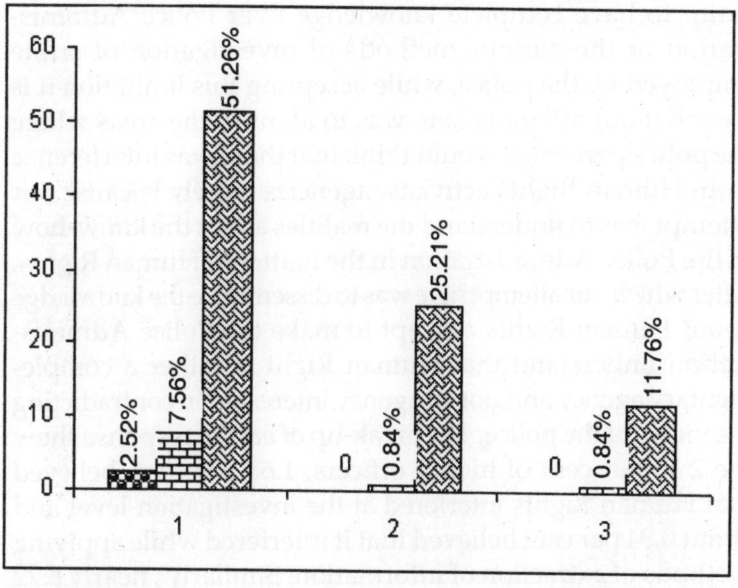

responsible for all Human Rights excesses. Nevertheless, when investigated into the levels of interference of Human Rights activism keeping in view the remarks, the police officials felt that with the increased interference of Human Rights, they will never be able to catch criminals. To investigate further it was enquired that whether respondents could identify the areas of interference of Human Rights in their administration. About 15.13 per cent of them identified that Human Rights interfered while applying various police methods to extract information from accused including the popularly known as third degree methods. About 6.72 per cent of them saw interference after imprisonment. While 5.04

per cent of them admitted that interference at the time of extending judicial rights/judicial custody. A large percentage of 33.61 responded as 'do not know' to this question, while a majority of the respondents, i.e., about 39.50 per cent of them felt its interference at the investigation level (See Graph. 5.12).

Although, as a researcher in political science, one cannot claim to have complete knowledge over Police Administration or the various methods of investigation of crime employed by the police, while accepting this limitation it is true that our attempts here was to identify the areas where the police personnel would think that there was interference from Human Rights activists/agencies merely because our attempt was to understand the realities about the know-how of the Police Administration in the matter of Human Rights. After which our attempt here was to disseminate the knowledge about Human Rights concept to make the Police Administration understand that Human Right is rather a complementary agency and not an agency interested in contradicting the views of the police. The break-up of earlier response show the 2.52 per cent of higher officers, 1.68 per cent believed that Human Rights interfered at the investigation level and about 0.84 per cent believed that it interfered while applying methods of extraction of information. Similarly , nearly 6.72 per cent of middle level officers believed that Human Rights interfered at investigation level and 0.84 per cent believed that Human Rights interfered after imprisonment and as 'do not know'. About 31.09 per cent from third category of constables believed that the Human Rights interfered at investigation level in police administration. 14.29 per cent said it interfered at that stage when various methods applying to extract information from the accused/criminals. 5.04 per cent of them said at the time of extending judicial rights/judicial custody and 5.88 per cent believed that after imprisonment Human Rights interfered. About 31.92 per cent replied as 'do not know'. Reacting to the interference of Human Rights, some top brass agreed that Indian Police still

Graph 5.12 : Can you identify the areas of their interference?

1.	At the investigation level	39.50%
2.	While applying methods of extraction of information	15.13%
3.	At the time of extending judicial rights/judicial custody	5.04%
4.	After imprisonment	6.72%
5.	Don't know	33.61%

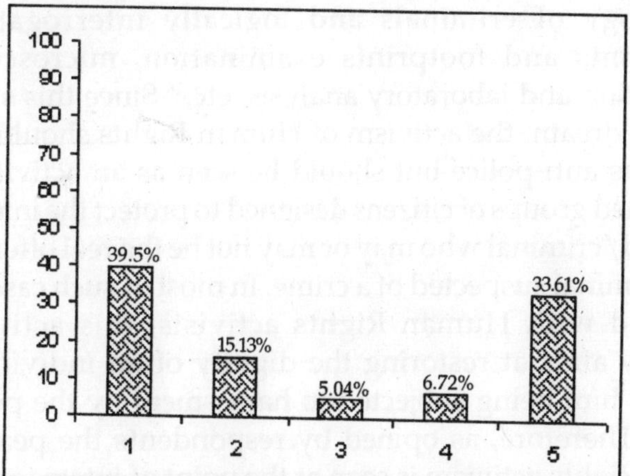

far away from accepting scientific methods of investigation and many of them suggested to bring about reforms in Police Administration (See Sub-Graph. 5.12.1)

Primarily, investigation in India begins with assumption and presumption that criminal activity except for the cases of murders begins with the criminal who has a track record. This kind of presumption leads to unwanted arrest of the alleged criminal depending on the nature and characteristics of crime committed. With the arrest of habitual offender/ criminal by the police, the work of extracting information starts initially with the third degree methods, which involves beating on toe, feet aeroplane method, i.e., hanging the person upside down, shock (treatment), punishment, etc., so that the police may find a clue to the crime committed. At this stage it is important to know what actually is criminal investigation. In fact, it simply means reconstructing the circumstances of an illegal act or omission and the mental state accompanying it. It is probing from the known to the unknown, backward in time and its goal is to determine truth as far as it can be discovered, in any *post factom* inquiry. As against this, scientific methods means application of forensic knowledge while investigating, using lie detector, studying psychology of criminals and logically interrogating, fingerprints and footprints examination, microscopic examination and laboratory analysis, etc.[26] Since this still a far away dream, the activism of Human Rights should not be seen as anti-police but should be seen as an activity of enlightened groups of citizens designed to protect the interest of alleged / criminal who may or may not be the real offender or the criminal suspected of a crime. In most of such cases as discussed with Human Rights activists, this activism primarily aims at restoring the dignity of an individual, avoiding him being subjected to harassment by the police agency. Therefore, as opined by respondents the peak of Human Rights activism is seen at the point of interrogation of the criminal itself. The second option is while applying methods to extract information although much is done behind the screen within the four walls of police station.

After identifying some of the areas of interference which the police believe the existence of Human Rights. An attempt was made to learn from the police if Human Rights were always a part of Police Administration, this question was posed relating it to the initial discussions held about the existence of components of Human Rights within Police Administration. As it happens in many cases, the hidden issue at the surface often hijacks the entire organization even here, Human Rights which were a wider part of Police Administration with its formal recognition has now come up into the mainstream, since Police Administration for quite a long period has been grounded by various criminal laws. This question was put to respondents to learn from them their responses. 35.30 per cent of respondents responded as 'do not know' for this question, 33.61 per cent have responded as positive stating that Human Rights had always been a part of Police Administration, without its formal recognition and 31.09 per cent respondents said that they had an idea about it (See Graph. 5.13). Keeping in view these responses,

Graph 5.13 : Do you think Human Rights without its formal recognition has always been a part of Police Administration?

1.	Yes	33.61%
2.	No	31.09%
3.	Don't know	35.30%

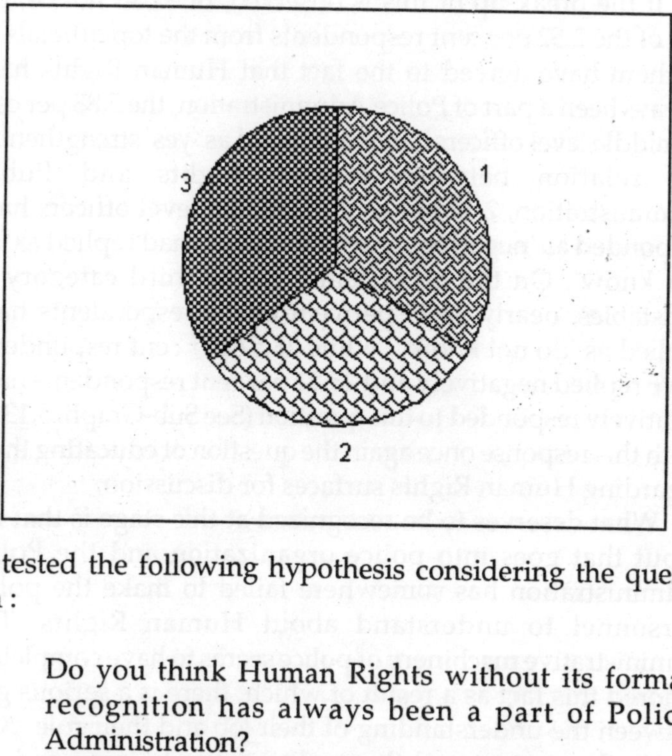

we tested the following hypothesis considering the question :

> Do you think Human Rights without its formal recognition has always been a part of Police Administration?
>
> A number of Police said 'Yes': 52% and 'No' : 48%. Based on this, the hypotheses to be tested are :

H_0: With or without formal recognition of Human Rights have always been a part of Police Administration

Against ;

H_1 : Without its formal recognition Human Rights have always been a part of Police Administration.

The table value of Z is 2.58 at 1 per cent level of significance and calculated value of Z statistic is 0.18898 > table value (procedure as described in previous test). Hence, alternative hypothesis is accepted implying that significant number of police personnel have accepted that without its formal recognition Human Rights have always been a part of Police Administration.

If the break-up of this is observed, one can notice that out of the 2.52 per cent respondents from the top officials all of them have agreed to the fact that Human Rights have always been a part of Police Administration, the 5.88 per cent of middle level officers have responded as 'yes' strengthening the relation between Human Rights and Public Administration, 2.52 per cent of middle level officers have responded as 'negative', and 0.84 per cent had replied as 'do not know'. On the other hand, in the third category of constables, nearly 34.45 per cent of the respondents have replied as 'do not know,' while 28.57 per cent respondents have replied negatively and 25.21 per cent respondents have positively responded to this question (See Sub-Graph. 5.13.1). With this response once again the question of educating them regarding Human Rights surfaces for discussion.

What deserves to be recognized at this stage is that the input that goes into police organization and the Police Administration has somewhere failed to make the police personnel to understand about Human Rights. The administrative machinery of police seems to have completely ignored this fact as a result of which, there is a serious gap between the understanding of their job and their role. As a result, the content and the quality police training and the realities of Police Administration are often found at contradicting positions. While on the one hand, the content of Police training speaks of its rules/regulations/procedures,

Sub-Graph 5.13.1 : Do you think Human Rights without its formal recognition has always been a part of Police Administration?

	Category I	*Cetegory II*	*Cetegory III*
1.	2.52%	5.88%	25.21%
2.	0.00%	2.52%	28.57%
3.	0.00%	0.84%	34.45%

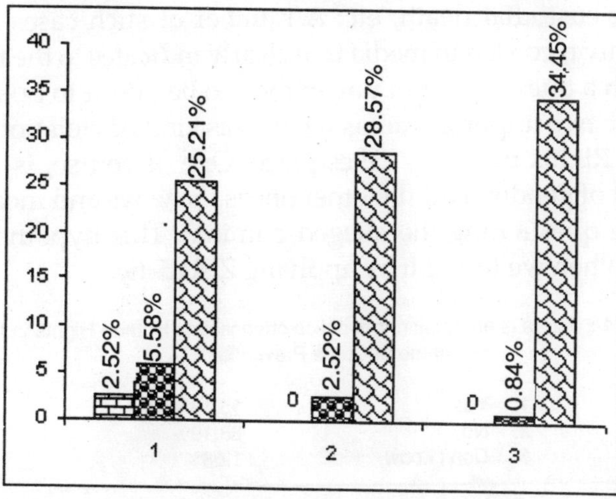

etc., and seems to completely give well-versed versions. The components of Human Rights and their practice that are to be put to use at the practical level seems to be totally neglected.[27]

In order to explicitly find out these gaps, a very intriguing question was put to the respondents in the form of a general opinion exercise. But this question was put in its negative tone stating that police often violate Human Rights in the name of crime prevention with options of 'yes' or 'no'. Out of 119 respondents nearly 83.19 per cent of respondents disagreed to this view. 15.13 per cent of them agreed to this, and about 1.68 per cent of respondents replied as 'do not know' (See Graph. 5.14). It is true that this is a very sensitive question and also a kind of indirect attack on the police, although, it is not hypothetical since there are many studies[28] undertaken in this direction which hints at such a thing as happening. These studies also clearly narrate the incidents of violation of Human Rights by the police in the name of crime prevention. Cases such as that of victims rape within the police station, inhuman degrading treatment, unnatural ways of harassing and also the violent methods of extracting information, cases like blinding custodial death, etc. A number of such cases are commonly recorded in media that clearly indicates to the fact that such a question is not uncommon to be posed to police. There are two important areas where this kind of violation of Human Rights normally takes place. One of course, is the question of gender, and the other one is the ways and means of police questioning the alleged criminal. This hypothesis proved when we tested it by applying Z statistic.

Graph 5.14 : There is an opinion that police often violate Human Rights in the name of Crime Prevention?

1.	Yes	15.13%
2.	No	83.19%
3.	Don't know	1.68%

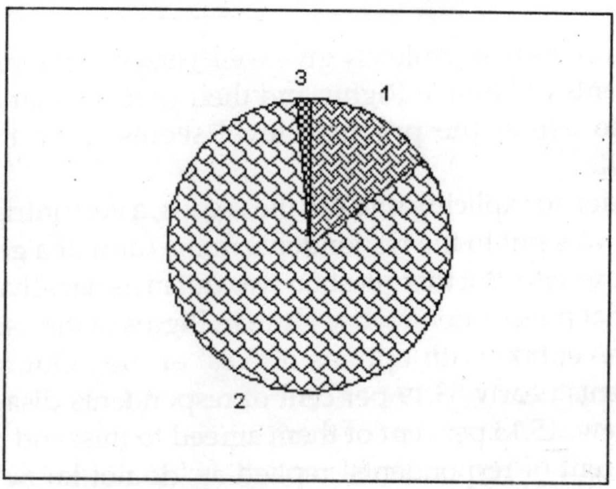

Considering the question :

> There is an opinion that police often violate Human Rights in the name of crime prevention.

15% have replied 'Yes' and 85% have replied as 'No'.

Based on this, the hypotheses to be tested are :

H_0: There may or may not be the opinion that police often violate Human Rights in the name of crime prevention

Against :

H_1: There is no such opinion about police.

The calculated value of Z statistic is 2.29643 (procedure as described in previous test) and table of Z is 2.58 at 1 per cent level of significance. Calculated Z value< Z table value, means H_0 null hypothesis is rejected and H_1 alternative hypothesis is accepted.

In the latter case, means adopted is always targeted in terms of violation of Human Rights. It is observed that despite 83.19 per cent of the respondents registering their dissension to this kind of allegation, in the course of the discussion, it was noticed that they were not completely obsessed with the information that could help them to defend their arguments. On the other hand, it was observed that police personnel only attempted to shield their image rather than substantially defend themselves against the allegations. Amongst higher officers, about 1.68 per cent disagreed to this, while 0.84 per cent have agreed that they often violate Human Rights in their functioning. However, much of their argument was in favour of protecting the image of police in Karnataka rather than the image of police in India. Amongst middle rank, about 6.72 per cent replied negatively to this allegation of violating Human Rights in the name of crime prevention. While 2.52 per cent respondents agreed to this. Of the 2.52 per cent, most of them agreed to the fact that majority of the cases of violation of Human Rights is unintentional but it has become a vital aspect about which there is need to sensitise the police, who otherwise not being intentional may commit this violation. Especially during the process of interrogation they said, such a violation is necessitated resulting in unexpected turn in the cases. Those who disagreed that police violates Human Rights argued that this kind of allegation is a kind of smear, campaign against police organization because Human Right activists instead of enlarging their operations to other areas, such as problems of poverty, hunger, right to education, etc., want to catch on with police to claim their success to see themselves as progressive. In other words, they were of the opinion that Human Right encompassed the issue like poverty, hunger, gender discrimination in public places, violence against women, etc., and most of the organizations including the Women Commission, National Human Rights Commission and such other Commissions concerned with protection of civil liberties, including the Civil Liberty Movement itself aim mostly at targeting the police which is rather easily accessible. While the messages about police violence gets or is given so much publicity, the same thing is not true of women exploitation, gender discrimination or the issues of poverty or hunger. This kind of one sided and excessive publicity they said now often made it difficult for the police to perform or defend themselves.

The middle level officers and top brass offcials, therefore, put forth a challenge before Human Rights groups to work successfully in locating on their own either problem of bonded labour or the people subjected to humiliation by virtue of caste, creed and gender discrimination or to locate the problems of poverty which are difficult subjects and which needs the force behind Human Right Groups to locate these problems they once again said that it is easy for the Human Rights groups to accuse the police whose support is always needed even by Human Rights groups and in their efforts at restoring the so-called rights.

While it is a fact that this kind of criticism against Human

Rights in a country like India. Where the published stories speak more of Human Rights in relation to Police Administration, while not many stories seem to be coming in the purview of Human Rights jurisdiction itself, although, the operational areas of Human Rights cover wider space, i.e., from poverty to right to life. Even to this day many of the studies reveal[29] that there are bonded labour activity within the reach of Human Rights and not much has been done by them. The activity of Human Rights Groups also seem to restrict itself within the academic territory or taking the cause of much published cases rather than working on its own merit investigating into these issues.

In the areas of Hubli-Dharwad, there are hardly one or two Human Rights groups. One is "Society for Human Rights Law" which is indulging in conducting annual seminars on Human Rights but not really active in terms of field level activism. The office bearers of this organization believe that Human Rights are still to catch up with public imagination. Therefore, right now they are concentrating only on popularizing Human Rights through academic activities. Another organization is run by lawyers which is also concentrating on conducting seminars and bringing in various academic and other guilds who are concerned about Human Rights together. Apart from these, in the recent years Rotary Clubs around Hubli-Dharwad are having small groups for Human Rights and they are also involved in undertaking this kind of academic activity. Since these are not activists groups here they have little data with them to argue in either way with the police. Most of the respondents belonging to this group, therefore, simply concede to the police accusations that the Human Rights has been active only in terms of finding fault with police than to function on their own merit to fight for real issues like, child labour or clean environment. Even when they address these issues in public the Human Rights Groups agreed that they do so with the support of secondary sources and nothing from their own efforts or through their investigations. This being the reality at ground level, Human Rights groups wish to take on the criticism of the police without vindicating it. At the third level, respondents consisting of police constables nearly 74.79 per cent of respondents negate this view that police often violate Human Rights. About 11.76 per cent of them agreed to the fact that there is violation of Human Rights. Once again their plea is that it happens without intention and that they are not guilty of it. About 1.68 per cent of respondents have replied as 'do not know'. One reason for this acceptable view that it happens without intention is that the police in this society are not fully aware of their rights and duties and, hence, violation of Human Rights is often seen as a common thing happening. Amongst 2.52 stratified groups (see sub-graph. 5.14.1), it is clear that there is still need for inclusion of component of Human Rights information in the police echelons and to disseminate amongst the police force.

In order to learn and to locate exactly where the police personnel see the component of Human Right in their organization structure, it was noticed that nearly 47.90 per cent respondents located this at the official/administrative procedure level. This in other words would amount to saying that the Human Rights component is more a procedural issue and not really an empirical issue connected with the day-to-day activities of police personnel. Quite possibly, perhaps this is the reason why today it is very difficult to identify or build a database about the police atrocities or their violations against Human Rights. 26.89 percent believed that Human Right component is given cognizance at the level of implementation of judicial proceedings. Since Judiciary is likely to observe the drawback of the police in matters relating to violations by police. While for an option 'any other reason', nearly 7.65 per cent respondents responded and said that at the time of investigation and handling the accused/ criminals that Human Right importance is felt. 6.72 per cent

Sub-Graph 5.14.1 : There is an opinion that Police often Violate Human Rights in the name of Crime Prevention?

	Category I	*Category II*	*Category III*
1.	0.84%	2.52%	11.76%
2.	1.68%	6.72%	74.79%
3.	0.00%	0.00%	1.68%

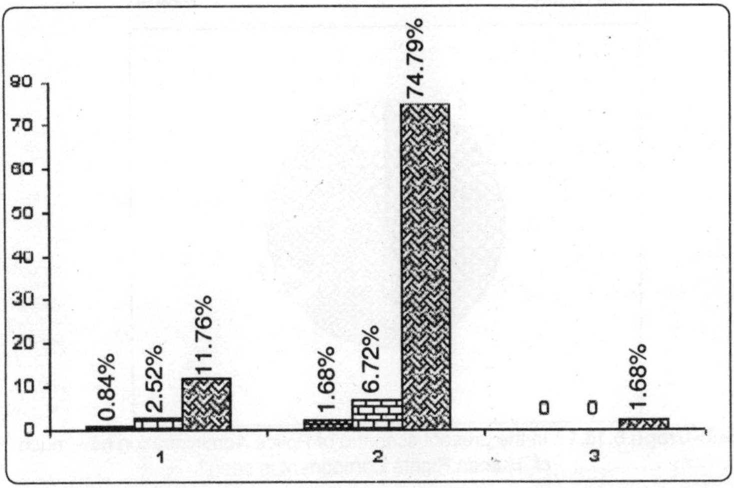

believed that Human Rights component is seen connected to the police training/curriculum procedure. So it is apparent that Police Administration does not on its own see the component of Human Right as a guiding star. They seem to notice the violation of Human Rights in their organization only at a stage when actually the police is made conscious of it at several stages of dealing with the alleged/criminal (See Graph. 5.15). The response of 3 stratified categories also given in Sub-Graph. 5.15.1 given a break-up of the total responses. With this being the status of the component of Human Rights within police organization, it would be redundant to stress on the fact that there is need to strengthen Human Rights matters *vis-à-vis* police force. However, the above argument also gives enough scope to speak the fact that Human Rights are not merely the concern of police alone and that action

Graph 5.15 : In the present scenario of Police Administration how much of Human Rights Component is seen?

1.	Only in training/curriculum procedure	6.72%
2.	At official/administrative procedure	47.90%
3.	While implementing judicial proceedings	26.89%
4.	Any other	17.65%
5.	Don't know	0.84%

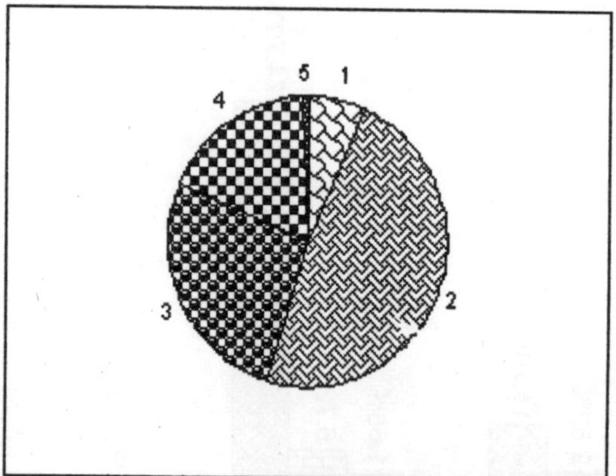

Sub-Graph 5.15.1 : In the present scenario of Police Administration how much of Human Rights Component is seen?

	Category I	*Category II*	*Category III*
1.	0.84%	0.00%	5.88%
2.	1.68%	5.88%	40.34%
3.	0.00%	1.68%	25.21%
4.	0.00%	0.84%	16.81%
5.	0.00%	0.84%	0.00%

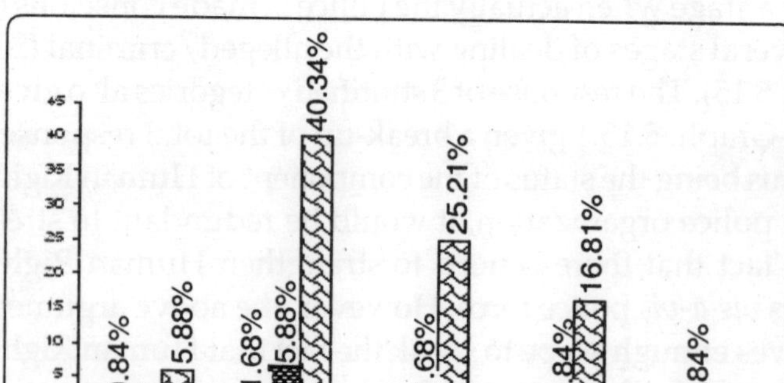

not seen by police themselves could be brought to the notice of police and that this Human Rights organization itself could do this job. While there is no second opinion about the need to concerntrate on the issue of educating the police in matters of Human Rights. There is also need for the larger group for citizens to be aware of Human Rights in the event of themselves being caught by surprise for violations of Human Rights in their day-to-day life. In this connection, to examine the response of the police and the Human Rights activist's groups were served with a question to learn from them how they see this issue. An overhauling 83.19 per cent police personnel have agreed that it is not the concern of police alone, 12.61 per cent agreed that it is the concern of police and 4.20 per cent replied as 'do not know', to this question (See Graph. 5.16). A break-up of this question for their faith in this aspect whether Human Rights are the concern of others other than the police is represented in (Sub-Graph. 5.16.1). Considering the question: Do you think Human Rights is a concern of police alone?

Graph 5.16 : Do you think the Concept of Human Rights is the concern of Police alone?

1.	Yes	12.61%
2.	No	83.19%
3.	Don't know	4.20%

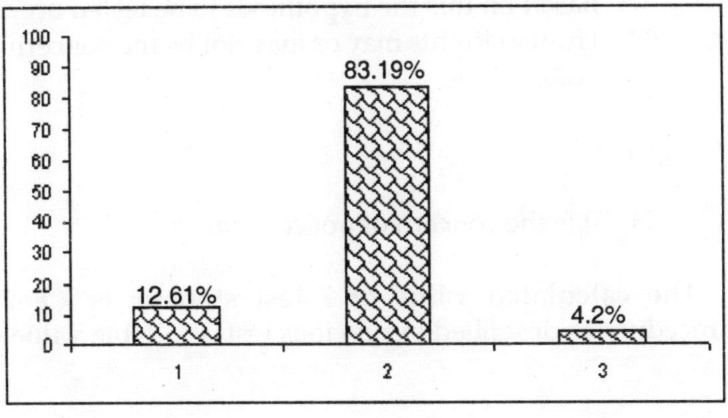

Sub-Graph 5.16 .1: Do you think the Concept of Human Rights is a concern of Police alone?

	Category I	*Category II*	*Category III*
1.	0.84%	1.68%	10.08%
2.	1.68%	7.56%	73.95%
3.	0.00%	0.00%	4.20%

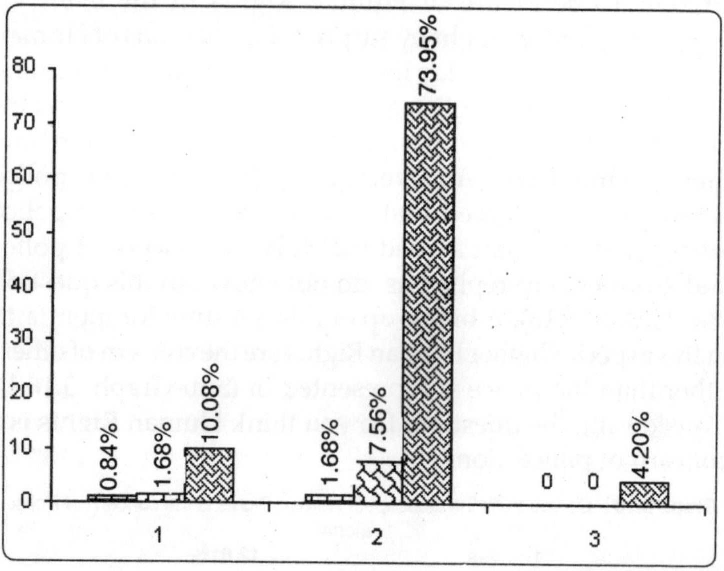

13 per cent of police said 'Yes' and 87 per cent said 'No' to this question.

Based on this the hypotheses to be tested are :

H_0: Human Rights may or may not be the concern of police alone

Against,

H_1: It is the concern of police alone.

The calculated value of Z-test statistic is 7.8672, (Procedure as described in previous test) is > table value of

Z=2.58 at 1 per cent level of significance. Hence, null hypothesis is accepted implying that significant number of police have not accepted that Human Rights is only the concern of police alone.

In the last part of the schedule a fast run test of understanding the relation between Human Rights and Police Administration and re-emphasizing their relationship was attempted with statements having options relating to the relation between Human Rights and Police Administration as positive, negative, mutually beneficial and neutral etc., were posed (see Graph. 5.17). Out of total 119 respondents, nearly 50.42 per cent opined that the relationship is positive. While 0.84 per cent of top officers, 1.68 per cent of middle level officers and 47.06 per cent of lower category believed in this opinion, 13.45 per cent of total respondents believed that this relationship is negative. 0.84 per cent of top brass, 0.84 per cent of middle level officers and 11.76 per cent of respondents from the constabulary level believed in this opinion. About 24.37 per cent believed in a kind of mutually beneficial relationship. This response had about 0.84 per cent of top brass, 4.20 percent of middle level officers and 19.33 per cent of constabulary. While 5.88 per cent each from the total respondents believed that the relationship between Human Rights and Police Administration is neutral and do not know respectively (see sub-graph. 5.17.1).

An overall total percentage indicates the fact that there is positive, negative and mutual beneficial relationship between Human Right and Police Administration. One observation that can be made here is that there is need to make this relationship neutral, in order to drive home the point neither of them work against each other. Further, another statement was put before them hinting at 3 possible replies, i.e., 'agree', 'disagree' and 'do not know', in relation to the idea that Human Right should be a part of Police Administration. The responses are represented in Graph. 5.18. About 76.47 per cent of police constabulary, 9.24 per cent middle level officers and 2.52 per cent of higher officers,

Graph 5.17 : The relationship between Human Rights and Police Administration is ....

1. Positive 50.42%
2. Negative 13.45%
3. Mutually beneficial 24.37%
4. Neutral 5.88%
5. Don't know 5.88%

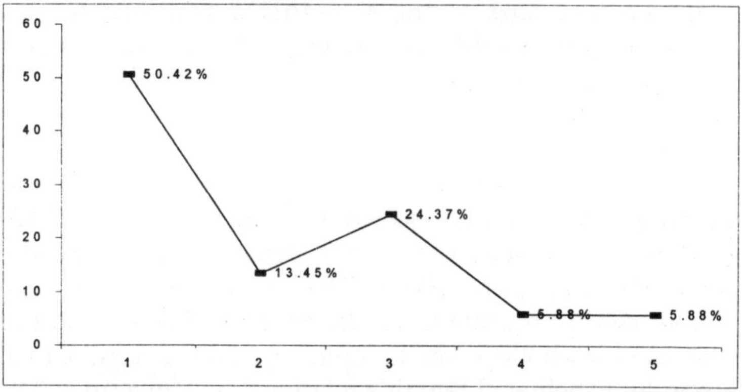

Sub-Graph 5.17.1 : The relationship between Human Rights and Police Administration is :

	Category I	*Category II*	*Category III*
1.	0.84%	2.52%	47.06%
2.	0.84%	0.84%	11.76%
3.	0.84%	4.20%	19.33%
4.	0.00%	0.84%	5.04%
5.	0.00%	0.84%	5.04%

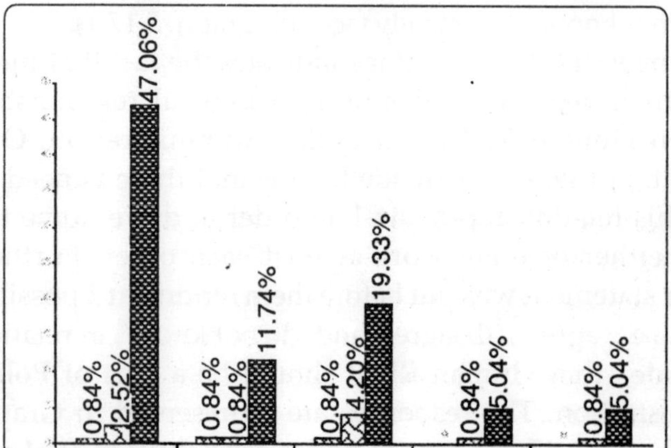

Graph 5.18 : Human Rights should be a part of Police Administration

1.	Agree	88.24%
2.	Disagree	7.56%
3.	Don't know	4.20%

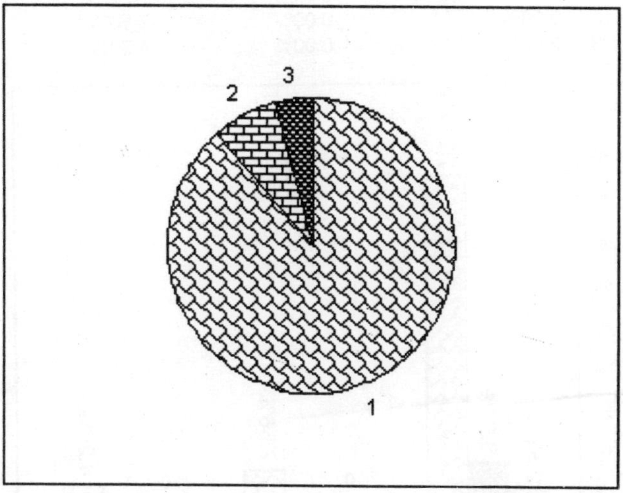

have agreed to the suggestive statement. While 7.56 per cent of police constabulary category disagree to this idea without any valid reason and 4.20 per cent said 'do not know' (See Sub-Graph. 5.18.1). This question is also put under hypothesis testing by applying Z-statistic.

Considering the question

Human Rights should be a part of Police Administration?

To this question 92 per cent have replied 'Yes' and 8 per cent have replied 'No'.

Based on this hypotheses to be tested are :

H_0: Human Rights may or may not be a part of Police Administration

Against;

Sub-Graph 5.18.1 : Human Rights should be a part of Police Administration.

	Category I	*Category II*	*Category III*
1.	2.52%	9.24%	76.47%
2.	0.00%	0.00%	7.56%
3.	0.00%	0.00%	4.20%

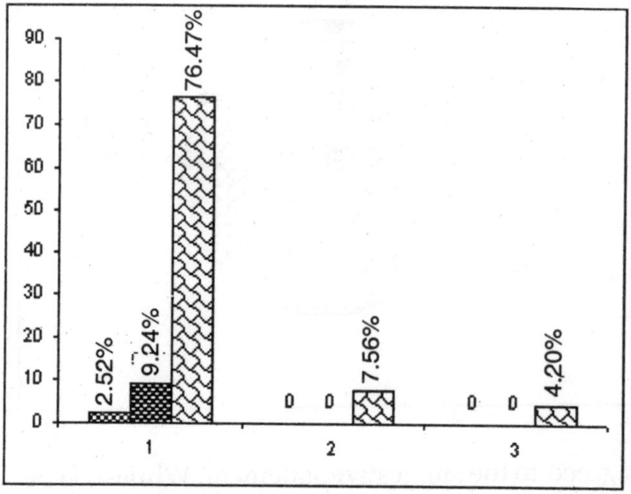

H_1: It should be a part of Police Administration

The computed test statistic Z. Value (procedure is as described in previous test) is 8.99.116, which is table value 2.58 at 1 per cent level of significance. Hence, the H_1 alternative hypothesis is accepted, implying that significant number of police preferred that Human Rights should be a part of Police Administration.

Similarly, another question was posed to learn from respondents whether they agree or disagree for the statement that Human Rights concept is functioning as catalytic agent for Police Administration. Nearly 90.76 per cent of respondent have agreed to this question, 5.04 per cent disagreed to this, and 4.20 per cent replied as 'do not know' (See Graph. 5.19). However, category-wise only 1.68 per cent of top brass agreed to this, 9.24 per cent middle level officers, and 79.84 per cent of third category agreed to this factor.

Graph 5.19 : Human Rights Concept is functioning as Catalytic Agent for Police Administration?

1. Agree 90.76%
2. Disagree 5.04%
3. Don't know 4.20%

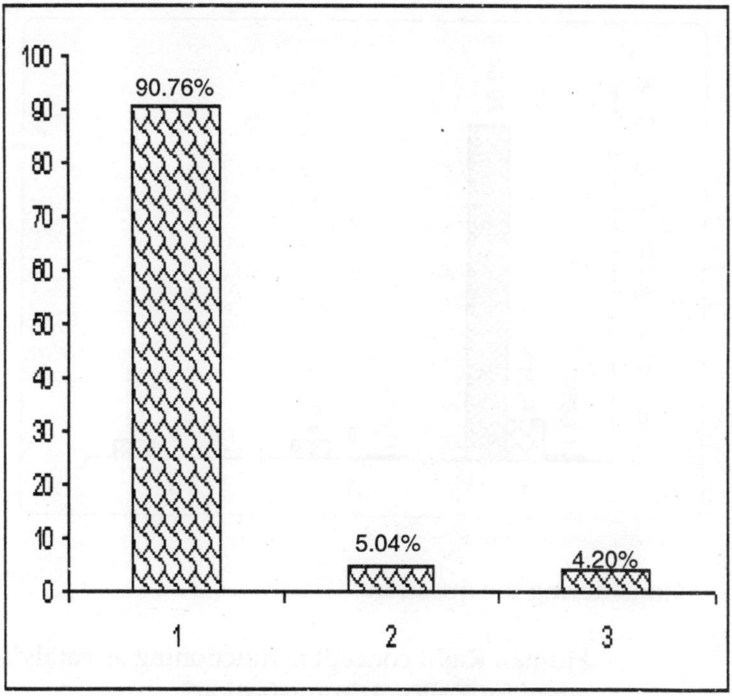

4.20 per cent from third category and 0.84 per cent of first category disagree to this and 4.20 per cent from third category replied as 'do not know'. The discussion in this regard was aiming at presenting the view that police organization have taken Human Rights as a count which had made them rather more conscious of their own activity and catching them at very stage of decision-making (See Sub-Graph. 5.19). We tested this question through Z statistic test.

Sub-Graph 5.19 : Human Right Concept is functioning as Catalytic Agent for Police Administration?

	Category I	*Category II*	*Category III*
1.	1.68%	9.24%	79.84%
2.	0.84%	0.00%	4.20%
3.	0.00%	0.00%	4.20%

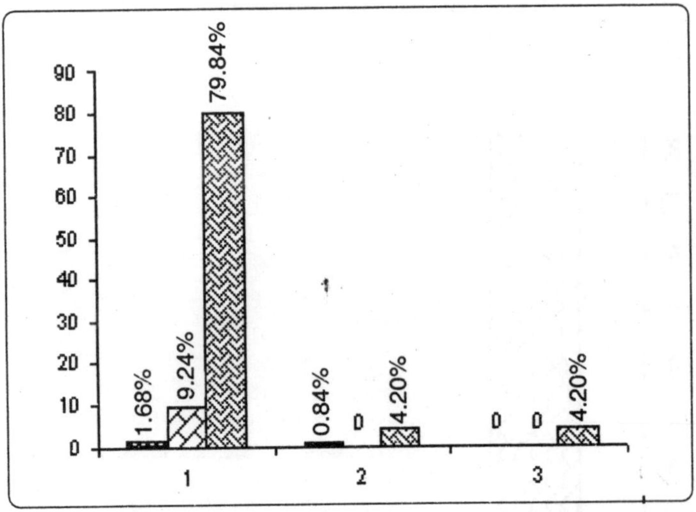

Considering the question :

Human Right concept is functioning as catalytic agent for Police Administration?
95 per cent of police said 'Yes' and 5 per cent said 'No'.
Based on this, the hypotheses to be tested are :

H_0: Human Rights may or may not function as catalytic agent in Police Administration.

Against,

H_1: It is functioning as catalytic agent for Police Administration.

The computed value of Z-statistic is 0.9552 (procedure described in previous test) which is > table value of Z is 2.58 at 1 per cent level of significance. Therefore, H_0 the null hypothesis is accepted.

Which indicates the aspect that Human Rights are not seen as positive factor supporting Police Administration. To a last question whether they would prescribe any limitations to Human Rights activism *vis-à-vis* Police Administration, 12.61 per cent of the total respondents have expressed that Human Rights activism should co-operate with police. Police did accept that teaching about Human Rights for themselves is far most essential. 1.68 per cent of respondents said that police personnel are also human beings and society should consider their rights. 11.76 per cent of police personnel were keen on their functioning and expressed that their investigative method should be free from any interference such as Human Rights activists, public, political pressure, lawyer, etc. Further, they aspired for betterment of police organization by establishing Human Rights cell at all levels of administration so that checks and balances will go hand in hand. Human Rights cells according to them should keep link with police activities/duties. 9.24 per cent of total respondents have said that Human Rights cannot be insisted upon to all the sections of criminals. Force is essential to put down the crime. Regarding this, studies conducted by Vadackumchery (1998) in his book *"Indian Police 2001:What Went Wrong Here?"*[30] clearly has hinted at reasons for the above statement. The cumulative effect of less knowledge, vague information, confused ideas and wrong side of concepts is what has promoted the police to perform their job exactly as they used to do them in the past. Fear as to whether or not they will be prosecuted because of Human Rights violations is a newly created fear amongst them that has not really contributed qualitatively to Police Administration. In continuation of the discussion with the police personnel they expressed that interrogation hours (24 hours) should be enhanced because according to them, 24 hours is not enough to get the needed information. Sometimes they said accused does not open his mouth or does not express anything to this effect, a police officer of higher rank even demonstrated this thing before a group which the researcher had led. In this context, organizational changes are essential to set right the functioning of police. Human Rights activists should also keep in contact with police regarding the cases handled by the police and must guide them on Human Rights issues and not threaten them. Nearly half of the total respondents, i.e., 49.58 per cent replied as 'do not know' to this question. 0.84 per cent of respondents from lower cadre expressed that Human Rights should be respected by higher officers. Apart from these opinions, police personnel have also expressed that their basic needs such as their welfare facilities, service conditions, qualifications, etc., should be taken care of by the organization and administration. Time schedule in duty hours, supply of advanced equipment (scientific methods). There should be medical facility and school facility to the police families like Railway employees who have separate hospital/school, and it would all go a long way to make their profession interesting. If the welfare facilities are given to them properly, people/government can demand efficiency from this organization (See Graph. 5.20).

2.52 per cent of respondents have opined that Human Rights can not be applied to all sections of criminals and the police should be given certain amount of freedom in choosing the investigative methods. Interrupting crucial activities through these pressure tactics in the name of Human Rights would only stall the activity of an organization and its objectives they said. About 1.68 per cent of respondents have in fact supported the above argument although their expressions differed. The other 2.52 per cent of respondents stated that both Human Rights and Police Organizations should work as partners having mutual co-operation and they should set their limits clearly and critically thereby

Graph 5.20 : Do you prescribe any limitations for Human Rights activities *vis-a-vis* in Police Administration?

1. 12.61%	6. 2.52%	11. 0.84%
2. 1.68%	7. 1.68%	12. 0.84%
3. 11.76%	8. 0.84%	13. 0.84%
4. 9.24%	9. 2.52%	14. 1.68%
5. 49.58%	10. 1.68%	

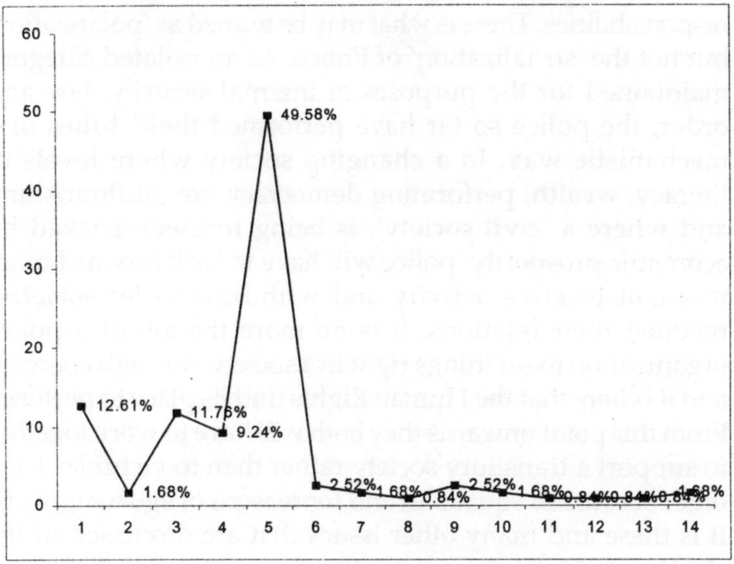

avoiding crossing over the fence of each other and unless it is done, they opined this lukewarm attitude between them would peddle on to create fatigue amongst them both. 1.68 per cent of respondents belonging to police organization agreed to the above and argued for protection of their rights by society, which they felt, was eroding because of too much pampering of Human Rights. 0.84 per cent of police personnel in other words were emotional about it and called for a healthy organizational relationship. 0.84 per cent of the respondents wanted Human Rights also to be disciplined within a formal structural set-up with minimum responsibilities and accountability fixed like any other Government or

Para Government agency/organization. They felt that the NGO style of Human Rights functioning was itself a botheration for them (See Graph. 5.20).

Thus, the study shows that these are serious defects and handicaps in many areas of Human Rights and Police Administration in general and in their interaction in particular. The failure of Police if any, so far has its roots in the 'conception', of their duties, functions and responsibilities. There is what may be termed as 'polarization' but not the 'socialization' of Police. As an isolated category maintained for the purposes of internal security, law and order, the police so far have performed their duties in a mechanistic way. In a changing society where levels of literacy, wealth, performing democracy are all flourishing and where a 'civil society', is being foreseen backed by economic prosperity, police will have to look forward more to a constructive activity and withdraw to let societies readjust their relations. It is no more the job of a police organization to set things right in a society through coercion and it is here that the Human Rights find its place to perform. From this point onwards they both will have to work together to support a transitory society rather than to victimize each other because of squabbles and for reasons of ego hangovers. It is these and many other issues that are discussed in the chapter that follows.

References

1. 'Police', *The New Encyclopaedia Britannica*, London, 1968.
2. Srivastav,V.P., ed. *Indian Police: Law and Reality*. New Delhi, Manas Publications, 1997.
3. *Ibid.*,
4. In his work *'The Social Contract*, Gauba, O.P. *An Introduction to Political Theory*, New Delhi, Macmillan India Ltd., 1995.
5. In his work *"The State and Revolution"*. *Ibid.*
6. SSLC is equivalent to 10th Standard.
7. Commissioner of Police, Deputy Commissioner of Police and Assistant Commissioner of Police.

8. Police Inspector, Police Sub-inspector and Assistant Sub-Inspector.
9. Head Constables and Police Constables irrespective of the gender.
10. Tyagi, A.R., *Public Administration*, Delhi, Atma Ram & Sons, 1975.
11. Vadackumchery, J., *The Police, the Accused and Criminal Injustice*, New Delhi, APH Publishing Corporation, 1997.
12. Vadackumchery, J., *Indian Police-2001:What Went Wrong Here?* New Delhi, APH Publishing Corporation, 1998.
13. *Op. cit* Tyagi, A.R. (1975).
14. Protection of Human Rights Act, 1993.
15. United Nations, Universal Declaration of Human Rights.
16. *Op. cit.*, Srivastav, V.P. (1997).
17. Chaturvedi, S.K. ed., *Role of Police in Criminal Justice System*, New Delhi, B.R. Publishing Corporation, 1996.
18. *Op. cit.*, Srivastav, V.P. (1997).
19. *Op. cit.*, Vadackumchery. J., (1998).
20. Deccan Hearld (1996) 16th August, 1996.
21. *Ibid*, also *op. cit.*, Chaturvedi (1996).
22. *Sixth Report of National Police Commission*, Ministry of Home Affairs, Government of India, March 1981.
23. Kapoor, H.L., *Police Administration*, Police Commission, Ministry of Home Affairs, Government of India, March 1981.
24. *Second Report of National Police Commission*, Ministry of Home Affairs, Government of India, August 1979.
25. Cases of Hubli-Dharwad such as communal riots, Idgah Maidan issue and Police firging in Mall, Lawyers strike.
26. Weston *et al.*, ed., *Criminal Investigation:Basic Perspectives*, New Jersey, Prentice Hall, Inc., Eagelwood Cliffs, 1986.
27. Shankar Sen. *et. al.*, ed., *Police Training* : Problems *and Perspectives*, New Delhi, Ashish Publishing House, 1994.
28. *Op. cit.*, Vadackumchery (1997).
——, *The Police, The People and Criminal Justice*, New Delhi, APH Publishing Corporation, 1997.
29. Kaul, J.L., ed., *Human Rights: Issues and Perspectives*, New Delhi, Regency Publications, 1995.
30. *Op. cit.*, Vadackumchery (1998).

6

Conclusion

The concept of rights provides for an essential tool of analysis of the relations between individual and state, while the state has been claiming authority over the individual despite, odds over the past centuries, the individual is doing his best to protect himself. However, when the state is viewed as an instrument of society, it is essential that the authority of the state is made to depend on the function it performs. It is this idea which is expressd when one regards state as a means, and the individual as the end. At this point the state can not be armed with absolute authority over the individual. In other words, if the state claims authority, the individual clings on to the rights. This kind of relationship thus can be termed as co-existing, co-operating and mutually beneficial. Questions like what does the individual claim from the state? or why individual owes allegiance to the state and obeys it, etc., will drive us to elucidate more discussion on the concept of rights.

It is a known fact that the rights essentially belong to the sphere of conflicting claims between individual and the state. Any political theory invariably holds on to the view that, an individual has rights "against the state", but this is no theory of rights. It is important to note here that the benefits which flow automatically from existence of the state do not constitute rights. Rights come into the picture only when authority of the state is sought to be limited when the society demands a positive role from the state. Thus, from Hobbes to Hegel, the rich tributes paid to the state, therefore, fell out of the congenial conditions created by state for the happiness of men. However, absence of rights in these theories invariably makes the individual dependent on the "benevolent nature of the state". It is, therefore, essential to argue that rights will only help to curb the authority of the state from claiming its absolutist state and degenerating into a regime of authoritarianism, despotism or tyrannical state, which not only subordinates the individual without giving him an opportunity to restrain the authority of the state but leads to the rise in social pathologies like oppression, exploitation and injustice, etc., subjecting the individual to hardships of life.[1]

The concept of 'Human Rights', therefore, originate from the voice of protest against the oppression, exploitation and injustice perpetuated by the dominating groups within the society. Therefore, Human Rights are seen as safeguards to the individual from the irresponsible and arbitrary use of power by the dominant groups with the society and by the ruling class. Emphasizing on this pathetic condition of the human society in the absence of Human Rights, *MacIver* significantly observed :

> *"Over most part of the earth and throughout the major range of recorded history the masses of men have lived in a condition of misery and oppression. Nearly everywhere small dominating groups acquired the techniques of power and used them to keep in subjection their fellowmen. In every age the vision of human liberation has been heard. In every age, the vision of human liberation has been glimpsed.*[2]

In modern times, however, this vision of human liberation has been developed into the concept of human rights, which are no longer expressed merely as certain demands but are sought to be enshrined in the structure of the government so as to prevent it from using its power in an arbitrary and irresponsible manner. As *MacIver* once again noted at this point, "the cry for Human Rights has now become more than an exhortation or protest, but it becomes the precise demand for the legal and constitutional embodiment of specific claims to liberties and then to opportunities.[3]

In simple terms, Human Rights today consist in claims of individuals and groups, on and against the state which are sought to be secured through legal and constitutional mechanism. In the current study this dynamic concept of Human Rights, which are subjected to continual review and redefinition, is taken up once again and presented in a new dimension having a reference to the police organization.[4] However, with spread of modern consciousness even among the police this concept of rights in general and Human Rights in particular, has taken two important directions :

(a) To avoid confining the advantages of rights to any tiny class which is placed in a privileged position by virtue of its manipulative power; and
(b) To avoid rights being confined to delimiting sphere of state activity and authority and prescribing functions and responsibilities of the state and also to make rights meaningful in the context of the bulk of the society when there will be a shift of focus from negative to positive rights.

The illustration of the case of 'right to life' where the state shall be directed in the formal sense, not to deprive men of their life except as measure of punishment for a crime, in accordance with the law and the principles of natural justice, provided the crime has been duly proved in a court of law or an illustration of the same case of 'right to life,' in its positive sense, when the state that shall provide for protection of man's life, without which right to life has no meaning, brings into the picture the question of whether or not the state should provide for 'police' and 'defence', only calls for minimum functions by the state even through these agencies in a society so complex as the one that we are witnessing today are here to stay and perform in either conditions of extremity. Similarly, threat to an individual may come from variety of sources, starting from tyrannical state, from assaults by other individuals and so on and so forth. Under these circumstances, police invariably becomes a necessary part of a transitory state into a welfare state. Apart from 'right to life', there are many other issues that call for restrain on the part of the state. While the coercive force of the state is not completely taken out of sight.[5]

Keeping such a debate about the question of rights in a welfare state *Vs.* the protection of the rights of citizens, the current study was thought about. Being aware of the difficulties of intruding into the police organization for collection of data and also eliciting their true and honest opinion as against the much publicized Human Rights resources, the current study was designed after entering into elaborate discussion with authorities concerned and explaining to them the purpose of this work. Once again it was ascertained that we would have no difficulties to access the information from both organizations concerned. A brief survey was undertaken to find out the potential of this research work, both at the empirical level and at the level of current availability of the literature. This was followed by a series of discussions with officers from the two organizations and other legal experts to finalise a framework for the study. Once again this was done with support and guidance from the professionals in the area of statistical methods and necessary research tools were prepared as can be seen in the chapter one. Formal methods of research were also employed in this study. The result of such an extensive study is presented in the form of Research Findings and Suggestions.

After designing the study and establishing the purposes, problems, objectives and hypotheses followed by a brief survey of literature and methodology and placing them under chapter one, the study was further divided into five more chapters. In chapter two, followed by introduction, the concept of Human Rights with a historical perspective was taken up employing historical and descriptive approaches. A series of important theories have been identified in this chapter before focusing on the concept of Human Rights. Much of it invariably gives an idea that the concept of Human Rights although is a part of Indian classical thinking, is more or less a western concept and this has been exposed clearly in this chapter. The chapter further brings into the picture the role of United Nations Organization in popularizing Human Rights concept, as a concept that has gained universal acceptance today.

Followed by this, once again employing the historical approach, Police Administration in chapter three has been discussed. Intertwining in this chapter we have discussed the western and the eastern concept of Police Administration together. This chapter also deals with the establishment of Police Administration in its historical time frame thus helping to trace the stages of growth of Police Administration in India.

Chapter four, titled Human Rights *vis-à-vis* Police Administration is an attempt to synchronise the two concepts. This chapter also brings out the commonality between these two agencies and also the areas of differences between the two, keeping in view only its operational aspects, thus bringing into the picture the Constitution of India as a document that has provided intertwining of these two concepts.

Entitled as "Human Rights and Police Administration'—An Empirical Analysis", this is chapter five, which has been carefully written with stress on analysis and presentation of facts supported by the available documents and secondary resources. Substitution of results obtained after serving the schedules to the designated officers, NGOs and those who matter for the study is done after duly collecting the information from the Police Administration and Human Rights documents. The details of methodology can be seen in chapter one. The results of this study after ensuring the covariant and intrinsic between the two concepts is presented in this chapter.

Findings of the Study

It is true that the Police Administration in India has been one of the acclaimed efficient units of administration even to this day. However, the major criticism against this unit of administration is in terms of its ability to accept change and to adapt itself to the new circumstances. On the other hand, the concept of Human Rights being enshrined in the Constitution in different forms (fundamental rights) is seen as rather recent phenomena. This supposedly new concept of Human Rights among the Police thus has made the Police more conscious of the presence of Human Rights. The larger publicity, exposure and the social base for Human Rights as compared with Police Administration, is seen by the Police Administration as a matter of concern. This is the first and most important finding of our study, since this kind of apprehension has led to a thorough change in the attitude of police towards Human Rights, while Human Rights seem to work to find faults with police rather than working towards other contents falling under Human Rights such as poverty, disaster, etc.

Keeping awareness as a yardstick the study conducted amongst the Police Officers, who consist of graduates and post-graduates in subjects ranging from science to history, it was noticed that the response of police personnel was quite overwhelming so far as their awareness about Human Rights was concerned.

Most of the police personnel had heard of Human Rights (85.71 per cent) from various media and less from their own in-service training or through routine circulars. This clearly demonstrated the fact that the change setting in the society has been noticed by the Police Administration by being alert leading to a sense of responsibility amongst them. The hypothesis test applied to this question clearly indicates that a significant number of police personnel were rather aware of the Human Rights. This of course is scientifically proved in the chapter concerned. However, a break-up of these responses clearly indicates that majority of the respondents at all the three levels chosen for the study were aware of Human Rights.

Of the sources from which this awareness about Human Rights has come, the study revealed that media had played a vital role in bringing about this awareness with majority of officers at all the three levels accepting this. This in fact indicates three important findings :

(a) That the level of education has a direct link with the level of understanding amongst the police personnel;
(b) That the information sources within Police Organization right from period of training up to the internal circulars, etc., are to be updated and socialized well by circulating in a proper fashion, so that it would facilitate this organization as an important input, and
(c) That it is the media which is still the largest socializing agent of Human Rights.

While the training for higher officers is quite updated, this study believes that there is lot to be done to update training programme to the lower level officers. This is evidenced by the fact that of the 74.79 per cent of respondents belonging to third category, viz., Police Constables, only 16.81 per cent had heard about Human Rights during in-service training and nearly 47.90 per cent had heard of it from the media.

To ascertain the weakness of training as discussed above, specific question on training/orientation *vis-à-vis* Human Rights give us nearly 82.35 per cent of respondents informing that they had not heard anything about Human Rights during the traning period as against a merely 15.13 per cent of respondents saying that they had learnt about it during their training. Once again it was a small group (6 to 9 per cent) of middle level officers who had been imparted refresher course in Human Rights in the recent years. This was further ascertained when nearly 35.29 per cent of respondents said that they had heard of the concept of Human Rights only recently.

To another question about the time period when the respondents belonging to various groups had heard of Human Rights, as discussed earlier, the respondents indicated that most of them had only heard of it in the period ranging between 5 to 10 years. This clearly speaks of weak input of Human Rights amongst Police Administration.

In their response to defining the concept of Human Rights, most of them attempted to locate the concept of Human Rights within the framework of Indian Constitution which falls under the Protection of Human Rights Act 1993. Although, many of them were unable to identify it precisely with Police Administration it is only a solace that they were able to lay hand on something closer to the concept of Human Rights, while defining it but at the same time this also indicated that they were not very familiar with the Universal Declaration of Human Rights and textual definition of Human Rights as enshrined within it. Even amongst senior officers belonging to the Indian Police Service, this differentiation is not clearly known, even the middle level officers only had a fair idea and the lower level officers also were not clear about the differences.

Being a comprehensive concept, Human Rights, it is noticed are rather elusive. This is clearly noticed when the respondents were asked to identify the various Acts/ Declarations that govern Human Rights. 84.87 per cent nearly accepted that they were unaware of these Acts/Declarations, while only a meagre 10.92 per cent of respondents were able to name the Fundamental Rights even amongst 2.52 per cent of higher officers, this was clearly divided.

Further, to a much focused question of identifying more specific Acts/Declarations governs Human Rights *vis-à-vis*

Police Administration, nearly 94.12 per cent of respondents replied 'do not know' and a meagre per cent of respondents were able to identify these Acts/Declarations although, they form the core of the Police Administration under the blanket of Criminal Justice System.[6]

Ignorance on their part in these matters is no doubt seen as a negative point in our study. Despite, the fact that the poor response of police personnel to identify the various acts that fall within broader framework of Human Rights having specific relation to Police Administration. To a further question regarding contents of Declarations, a supportive 5.04 per cent responded saying that the contents of these Declarations as being satisfied which of course consists of a very minor percentage of respondents, indicating to the fact that there is a need for some of these police officers to update themselves about the Acts/Declarations that govern Police Administration. And most of them who responded 'negatively', to this question were of the opinion that the contents of these Acts/Declarations were not in consonance with the Indian conditions. In fact the entire preceding paragraphs clearly brings out two major findings :

(a) That the Police organization needs to help their personnel to be updated in the worldwide changes that are taking place.
(b) Is supportive of the first of our hypothesis which spells out that the concept of Human Rights may be too complex for specific application in Police Administration.

This is so because there are today a number of development in Human Rights that have an application value to the state in general both at the national and at the international level of which sub-systems like Police Administration will have to draw out in their functioning. Since this is too large for a smaller organization to draw from the question of specific application is put into debate, and hence, the confusion and weakness within the Police Administration.

On the issue of relationship between Human Rights and Police Administration, there was consensus. The hypothesis test indicated this as a positive response. While to a rejoinder about defining this relationship most of them saw it as a co-operative kind of relationship followed by Human Rights as dominating over Police Administration and friendly also. The respondents firmly believed that Human Rights were dominant over Police Administration (84.03%) and considered Human Rights as a stumbling block but at the same time they also saw it as a humanizing one. While they also said it was bottleneck too.

Accepting the fact that Human Rights interferes in Police Administration, the respondents saw the intervention of Human Rights in Police Administration at the investigation level and they also felt that it interrupted the investigations of Police Administration while applying the methods of extraction of information at the second stage of interference by Human Rights in Police Administration. A majority of them agreed that Human Rights were a part of Police Administration and disagreed to the view that Police often violates Human Rights in the name of crime prevention. It is at this stage that the difference in opinion amongst the two agencies crops up, throwing up the fact that Police Administration is not receptive to Human Rights. This of course is our second hypothesis which is proved. Though they were not agreeable to the idea that crime prevention lead to violation of Human Rights, they only accepted the fact Human Rights invariably targets Police Administration and, therefore, this bitterness amongst Police Administration towards Human Rights.[7]

Accepting the fact that Human Rights were a component of Police Administration in matters connected to official/ administrative procedure even in implementing judicial proceedings they say Human Rights as a weak component in the training curriculum of police.

Human Rights on the other hand are seen as a concern

beyond the police and this fact is represented in graph. 5.16. Nearly 83.19 per cent have disagreed to the view that Human Rights are the concern of police alone.

Despite this, Police Administration believes that Human Rights have a positive as well as mutually beneficial relationship and agrees to the fact that Human Rights should be a part of Police Administration. They also see Human Rights as a catalytic agent to put Police Administration on its toes. They firmly believed that necessary interruption of Human Rights is a must to work efficiently in their administration. However, it is important to note here that most of the police personnel at all the three stratified levels are agreeable to the fact that there is a positive relationship between Police Administration and Human Rights. Our hypotheses were inclined to put this issue rather as a doubtful cases but with this response our analysis in fact favours this mutually contributory relationship. Hence, our third hypothesis is also accepted.

With these being the findings, it is clearly seen that Human Rights and Police Administration are not anti-thesis but definitely are at logger heads depending upon the issues that they confront and what is required is a careful mode of inter-twining and combining these two, keeping in view the larger welfare of the society.

The following suggestions emerges from the study which may not be a complete recipe for revamping Police Administration, but is definitely responsible attempt to speak out about the needed changes in Police Administration as well as Human Rights application. These suggestions include :

- That there is a need to prescribe higher education for entry into the Police irrespective of caste, creed, etc., to facilitate better understanding of their job.
- That the on-job training and in-service training imparted in Police Administration with futuristic perceptions would go a long way in contributing to the efficiency of this organization.

- That it is not only important that top officials have necessary training or higher qualification but this facility must be horizontally extended to other officers for ensuring an improved and effective command of operation and performance among the police.
- That there is need for improvement and upgradation in the training components of Police Administration.
- That the police manuals must be updated to facilitate greater perceptibility among all the levels of officers and compulsory reading and regular orientation to all these officers at all levels should be made a must.
- That there should be meetings at regular intervals of officers at different levels by the hierarchy and external experts should be brought into the organization to help the organization perform effectively.
- That regular interface of these two organizations, Human Rights and Police Administration, through a state level mediating agencies and NGOs for cross pollination of ideas should be made a must.
- Since automation has invaded every stream of life, equipping every police station with accessibility to all the levels of officers and training to handle them would greatly benefit to understand the consequences of new development.
- Socializing the new Acts/Declarations by calling regular academic sessions from the Universities activists would thus contribute to internalizing the new developments in the areas directly connected to police organization.
- Similarly, orientation in law and elaborate discussions on the Constitution, the important case in focus would greatly benefit the enlargement of knowledge among the functionaries in the police organization.

- As is being done in case of Inspector and Sub-Inspector levels, refresher course would go a long way in contributing to expansion of knowledge at all the levels of police officers.
- Personality Development Programme, Human Resources management, techniques and newer managerial approaches for those incharge of day-to-day administration would thus make Police Administration change receptively. This further enables the organization to be appreciative of the new thoughts and progressive thinking thus helping to improve the organizational aspects contributing to changing their old and outdated styles of functioning.
- Exposure to western and newer modes of investigation, extraction of information and corrective administrative aspects would go a long way in changing the face of Police Administration. These changes would, therefore, effectively contain violation if any, of Human Rights in the modes of these investigations.
- Exemplifying the police with reverence and identifying their achievement in the media and representing them properly in media without any pervasions giving them greater scope as heroes and law abiding citizens would help to remove greatly the disrepute they have earned so far.
- Personnel and other service conditions must be improved to alienate police to certain extent above the society would also greatly bring value to Police Adminstration. Amongst Human Right, focus of Human Rights activists must be enlarged to other social actions of state and not only target police always. Failures of crisis management and disaster management should be brought within their purview. The Human Rights Groups must be educated on the

issues of human failures, poverty administrative negligence, etc., so that they concentrate and work towards improving life situations. Perhaps, this and many more constructive suggestions if are brought together as a set of reforms in Public Administration, the social change contemplated in and through the Constitution could be achieved.

More precisely, the current rate of uneasiness between Police Administration and Human Rights would thus shrink further. If only a civic society precedes the current standards of society them things as desired in an 'ideal' atmosphere would no longer be a myth in a developing society like India. In this regard, Police Administration seems to be positive about it. This itself is a sign of hope for a better tomorrow and for a better society. In conclusion, it may be said that Police Administration and Human Rights are like the bridegroom and the bride, whose marriage of course is a necessity, especially in the light of a brighter prospect for the society as a whole. So long as they are seen as opposing to each other, accusations against each other would only cause stress within the society, which is not in the interest of the society.

This study is only an humble attempt to bring these concepts and issues into focus and this study may have left many more questions unanswered in it and it is hoped that this would generate further research. Thus, this study has helped us to prove our hypotheses in a scientific manner.

APPENDIX-I

Position/Category	*Strength of Police in Hubli-Dharwad*		*Police Personnel Chosen for Study*	*Respondents chosen in percentage*
	Sanctioned Strength	*Present Strength*		
Commissioner of Police	01	01	01	100
Deputy Commissioner of Police	02	02	02	100
Assistant Commissioner of Police	04	04	02	50
Police Inspector	23	23	02	10
Police Sub-Inspector	32	27	03	10
Assistant Sub-Inspector	56	56	06	10
Head Constable	232	209	23	10
Women Head Constable	19	14	02	10
Police Constable	754	751	75	10
Women Police Constable	66	61	07	10
Total	**1189**	**1148**	**123**	

APPENDIX-II

Universal Declaration of Human Rights

On 10th December, 1948, the General Assembly of the United Nations adopted and proclaimed the Universal Declaration of Human Rights. The list of Human Rights elaborated in the Declaration provides a common standard of 'achievement for all peoples and all nations. Considering the worldwide historic significance of this Declaration, the full text of which is reproduced below, 10th December is observed as the World Human Rights Day every year.

PREAMBLE

WHEREAS recognition of the inherent dignity and of the equal and inalienable rights of all members of the human family is the foundation of freedom, justice and peace in the world;

WHEREAS disregard and contempt for Human Rights have resulted in barbarous acts which have outraged the conscience of mankind and the advent of a world in which human beings shall enjoy freedom of speech and belief and freedom from fear and want has been proclaimed as the highest aspiration of the common people;

WHEREAS it is essential if man is not to be compelled to have resource, as last resort, to rebellion against tyranny and oppression, that Human Rights should be protected by the rule of law;

WHEREAS the people of the United Nations have in the Charter reaffirmed their faith in fundamental Human

Rights, in the dignity and worth of the human person and in the equal rights of men and women and have determined to promote social progress and better standards of life in large freedom;

WHEREAS Member-States have pledged themselves to achieve in co-operation with the United Nations, the promotion of universal respect for and observance of Human Rights and fundamental freedoms; and

WHEREAS a common understanding of these rights and freedom is of the greatest importance or full realization of this pledge.

Now, therefore :

The General Assembly

Proclaims this Universal Declaration of Human Rights as a common standard of achievement for all peoples and all nations, to the end that every individual and every organ of society, keeping this Declaration constantly in mind, shall strive by teaching and education to promote respect for these rights and freedoms and by progressive measures, national and international, to secure their universal and effective recognition and observance both among the peoples of Member-States themselves and among the peoples of territories under their jurisdiction.

Article 1

All human beings are born free and equal in dignity and rights. They are endowed with reason and conscience and should act towards one another in a spirit of brotherhood.

Article 2

Everyone is entitled to all the rights and freedoms set forth in this Declaration, without distinction of any kind, such as race, colour, sex, religion, language, political or other opinion, national or social origin, property, birth or other status.

Furthermore, no distinction shall be made on the basis of the political, jurisdictional or international status of the country or territory to which a person belongs, whether it is independent, trust, non-self-government or under any other limitation of sovereignty.

Article 3

Everyone has the right to life, liberty and security of person.

Article 4

No one shall be held in slavery or servitude; slavery and the slave trade shall be prohibited in all their forms.

Article 5

No one shall be subjected to torture or to cruel, inhuman or degrading treatment or punishment.

Article 6

Everyone has the right to recognition everywhere as a person before the law.

Article 7

All are equal before the law and are entitled without any discrimination to equal protection of the law. All are entitled to equal protection against any discrimination in violation of this Declaration and against any incitement to such discrimination.

Article 8

Everyone has the right to an effective remedy by the competent national tribunals for acts violating the fundamental rights granted to him by the constitution or by law.

Article 9

No one shall be subjected to arbitrary arrest, detention or exile.

Article 10

Everyone is entitled in full equality to a fair and public hearing by an independent and impartial tribunal, in the determination of his rights and obligations and of any criminal charge against him.

Article 11

1. Everyone charged with a penal offence has the right to be presumed innocent until proved guilty according to law in a public trial at which he has had all the guarantees necessary for his defence.

2. No one shall be held guilty of any penal offence on account of any act or omission which did not constitute a penal offence under national or international law, at the time when it was committed. Nor shall a heavier penalty be imposed than the one that was applicable at the time the penal offence was committed.

Article 12

No one shall be subjected to arbitrary interference with his privacy, family home or correspondence, or to attacks upon his honour and reputation. Everyone has the right to the protection of the law against such interference or attacks.

Article 13

1. Everyone has the right to freedom of movement and residence within the borders of each State.

2. Everyone has the right to leave any country, including his own, and to return to his country.

Article 14

1. Everyone has the right to seek and to enjoy in other countries asylum from persecution.
2. This right may not be invoked in the case of prosecutions genuinely arising from non-political crimes or from acts contrary to the purpuses and principles of the the United Nations.

Article 15

1. Everyone has the right to a nationality.
2. No one shall be arbitrarily deprived of his nationality nor denied the right to change his nationality.

Article 16

1. Men and women of all age, without any limitation due to race, nationality or religion, have the right to marry and to form a family. They are entitled to equal rights as to marriage, during marriage and as to its dissolution.
2. Marriage shall be entered into only with the free and full consent of the intending spouses.
3. The family is the natural and fundamental group unit of society and is entitled to protection by society and the states.

Article 17

1. Everyone has the right to own property alone as well as in association with others.
2. No one shall be arbitrarily deprived of his property.

Article 18

Everyone has the right to freedom of thought, conscience and religion, this right includes freedom to change his religion or belief, and freedom, either alone or in community with others and in public or private, to manifest his religion or belief in teaching, practice, worship and observance.

Article 19

Everyone has the right to freedom of opinion and expression; this right includes freedom to hold opinions without interference and to seek, receive and impart information and ideas through any media and regardless of frontiers.

Article 20

1. Everyone has the right to freedom of peaceful assembly and association.
2. No one may be compelled to belong to an association.

Article 21

1. Everyone has the right to take part in the Government of his country directly or indirectly or through freely chosen representatives.
2. Everyone has the right to equal access to public services in his country.
3. The will of the people shall be the basis of the authority of government; this shall be expressed in periodic and genuine elections which shall be by universal and equal suffrage and shall be held by secret vote or by equivalent free voting procedures.

Article 22

Everyone, as a member of society, has the right to social security and is entitled to realization, through national effort and international co-operation and in accordance with the organization and resources of each state, of the economic, social, cultural rights indispensable for his dignity and the free development of his personality.

Article 23

1. Everyone has the right to work, to free choice of employment, to just and favourable conditions of work and to protection against unemployment.
2. Everyone, without any discrimination, has the right to equal pay for equal work.
3. Everyone who works has the right to just and favourable remuneration ensuring for himself and his family an existence worthy of human dignity, and supplemented, if necessary, by other means of a social protection.
4. Everyone has the right to form and to join trade unions for the protection of his interests.

Article 24

Everyone has the right to rest and leisure, including reasonable limitation of working hours and peiodic holidays with pay.

Article 25

1. Everyone has the right to a standard of living adequate for the health and well-being of himself and of his family, including food, clothing, housing and medical care and necessary social services, and the right to security in the event of unemployment, sickness, disability, widowhood, old age or other lack of livelihood in circumstance beyond his control.
2. Motherhood and childhood are entitled to special care and assistance. All children, whether born in or out of wedlock, shall enjoy the same social protection.

Article 26

1. Everyone has the right of education. Education shall be free, at least in the elementary and fundamental stages. Elementary education shall be compulsory. Technical and professional education shall be made generally available and higher education shall be equally accessible to all on the basis of merit.
2. Education shall be directed to the full development of the human personality and to strengthening of respect for human rights and fundamental freedoms. It shall promote understanding, tolerance and friendship among the nations, racial or religious groups, and shall further the activities of the United Nations for the maintenance of peace.
3. Parents have a prior right to choose the kind of education that shall be given to their children.

Article 27

1. Everyone has the right freely to participate in the cultural life of the community, to enjoy the arts and to share in scientific advancement and its benefits.
2. Everyone has the right to the protection of the moral and material interest resulting from any scientific literary or artistic production of which he is the author.

Article 28

Everyone is entitled to a social and international order in which the right and freedoms set forth in this Declaration can be fully realized.

Article 29

1. Everyone has duty to the community in which alone

the free and full development of his personality is possible.

2. In the exercise of his right and freedoms, everyone shall be subject only to such limitations as are determined by law solely for the purpose of securing due recognition and respect for the right and freedoms of others and of meetig the just requirements of morality, public order and the general welfare in a democratic society.
3. These rights and freedoms may in no case be exercised contrary to the purposes and principles of the United Nations.

Article 30

Nothing, in this Declaration be interpreted as implying for any state, group or person any right to engage in any activity or to perform any act aimed at the destruction of any of the rights and freedoms set forth herein, well-being which are necessary for peaceful and friendly relations among nations based on respect for the principle of equal rights and self-determination of peoples, the United Nations shall promote :

(a) Higher standards of living, full employment, and conditions of economic and social progress and development;

(b) Solutions of international economic, social, health, and related problems; and international cultural and educational co-operation; and

(c) Universal respect for and observance of human rights and fundamental freedoms for all without distinction as to race, sex, language or religion.

APPENDIX-III

International Covenant on Civil and Political Rights

Reproduced below are excerpts from the *International Covenant on Civil and Political Rights* which was adopted by the General Assembly of the United Nations on 16th December, 1966 and came into force on 23rd March, 1976.

PREAMBLE

The States parties to the present Covenant

Considering that, in accordance with the principles proclaimed in the Charter of the United Nations, recognition of the inherent dignity and of the equal and inalienable rights of all members of the human family is the foundation of freedom, justice and peace in the world.

Recognizing that these rights derive from the inherent dignity of the human person.

Recognizing that, in accordance with the Universal Declaration of Human Rights, the ideal of free human beings enjoying civil and political freedom and freedom from fear and want can only be achieved if conditions are created whereby everyone may enjoy his civil and political rights as well as his economic, social and cultural rights.

Considering the obligation of states under the Charter of the United Nations to promote universal respect for an observance of human rights and freedoms.

Realizing that the individual, having duties to other individuals and to the community to which he belongs is under a responsibility to strive for the promotion and observance of the rights recognized in the present Covenant.

Agree upon the following Articles :

PART-I

Article-1

1. All peoples have the right of self-determination. By virtue of that right they freely determine their political status and freely pursue their economic, social and cultural development.
2. All peoples may, for their own ends, freely dispose of their natural wealth and resources without prejudice to any obligations arising out of international economic co-operation based upon the principle of mutual benefit, and international law. In no case may the people be deprived of its own means of subsistence.
3. The State Parties to the present Covenant, including those having responsibility for the administration of Non-self-governing and Trust Territories, shall promote the realization of the right of self-determination, and shall respect the right in conformity with the provisions of the United Nations.

PART-2

Article-2

1. Each State Party to the present Covenant undertakes to respect and to ensure to all individuals within its territory and subject to its jurisdiction the rights recognized in the present Covenant, without distinction of any kind, such as race, colour, sex, language, religion, political or other opinion, national or social origin, property, birth or other status.

2. Where not already provided for by existing legislative or other measures, each State Party to the present Covenant undertakes to take the necessary steps, in accordance with its constitutional processes and other measures as may be necessary to give effect to the rights recognized in the present Covenant.

Article - 3

The States Parties to the present Covenant undertake to ensure the equal right of men and women to the enjoyment of all civil and political rights set forth in the present Covenant.

Article - 4

1. In time of public emergency which threatens the life of the nation and the existence of which is officially proclaimed, the State Parties to the present Covenant may take measures derogating from their obligations under the present Covenant to the extent strictly required by the exigencies of the situation, provided that such measures are not inconsistent with their other obligations under international law and do not involve discrimination solely on the ground of race, colour, sex, language, religion or social origin.
2. No derogation from articles 6, 7, 8 (pragraphs 1 and 2), 11, 15, 16 and 18 may be made under this provision.
3. Any State Party to the present Convenant availing itself of the right of derogation shall immediately inform the other States Parties to the present Covenant, through the intermediary of the Secretary-General of the United Nations, of the provisions from which it has derogated and of the reasons by which it was actuated. A further communication shall be made, through the same intermediary, on the date on which it terminates such derogation.

PART - 3

Article - 6

1. Every human being has the inherent right to life. This right shall be protected by law. No one shall be arbitrarily deprived of his life.
2. In countries which have not abolished the death penalty, sentence of death may be imposed only for the most serious crimes in accordance with the law in force at the time of the commission of the crime and not contrary to the provisions of the present Covenant and to the Convention on the Prevention and Punishment of the Crime and Genocide.
3. Anyone sentenced to death shall have the right to seek pardon or commutation of the sentence. Amnesty, pardon or commutation of the sentence of death may be granted in all cases.
4. Sentence of death shall not be imposed for crimes committed by persons below eighteen years of age and shall not be carried out on pregnant women.

Article-7

No one shall be subjected to torture or to cruel, inhuman or degrading treatment or punishment. In particular, no one shall be subjected without his free consent to medical or scientific experimentation.

Article-8

1. No one shall be held in slavery; slavery and the slave-trade in all their forms shall be prohibited.
2. No one shall be held in servitude.
3. No one shall be required to perform forced or compulsory labour.

Article-9

1. Everyone has the right to liberty and security of person. No one shall be subjected to arbitrary arrest or detention. No one shall be deprived of his liberty except on such grounds and in accordance with such procedure as are established by law.
2. Anyone who is arrested shall be informed, at the time of arrest, of the reasons for his arrest and shall be promptly informed of any charges against him.
3. Anyone arrested or detained on a criminal charge shall be brought promptly before a Judge or other officer authorized by law to exercise judicial power and shall be entitled to trial within a reasonable time or to release. It shall not be the general rule that persons awaiting trial shall be detained in custody, but release may be subject to guaratees to appear for trial, at any other stage of the judicial proceedings, and, should occasion arise, for execution of the judgement.
4. Anyone who is deprived of his liberty by arrest or detention shall be entitled to take proceedings before a court in order that court may decide without delay on the lawfulness of his detention and order his release if the detention is not lawful.
5. Anyone who has been the victim of unlawful arrest or detention shall have an enforceable right to compensation.

Article-10

1. All persons deprived of their liberty shall be treated with humanity and with respect for the inherent dignity of the human person.
2. Accused persons shall, save in exceptional circumstances, be segregated from convicted persons

and shall be subject to separate treatment appropriate to their status as unconvicted persons.

3. Accused juvenile persons shall be separated from adults and brought as speedily as possible for adjudication.
4. The penitentiary system shall comprise treatment of prisoners the essential aim of which shall be their reformation and social rehabilitation. Juvenile offenders shall be segregated from adults and be accorded treatment appropriate to their age and legal status.

Article-11

No one shall be imprisoned merely on the ground of inability to fulfil a contractual obligation.

Article-12

1. Everyone lawfully within the territory of a state shall, within that territory, have the right to liberty of movement and freedom to choose his residence.
2. Everyone shall be free to leave any country, including his own.
3. The above mentioned rights shall not be subject to any restrictions except those which are provided by law, are necessary to protect national security, public order (order public), public health or morals or the rights and freedoms of others, and are consistent with the other rights recognized in the present Covenant.
4. No one shall be arbitrarily deprived of the right to enter his own country.

Article-13

An alien lawfully in the territory of a State Party to the present Covenant may be expeelled therefrom only in pursuance of a decision reached in accordance with law and shall, except where compelling reasons of national security otherwise require, be allowed to submit the reasons against his expulsion and to have his case reviewed by, and be represented for the purpose before, the competent authority or a person or persons expecially designated by the competent authority.

Article-14

1. All persons shall be equal before the Courts and Tribunals. In a determination of any criminal charge against him, or of his rights and obligations in a suit of law, everyone shall be entitled to a fair and public hearing by a competent, independent and impartial Tribunal established by law.
2. Everyone charged with a criminal offence shall have the right to be presumed innocent until proved guilty according to law.
3. In the determination of any criminal charge against him, everyone shall be entitled to the following minimum guarantees, in full equality :
   (a) To be informed promptly and in detail in a language which he understands of the nature and cause of the charge against him;
   (b) To have adequate time and facilities for the preparation of his defence and to communicate with counsel of his own choosing;
   (c) To be tried without undue delay;
   (d) To be tried in his present, and to defend himself in person or through legal assistance of his choosing.

   • • • • • •

   (g) Not to be compelled to testify against himself or to confess guilt.
4. In the case of juvenile persons, the procedure shall

be such as will take account of their age and the desirability of promoting their rehabilitation.

Article-15

1. No one shall be held guilty of any criminal offence on account of any act or omission which did not constitute a criminal offence, under national or international law, at the time when it was committed. Nor shall a heavier penalty be imposed than the one that was applicable at the time when the criminal offence was committed. If, subsequent to the commission of the offence, provision is made by law for the imposition of the lighter penalty, the offender shall benefit thereby.
2. Nothing in this article shall prejudice the trail and punishment of any person for any act or omission which, at the time when it was committed, was criminal according to the general principles of law recognized by the community of nations.

Article-16

Everyone shall have the right to recognition everywhere as a person before the law.

Article-17

1. No one shall be subjected to arbitrary or unlawful interference with his privacy, family, home or correspondence, nor to unlawful attacks on his honour and reputation.
2. Everyone has the right to the protection of the law against such interference or attacks.

Article-18

1. Everyone shall have the right to freedom of thought

conscience and religion. This right shall include freedom to have or to adopt a religion or belief of his choice, and freedom, either individually or in community with others and in public or private, to manifest his religion or belief in worship, observance, practice and teaching.

2. No one shall be subject to coercion which would impair his freedom to have or to adopt a religion or belief of his choice.
3. Freedom to manifest one's religion or beliefs may be subject only to such limitations as are prescribed by law and are necessary to protect public safety order, health, or morals or the fundamental rights and freedoms of others.
4. The States Parties to the present Covenant undertake to have respect for the liberty of parents and, when applicable legal guardians to ensure the religious and moral education of their children in conformity with their own convictions.

Article-19

1. Everyone shall have the right to hold opinions without interference.
2. Everyone shall have the right to freedom of expression, this right shall include freedom to seek, receive and impart information and ideas of all kinds regardless of frontiers, either orally, in writing or in print, in the form of art, or through any other media of his choice.
3. The exercise of the rights provided for in paragraph 2 of this Article carried with it special duties and responsibilities. It may, therefore, be subject to certain restrictions but these shall only be such as are provided by law and are necessary;
   (a) For respect of the rights or reputations of others; and

(b) For the protection of national security or of public order (order public), or of public health or morals.

Article-20

1. Any propaganda for war shall be prohibited by law.
2. Any advocacy of national, racial or religious hatred that constitutes in incitement to discrimination, hostility or violence shall be prohibited by law.

Article-21

The right of peaceful assembly shall be recognized. No restrictions may be placed on the exercise of this right other than those imposed in conformity with the law and which are necessary in a democratic society in the interest of national security or public safety, public order (order public) the protection of public health morals or the protection of the rights and freedoms of others.

Article-22

1. Everyone shall have the right to freedom of association with others, including the right to form and join trade unions for the protection of his interests.
2. No restrictions may be placed on the exercise of this right other than those which are prescribed by law and which are necessary in a democratic society in the interest of national security or public safety, public order (*ordre public*), the protection of public health or morals or the protection of the rights and freedoms of others. This article shall not prevent the imposition of lawful restrictions on members of the armed forces and of the police in their exercise of this right.
3. Nothing in this article shall autorize States Parties to the International Labour Organization Convention of 1948 concerning Freedom of Association and

Protection of the Right of Organize to take legislative measures which would prejudice, or to apply the law in such a manner as to prejudice, the guarantees provided for in the Convention.

Article-23

1. The family is the natural and fundamental group unit of society and is entitled to protection by society and the state.
2. The right of men and women of marriageable age to marry and to found a family shall be recognized.
3. No marriage shall be entered into without the free and full consent of the intending spouses.
4. State Parties to the present Covenant shall take appropriate steps to ensure equality of rights and responsibilities of spouses as to marriage, during marriage and after its dissolution. In the case of dissolution, provision shall be made for the necessary protection of any children.

Article-24

1. Every child shall have without any discrimination as to race, colour, sex, language, religion, national or social origin, property or birth, the right to such measures of protection as are required by his status as a minor, on the part of his family, society and the state.
2. Every child shall be registered immediately after birth and shall have a name.
3. Every child has the right to acquire a nationality.

Article-25

Every citizen shall have the right and the opportunity without any of the distinctions mentioned in Article 2 and without unreasonable restrictions :

(a) To take part in the conduct of public affairs, directly or through freely chosen representatives;
(b) To vote and to be elected at genuine periodic elections which shall be by universal and equal suffrage and shall be held by secret ballot, guaranteeing the free expressions of the will of the elections; and
(c) To have access, on general terms of equality, to public service in his country.

Article-26

All persons are equal before the law and are entitled without any discrimination to the equal protection of the law. In this respect, the law shall prohibit any discrimination and guarantee to all persons equal and effective protection against discrimination on any ground such as race, colour, sex, language, religion, political or other opinion, national or social origin, property, birth, or other status.

Article - 27

In those states in which ethnic, religious or linguistic minorities exist, persons belonging to such minorities shall not be denied the right, in community with the other members of their group, to enjoy their own culture, to profess and practice their own religion or to use their own language.

PART - 4

Article-40

1. The States Parties to the present Covenant undertake to submit reports on the measures they have adopted which give effect to the rights recognized herein and on the progress made in the enjoyment of those rights:

(a) Within one year of the entry into force of the present Convenant for the States Parties concerned;

(b) Thereafter whenever the Committee so requests.

2. All reports shall be submitted to the Secretary-General of the United Nations, who shall transmit them to the committee for consideration. Reports shall indicate the factors and difficulties, if any, affecting the implementation of the present Convenant.
3. The secretary-General of the United Nations may, after consultation with Committee, transmit to the specialized agencies concerned copies of such parts of the reports as may fall within their field of competence.
4. The Committee shall study the reports submitted by the States parties to the present Covenant. It shall transmit its reports, and such general comments as it may consider appropriate, to the States Parties. The Committee may also transmit to the Economic and Social Council these comments along with copies of the reports it has received from States Parties to the present Covenant.
5. The State Parties to the present Convenant many submit to the Committee observations on any comments that may be made in accordance with paragraph 4 of this article.

Article-41

1. A State Party to the present Covenant may at any time declare under this article that it recognizes the competence of the Committee to receive and consider communications to the effect that a State party claims that another State Party is not fulfilling its obligations under the present Covenant. Communications under this article may be received and considered only if submitted by a State Party which has made a

declaration recognizing in regard to itself the competence of the Committee. No comunication shall be received by the Committee if it concerns a State Party which has not made such a declaration. Cummunications received under this article shall be dealt with in accordance with the following procedure :

(a) If a State Party to the present Covenant considers that another State Party is not giving effect to the provisions of the present Convenant, it may, by written communication, bring the matter to the attention of that State Party. Within three months after the receipt of the communication, the receiving State shall afford the State which sent the communication an explanation or any other statement in writing clarifying the matter, which should include, to the extent possible and paertinent, reference to domestic procedures and remedies taken, pending, or available in the matter;

(b) If the matter is not adjusted to the stisfaction of both States Parties concerned within six months after the receipt by the receiving State of the initial communication, either State shall have the right to refer the mater to the Committee, by notice given to the Committee and to the other State;

(c) The Committee shall deal with a matter referred to it only after it has ascertained that all available domestic remedies have been invoked and exhausted in the matter, in conformity with the generally recognized principles of international law. This shall not be the rule where the application of the remedies is unreasonably prolonged;

(d) The committee shall hold closed meetings when examining communications under the article.

APPENDIX-IV

International Covenant on Economic, Social and Cultural Rights

The Universal Declaration of Human Rights provided the basis for the formulation by the United Nations of Convenant and Conventions, declarations and recommendations on specific aspects. The two broad sets of Human Rights affirmed in the *Universal Declaration*—civil and political rights, and economic, social and cultural rights were elaborated and divided into two covenants—*the International Covenant on Economic, Social and Cultural Rights,* and *the International Covenant on Civil and Political Rights*. These three documents i.e., *the Universal Declaration of Human Rights, the International Covenant on Civil and Political Rights,* and *the International Covenant on Economic, Social and Cultural Rights* along with two protocols — the *optional protocol to the International Covenant on Civil and Political Rights, aiming at the abolition of the Death Penalty*— constitute *the International Bill of Human Rights.* These are the fundamental documents, which lay the basis for the protection and promotion of Human Rights throughout the world. Excerpts from this Covenant, which was adopted by the General Assembly of the United Nations on 16th December, 1966 and came into force on 3rd January, 1976, are reproduced below.

PREAMBLE

The States Parties to the present Covenant,

Considering that, in accordance with the principles proclaimed in the Charter of United Nations, recognition of the inherent dignity and of the equal and inalienable rights of all members of the human family is the foundation of freedom, justice and peace in the world.

Recognizing that, these rights derive from the inherent dignity of the human person.

Recognizing that, in accordance with the Universal Declaration of Human Rights, the ideal of free human beings enjoying freedom from fear and want can only be achieved if conditions are created whereby everyone may enjoy his economic, social and cultural rights, as well as his civil and political rights.

Considering the obligation of states under the Charter of the United Nations to promote universal respect for, and observance of, Human Rights and freedoms.

Realizing that the individual having duties to other individuals and to the community to which he belongs, is under a responsibility to strive for the promotion and observance of the rights recognized in the present Covenant.

Agree upon the following Articles :

PART-1

Article-1

1. All people have the right of self-determination. By virtue of that right they freely determine their political status and freely pursue their economic, social and cultural development.
2. All people may, for their own ends, freely dispose of their natural wealth and resources without prejudice to any obligations arising out of international economic co-operation, based upon the principle of mutual benefit, and international law. In no case may the people be deprived of their own means of subsistence.

PART-2

Article-2

1. Each State Party to the present Covenant undertakes to take steps, individually and through international assistance and co-operation, especially economic and technical, to the maximum of its available resources, with a view to achieving progressively the full realization of the rights recognized in the present Covenant by all appropriate means, including particularly the adoption of legislative measures.
2. The States Parties to the present Covenant undertake to guarantee that the rights enunciated in the Covenant will be exercised without discrimination of any kind as to race, colour , sex, language, religion, political or other opinion, national or social origin, property, birth or other status.
3. Developing countries, with due regard to Human Rights and their national economy, may determine to what extent they would guarantee the economic rights recognized in the present Covenant to non-nationals.

Article-3

The States Parties to the present Covenant undertake to ensure the equal right of men and women to the enjoyment of all economic, social and cultural rights set forth in the present covenant.

Article-4

The States Parties to the present Covenant recognize that, in the enjoyment of those rights provided by the State in conformity with the present Covenant, the state may subject such rights only to such limitations as are determined by law only insofar as this may be compatible with the nature of these rights and solely for the purpose of promoting the general welfare in a democratic society.

PART-3

Article-6

1. The States Parties to the present Covenant recognize the right to work, which includes the right of everyone to the opportunity to gain his living by work which he freely chooses or accepts, and will take appropriate steps to safeguard this right.
2. The steps to be taken by a State Party to the present Covenant to achieve the full realization of this right shall include technical and vocational guidance and training programmes, policies and techniques to achieve steady economic, social and cultural development and full and productive employment under conditions safeguarding fundamental political and economic freedoms to the individual.

Article-7

1. The State Parties to the present Covenant recognize the right of everyone to the enjoyment of just and favourable conditions of work which ensure, in particular :
2. Fair wages and equal remuneration for work of equal value without distinction of any kind, in particular women being guaranteed conditions of work not inferior to those enjoyed by men, with equal pay for equal work :

   (a) A decent living for themselves and their families in accordance with their provisions of the present Covenant;

(b) Safe and healthy working conditions;
(c) Equal opportunity for everyone to be promoted in his employment to an appropriate higher level, subject to no considerations other than those of seniority and competence; and
(d) Rest, leisure and reasonable limitation of working hours and periodic holidays with pay, as well as remuneration of public holidays.

Article-8

1. The States Parties to the present Covenant undertake to ensure :

    (a) The right of everyone to form trade unions and join the trade union of his choice, subject to the rules of the organization concerned, for the promotion and protection of his economic and social interests;
    (b) The right of trade unions to establish national federations or confederations and the right of the latter to form or join international trade union organization;
    (c) The right of trade unions to function freely subject to no limitations other than those prescribed by law and which are necessary in a democratic society in the interests of national security or public order or for the protection of the rights and freedoms of others; and
    (d) The right to strike, provided that it is exercised in conformity with the laws of the particular country.

Article-9

The States Parties to the present Covenant recognize the right of everyone to social security, including social insurance.

Article-10

The States Parties to the present Covenant recognize that :

1. The widest possible protection and assistance should be accorded to the family, which is the natural fundamental group unit of society, particularly for its establishment and while it is responsible for the case and education of dependent children. Marriage must be entered into with the free consent of the intending spouses;
2. Special protection should be accorded to mothers during a reasonable period before and after child birth. During such period working mother should be accorded paid leave or leave with adequate social security benefits; and
3. Special measures of protection and assistance should be taken on behalf of all children and young persons without any discrimination for reasons of parentage or other conditions. Children and young persons should be protected from economic and social exploitation. Their employment in work is harmful to their morals or health or dangerous to life or likely to hamper their normal development should be punishable by law. States should also set age limits below which the paid employment of child labour should be prohibited and punishable by law.

Article-11

1. The States Parties to the present Covenant recognize the right of everyone to an adequate standard of living for himself and his family, including adequate food, clothing and housing, and to the continuous improvement of living conditions. The States Parties will take appropriate steps to ensure the realization of this right, recognizing to this effect the essential

importance of international co-operation based on free consent.

2. The States Parties to the present Covenant, recognizing the fundamental right of everyone to be free from hunger, shall take, individually and through international co-operation, the measures, including specific programmes, which are needed;

   (a) To improve methods of production, conservation and distribution of food by making full use of technical and scientific knowledge, by disseminating knowledge of the principles of nutrition and by developing or reforming agrarian systems in such a way as to achieve the most efficient development and utilization of natural resources; and
   (b) Taking into account the problems for both food importing and food exporting countries, to ensure an equitable distribution of world food supplies in relation to need.

Article-12

1. The States Parties to the present Covenant recognize the right of everyone to the enjoyment of the highest attainable standard of physical and mental health.
2. The steps to be taken by the States Parties to the present Covenant to achieve the full realization of this right shall include those necessary for :

   (a) The provision for the reduction of the still birth rate and of infant mortality and for the healthy development of the child;
   (b) The improvement of all aspects of environmental and industrial hygiene;
   (c) The prevention, treatment and control of epidemic, endemic, occupational and other diseases; and

(d) The creation of conditions which would assure to all medical service and medical attention in the event of sickness.

Article-13

1. The States Parties to the present Covenant recognize the right of everyone to education. They agree that education shall be directed to full development of the human personality and the sense of its dignity, and shall strengthen the respect for human rights and fundamental freedoms. They further agree that education shall enable all persons to participate effectively in a free society, promote understanding, tolerance and friendship among all nations and all racial, ethnic or religious groups, and further the activities of the United Nations for the maintenance of peace.
2. The States Parties to the present Covenant recognize that, with a view to achieving the full realization of this right;

   Primary education shall be compulsory and available free to all :

   (a) Secondary education in its different forms, including technical and vocational secondary education, shall be made generally available and accessible to all by every appropriate means, and in particular by the progressive introduction of free education;

   (b) Higher education shall be made equally accessible to all, on the basis of capacity, by every appropriate means, and in particular by the progressive introduction of free education;

   (c) Fundamental education shall be encouraged or intensified as far as possible for those persons who have not received or completed the whole period of their primary education; and

(d) The development of a system of schools at all levels shall be actively pursued, an adequate fellowship system shall be established, and the material conditions of teaching staff shall be continuously improved.

3. The States Parties to the present Covenant undertake to have respect for the liberty of parents and when applicable legal guardians to choose for their children schools, other than those established by the public authorities, which conform to such minimum educational standards as may be laid down or approved by the State and to ensure the religious and moral education of their children in conformity with their own convictions.
4. No part of this Article shall be construed so as to interfere with the liberty of individuals and bodies to establish and direct educational institutions, subject always to the observance of the principles set forth in paragraph 1 of this Article and to the requirement that the education given in such institutions shall conform to such minimum standards as may be laid down by the State.

Article-15

1. The States Parties to the present Covenant recognize the right of everyone :

(a) To take part in cultural life;
(b) To enjoy the benefits of scientific progress and its applications; and
(c) To benefit from the protection of the moral and material interest resulting from any scientific, literary or artistic production of which he is the author.

2. The steps to be taken by the States Parties to the present Covenant to achieve the full realization of this right shall include those necessary for the conservation, the development and the diffusion of science and culture.
3. The States Parties to the present Covenant undertake to respect the freedom indispensable for scientific research and creative activity.
4. The States Parties to the present Covenant recognize the benefits to be derived from the encouragement and development of international contacts and co-operation in the scientific and cultural fields.

APPENDIX-V

International Convention on the Elimination of All Forms of Racial Discrimination

This Convention was adopted by the General Assembly of the United Nations on 21st December, 1965 and came into force on 4th January, 1969. Reproduced below are excerpts from this Convention.

The States Parties to this Convention,

Considering that the Charter of the United Nations is based on the principles of the dignity and equality inherent in all human beings, and that all Member-States have pledged themselves to take joint and separate action, in co-operation with the Organization, for the achievement of one of the purposes of the United Nations which is to promote and encourage universal respect for and observance of human rights and fundamental freedoms for all, without distinction as to race, sex, language or religion.

Considering that the Universal Declaration of Human Rights proclaims that all human beings are born free and equal dignity and rights and that everyone is entitled to all the rights and freedoms set out therein, without distinction of any particular as to race, colour or national origin,

Considering that all human beings are equal before the law are entitled to equal protection of law against any discrimination and against any incitement to discrimination,

Considering that the United Nations has condemned colonialism and all practices of segregation and discrimination associated therewith. In whatever forms and wherever they exist, and that the Declaration on the Granting of Independence to colonial countries and peoples of 14th December, 1960 (*General Assembly Resolution 1514* (XV) has affirmed and solemnly proclaimed the necessity of bringing them to a speedy and unconditional end,

Considering that the United Nations Declaration on the Elimination of all forms of Racial Discrimination of 20th November, 1963 (*General Assembly Resolution 1514* (XVIII) *solemnly* affirms the necessity of speedily eliminating racial discrimination through the world in all its forms and manifestations and of securing understanding of and respect for the dignity of the human person, Convinced that any doctrine of superiority based on racial differentiation is scientifically false, morally condemnable, socially unjust and dangerous, and that there is no justification for racial discrimination, in theory or in practice, anywhere,

Reaffirming that discrimination between human beings on the grounds of race, colour or ethnic origin is an obstacle to friendly and peaceful relations among nations and is capable of disturbing peace and security among peoples and the harmony of persons living side by side even within one and the same state.

Convinced that the existence of racial barriers is to represent the ideals of any human society.

Alarmed by manifestations of racial discrimination still in evidence in some areas of the world and by governmental policies based on racial superiority or hatred, such as policies or apartheid, segregation or separation,

Resolved to adopt all necessary measures for speedily eliminating racial discrimination in all its forms and manifestations, and to prevent and combat racist doctrines and practices in order to promote understanding between races and to build an international community free from all forms of racial segregation and racial discrimination.

Have agreed as follows :

PART-1

Article-1

1. In this convention, the term 'racial discrimination', shall mean any distinction, exclusion, restriction or preference based on race, colour, descent, or national or ethnic origin which has the purpose or effect of nullifying or impairing the recognition, enjoyment or exercise, on an equal footing, of human rights and fundamental freedoms in the political, economic, social, cultural or any other field of public life.
2. Special measures taken for the sole purpose of securing adequate advancement of certain racial or ethnic groups or individuals requiring such protection as may be necessary in order to ensure such groups or individual equal enjoyment or exercise of human rights and fundamental freedoms shall not be deemed racial discrimination, provided, however, that such measures do not as a consequence lead to the maintenance of separate rights for different racial groups and that they shall not be continued after the objectives for which they were taken have been achieved.

Article-2

1. States Parties condemn racial discrimination and undertake to pursue by all appropriate means and without delay a policy of eliminating racial discrimination in all its forms and promoting understanding among all races.
2. States Parties shall, when the circumstances so warrant, take, in the social, economic, cultural and other fields, special and concrete measures to ensure

the adequate development and protection of certain racial groups or individuals belonging to them, for the purpose of guaranteeing them the full and equal enjoyment of human rights and a consequence the maintenance of unequal or separate rights for different racial groups after the objective for which they were taken have been achieved.

Article-3

States Parties particularly condemn racial segregation and apartheid and undertake to prevent, prohibit and eradicate all practices of this nature in territories under their jurisdiction.

Article-4

States Parties condemn all propaganda and all organizations which are based on ideas or theories of superiority of one race or group of persons of one colour or ethnic, or which attempt to justify or promote racial hatred and discrimination in any form, and undertake to adopt immediate and positive measures designed to eradicate all incitement to, or acts of such discrimination and, to this end, with due regard to the principles embodied in the Universal Declaration of Human Rights and the rights expressly set forth in Article-5 of this convention *inter alia* :

(a) Shall declare an offence punishable by law all dissemination of ideas based on racial superiority or hatred, incitement to racial discrimination, as well as all acts of violence or incitement to such acts against any race or group of persons of another colour or ethnic origin, and also the provision of any assistance to racist activities, including the financing thereof;

(b) Shall declare illegal and prohibit organizations, and

also organized and all other propaganda activities which promote and incite racial discrimination, and shall recognize participation in such organizations or activities as an offence punishable by law;

(c) Shall not permit public authorities or public institutions, national or local, to promote or incite racial discrimination.

Article-5

In compliance with the fundamental obligations laid down in Article 2 of this convention, States Parties undertake to prohibit and to eliminate racial discrimination in all its forms and to guarantee the right of everyone, without distinction as to race, colour or national or ethnic origin, to equality before the law.

Article-7

States Parties undertake to adopt immediate and effective measures, particularly in the fields of teaching, educating culture and information, with a view to combating prejudices which lead to racial discrimination and to promoting understanding tolerance and friendship among nations and racial or ethnical group, as well as to propagating the purposes and principles of the Charter of the United Nations, the Universal Declaration of Human Rights, the United Nations Declaration on the Elimination of all forms of Racial Discrimination, and this Convention.

APPENDIX-VI

A Comparative Table

Subject	*Constitution of India*	Universal *Declaration of Human Rights (1948)*
(1)	*(2)*	*(3)*
(a) Equality Before Law FUNDAMENTAL RIGHTS	**Art. 14:** The State shall not deny to any person equality before the law or the equal protection of the laws within the territory of India. **Art. 7:** All are equal before	the Law and are entitled without any discrimination to equal protection of the Law. All are entitled to equal protection against any discrimination.
(b) Prohibition of discrimination on grounds only of religion, race, caste,	**Art. 15 (1) :** The State shall not discriminate against any citizen on grounds only.	**Art.2 para (1):** Everyone is entitled to all the rights and freedoms set forth in this
(c) Equality of opportunity in matters of public employment.	**Art. 16 (1) :** There shall be equality of opportunity for all citizens in matters relating to employment or appointment to any office under the State.	**Art.21(2) :** Everyone has a right to equal access to public service in his country.
(d) Freedom of Speech, Assembly, Association etc.	**Art. 19 (1):** All citizens shall have the (a) Right to freedom of speech and expression; Right to assemble peaceably and without arms; (b) Right to form Unions and Associations; (c) Right to move freely throughout the territory of India; (d) Right to reside and settle in any part of the territory of India.	**Art. 19 :** Everyone has the right to freedom of opinion and expression..... Everyone has the right to freedom of peaceful assembly and association. **Arti.23 (4):** Everyone has a right to form and to join trade unions for the protection of his rights; **Art. 20 (2):** No one may be compelled to belong to an Association. **Art.13 (1):** Everyone has the right to freedom of movement and residence within the borders of each state.

(e) Protection in respect of conviction for offences.	**Art.20(1) :** No person shall be convicted of any offence except for violation of law in force at the time of the commission of the act charged as an offence, nor be subjected to a penalty greater than that which might have been inflicted under the law in force at the time of the commission of the offence.	**Art.11(2) :** No one shall be held guilty of any penal offence on account of any act or omission which did not constitute a penal offence, under national or international law, at the time when it was committed. Nor shall a heavier penalty be imposed than the one that was applicable at the time the penal offence was committed.
(f) Protection of Life and personal Liberty	**Art.23 (1) :** Traffic in human beings and 'Beggar' and other similar forms of forced labour are prohibited and any contravention of this provision shall be an offence punishable in accordance with law. *Note :* Beggar is a form of forced labour under which a person is compelled to work without remuneration.	**Art. 4 :** No one shall be held in slavery or servitude; slavery and the slave trade shall be prohibited in all forms.
(h) Freedom of conscience and free profession, practice and propagation of religion.	**Art.25 (1):**Subject to public order, morality and health and to the provisions to this part, all persons are equally entitled to freedom of conscience and right freely to profess, practice and propagate religion.	**Art. 18:** Everyone has the right to freedom of thought, conscience and religion, this right includes freedom to change his religion or belief, and freedom, either alone or in community with others and in public or private, to manifest his religion or belief in teaching, practice, worship and observance.
(i) Protection of Interest of Minorities.	Any section of the citizens residing in the territory of India or any part thereof having a distinct language, script or culture of its own shall have the right to conserve the same.	Everyone as a member of society, has the right to social security and is entitled to through the national effort and the operation and the accordance with the organisation and resources of each state of the economic, social

		and cultural rights indispensable for the dignity and the free development of personality.
(j) Administer Education Institutions	**Art. 30 (1):** All minorities, whether based on religion or language shall have the right to establish and administer educational institutions of their choice.	**Art. 26 (3):** Everyone has the right to an effective remedy by the competent National Tribunals for acts violating the fundamental rights granted to him by the Constitution or by law.

APPENDIX-VII

In Standing Order No. 937 dated 31-12-1996 instructions have been issued on the subject cited here.

D.K.Basu *Vs.* State of West Bengal

The Supreme Court of India has ordered certain requirements to be followed by various authorities who are empowered to effect arrest or detention under the laws. In all cases of arrest and detention the following preventive measures are, therefore, required to be strictly followed and failure to follow the following requirements shall amount to contempt of court *vide* the Supreme Court WP (Criminal) Nos. 539 of 1986 and 592 of 1987 dated 18th December, 1996.

1. The police personnel carrying out the arrest and handling the interrogation of the arrestee should bear accurate, visible and clear identification and name tags with their destinations. The particulars of all such police personnel who handle interrogation of the arrestee must be recorded in a register.
2. That the police officer carrying out the arrest of the arrestee shall prepare a memo of arrest at the time of arrest and such memo shall be attested by at least one witness, who may be either a member of the

family of the arrestee or a respectable person of the locality from where the arrest is made. It shall also be countersigned by the arrestee and shall contain the time and date of arrest.

3. A person who has been arrested or detained and is being held in custody in a police station or interrogation centre or other lock-up shall be entitled to have one friend or relative or other person known to him or having interest in welfare being informed as soon as practicable, that he has been arrested and is being detained at the particular place, unless the attesting witness of the memo of arrest is himself such a friend or a relative of the arrestee.
4. The time/place of arrest and venue of custody of an arrestee must be notified by the police where the next friend or relative or the arrestee lives outside the district or town through the Legal Aid Organization in the District and the police station of the area concerned telegraphically within a period of 8 to 12 hours after the arrest.
5. The person arrested must be made aware of this right to have someone informed of his arrest or detention as soon as he is put under arrest or is detained.
6. An entry must be made in the diary at the place of detention regarding the arrest of the person which shall also disclose the name of the next friend of the person who has been informed of the arrest and the names and particulars of the police officials in whose custody the arrestee is.
7. The arrestee should, where he so requests, be also examined at the time of his arrest and major and minor injuries, if any present on his/her body, must be recorded at that time. The "Inspection Memo", must be signed both by the arrestee and the police officer effecting the arrest and its copy provided to the arrestee.

8. The arrestee should be subjected to medical examination by a trained doctor every 48 hours during his detention in custody by a doctor on the panel State or Union territory, Director, Health Services, should prepare such a panel for all Tehsils and Districts as well.
9. Copies of all the documents including the memo of arrest referred to above, should be sent to the village Magistrate for his record.
10. The arrestee may be permitted to meet his lawyer during interrogation, throughout the interrogation.
11. A police control room should be provided at district and State headquarters where information regarding the arrest and the place of custody of the arrestee shall be communicated by the officer causing the arrest, within 12 hours of effecting the arrest and at the police control room it should be displayed on a conspicuous notice board.

Failure to comply with the requirements herein above mentioned shall apart from rendering the concerned official liable for departmental action, also render him liable to be punished for contempt of court and the proceedings for contempt of court may be instituted in any High Court of the country, having territorial jurisdiction over the matter.

The requirements, referred to have flow from Articles 21 and 22 (1) of the Constitution and need to be strictly followed. These would apply with equal force to the other governmental agencies also to which a reference has been made earlier.

These requirements are in addition to the constitutional and statutory safeguards and do not detract from various other directions given by the courts from time to time in connection with the safeguarding of the rights and dignity of the arrestee.

Bibliography

Ackoff, R.L., *Design of Social Research*. Chicago, Chicago University Press, 1953.

Aiyar, K., *Constitution and Fundamental Rights*, Madras, Srinivas Shastri Institution Publication, 1955.

Aleem, Shamin, *Women Police and Social Change*, New Delhi, Ashish Publishing House, 1991.

Alston, Philip, *et al.*, *International Human Rights in Context*, New Delhi, Oxford University Press, 1996.

Alwin, *et al. Philosophical Foundation of Human Rights*, Paris, Unesco, 1986.

Ambedkar, B.R., *States and Minorities: What are their rights and how to secure them in the Constitution of Free India*, Bombay, Thacker Publications, 1947.

Arjun Dev, *et al.*, (eds.) *Human Rights: A Source Book*, New Delhi, National Council for Education and Research Training (NCERT), 1996.

Asghar Ali, *The Rights of Women in Islam*, New Delhi, Sterling Publications, 1992.

Ashworth, *et al. Principles of Criminal Law*, New Delhi, Oxford University Press, 1995.

Ashraf Nehal, *Police and Policing in India*, New Delhi, Commonwealth Publishers, 1992.

Avasti, *et al.*, (eds.), *Bureaucracy and Development: Indian Perspectives*, New Delhi, Asish Publishing House, 1978.

Barbalet, J.M., *Citizenship: Rights, Struggle and Class Inequality*, Milton Keynes, Open University Press, 1988.

Batra, T.S., *Human Rights : A Critique*, New Delhi, Metropolitan Book Company, 1979

Baxi, U., (ed.), *The Right to be Human*, New Delhi, Lancer International, 1987.

Baxi, U. *et al.*, (ed.), *The Rights of Subordinated People*, Delhi, Oxford University Press, 1994.

Baxi, U. *et al.*, *The Rights Subordinated Peoples*, New Delhi, Oxford University Press, 1997.

Benton Ted, *Natural Relations: Ecology, Animals Rights and Social Justice*, London, Verso, 1993.

Bhatia, H.S., (eds.), *Origin and Development of Legal'and Political System*, New Delhi, Deep & Deep Publications, 1978.

Black, *et.al.*, *Methods and Issues in Social Research*, New York, Wiley, 1976.

Blackburn, (ed.) *Rights of Citizenship*, London, Mansell, 1993.

Bogdan, R., *et al.*, *Introduction to Qualitative Research Methods: Phenomenological Approach to the Social Sciences*, New York, Willy *inter se*, 1975.

Borgonain, B., *Human Rights : Social Justice and Political Challenges*, New Delhi, Kanishka Publishers, 1999.

Britton, K., *John Stuart Mill*, Penguin, Melbourne, 1953.

Brownline Ian, *Basic Documents on Human Rights*, Oxford, Clarendon, 1981.

Bunyard, R.S., *Police: Organization and Command*, Plymouth, Macdonald and Evans, 1978.

Burtt, ed., *English Philosophers from Backon to Mill*, New York, Modern Publications, 1939.

Campbell, Tom, *et al.*, (ed.), *Human Rights from Rhetoric to Reality*, Oxford, Basic Blackwell, 1986.

Carr Hall, R.A., *et al.*, *Crime, the Police and Criminal Statistics: Analysis of Statistics for England and Wales using Econometric Methods*, London, Academic Publications, 1979.

Carruthers, Peter, *The Animals Issue: Moral Theory in Practice*, New York, Cambridge University Press, 1992.

Chakrabarty, M., *Human Rights and Refugees: Problems, Law and Practices*, New Delhi, Deep & Deep Publications, 1998.

Champbell, Don, *Police: The Exercise of Powers*, London, Macdonald and Evans, 1978.

Chander, Shailaja, *Justice V.R.Krishna Iyer on Fundamental Rights and Directive Principles,* New Delhi, Deep & Deep Publications, 1992.

Chatterjee, *et. al., Bengal Riots : Their Rights and Liabilities,* Calcutta, K.P., Bagchi, 1977.

Chaturvedi, D.C., *Indian Fundamental Rights,* Meerut, Saru Publishing House, 1992.

Chaturvedi, R.G., *States and the Rights of Men,* Delhi, Metropolitan Books Company, 1971.

....., *Metropolitan Police Administration in India,* Delhi, B.R., Publishing Corporation, 1985.

....., *Police and Emerging Challenges,* Delhi, B.R., Publishing Corporation, 1985.

....., (ed.) *Role of Police in Criminal Justice System,* New Delhi, B.R. Publishing Corporation, 1996.

Churchill, Winston Spencer, *The Peoples Rights,* London, Jonathan Cape, 1970.

Correa, Sonia, *Population and Reproductive Rights : Feminist Perspective from the South,* New Delhi, Kali for Women, 1996.

Cronin, Kieran, *Rights and Christian Ethics,* New York, Cambridge University Press, 1992.

Curry, J.C., *Indian Police,* London, Faber & Faber, 1932.

David, William, *Keeping the Peace : The Police Order,* London, Dhutchinson & Co., 1967.

Das, R.M., *Manu on Crime and Punishment,* Patna, Janki Prakashan, 1987.

Deb, R., *Police and Law Enforcement,* Calcutta, S.C. Sarkar & Sons Pvt. Ltd., 1988, 2nd ed.

Desai, A.R., (ed.), *Violation of Democratic Rights in India,* Bombay, Popular Prakashan, 1986, Vol. 1.

....., *Changing Profile of Rural India and Human Rights of Agricultural Poor : An Assessment to Strategy of Rural Development since Independence,* Chandigarh, Crrid, 1990.

....., *Repression and Resistance in India : Violation of Democratic Rights of the Working Class, Rural Poor, Adivasis and Dalits,* Bombay, Popular Prakashan, 1990.

Dewan, V.N., *Security Guide for Police and Public : Techniques of Criminal and Counter Measures for Safety*, New Delhi, Newman, 1977.

Dhagamwar Vasudha, *Law Power and Justice : Protection of Personal Rights under the Indian Penal Code*, Bombay, N.M. Tripathi, 1974.

Dhillon, K.S., "Police Reforms : An alternative Approach," *Indian Police Journal*, Jan.-March, 1999.

....., *Defenders of the Establishment Ruler Supportive Forces of South Asia*, Shimla, Indian Institute for Advance Study, 1998.

Doherthy, *et al.*, (eds.) *Democracy and Green Political Thought : Sustainability, Rights and Citizenship*, London Routledge, 1996.

Dwarkadas, R., *Role of Higher Civil Service in India*, Bombay, Popular Publication, 1958.

Dwivedi, K.C., *Right to Freedom and the Supreme Court*, New Delhi, Deep & Deep Publications, 1994.

Dunnil, F., *Civil Service: Some Human Aspects*, London, Allen and Unwin, 1956.

English, J., *et al.*, *Butterworth's Police Law*, Leicester, The British Psychological Society, 1987.

Ezorsky, ed., *Moral Rights in the Workplace*, Albany, State University of New York Press, 1987.

Favarau, *et al.*, *Modern Police Administration*, New Jersey, Prentice Hall, Inc., Englewood Cliff, 1978.

Fernando, Laksirid (ed.), *Academic Freedom 1990 : A Human Rights Report*, London, Zed Books, 1990.

Ferry, Luc., *The New Ecological Order*, Chicago, University of Chicago Press, 1995.

Fichte, J.G., *The Science of Rights*, New York, Harper and Row, 1970.

Flathman, Richard E., *The Practice of Rights*, Cambridge, Cambridge University Press, 1976.

Francis, Jacob, *European Convention on Human Rights*, London, OUP, 1975.

Freedom, Michael, *Rights*, Buckingham, Open University Press, 1991.

Friedman, Lawrence M., *The Republic of Choice : Law, Authority and Culture*, Cambridge, Harvard University Press, 1990.

Gadgil, D.R., *Human Rights in Multi-National Society*, Poona, Gokhale Institute of Politics and Economics, 1968.

Galligun B., *et al.*, (eds.), *Rethinking Human Rights*, Sydney, Third Federation Press, 1997.

Galtung, Johan, *Human Rights in another Key*, Cambridge, Polity Press, 1994.

Gaultung, J., *Theory and Methods of Social Research*, London, George Allen and Unwin Press, 1967.

Gautam, *Liberal Equality*, Cambridge, Cambridge University Press, 1980.

Gautam, D.N., *The Indian Police : A Study in Fundamentals*, New Delhi, Mittal Publications, 1993.

Gesschwender, J.A., (ed.), *The Black Revolts the Civil Rights Movement, Ghetto Uprisings and Separatism*, Englewood Cliffs, Prentice-Hall, 1971.

Ghosh, S.K., *Keeping the Peace : Police Then and Now*, New Delhi, Ashish Publications, 1989.

...., *et al.*, (eds.), *Encyclopaedia of Police in India*, New Delhi Oxford University Press, 1993, 3 vols.

...., (ed.), *Police Administration Reminiscences*, New Delhi, Ashish Publishing House, 1989.

...., *The Interpol International Criminal Police Organisation*, Calcutta, Eastern Law House, 1976.

...., *Violence in the Street Order and Liberty in Indian Society*, New Delhi, Light and Life Publications, 1981.

Ghoshal, A., *Civil Service in India under the East India Company : A Study in Administrative Development*, Calcutta, University Press, 1944.

Glaser, D., *Crime in Our Changing Society*, New York, HRW Publications, 1978.

Gleason, Gregory, *Federalism and Nationalism : The Struggle for Republican Rights in the USSR*, Gregory Gleason, Boulder, Westview Press, 1990.

Gledhill, Alan, *Fundamental Rights in India*, London, Stevens, 1956.

Goode, *et al.*, *Methods in Social Research*, Tokyo, NC Grow-Hill, 1952.

Grand, *The Strategy of Equality Redistribution and Social Services*, London, George Allen and Unwin, 1982.

Green, T.H., *Lectures on the Principles of Political Obligation*, London, Longmans, 1937, 2 vols.

Gupta, A., *Crime and Police in India upto 1861*, Agra, Sahitya Bhavan, 1974.

Gupta, A., *The Police in British India 1861-1947*, New Delhi, Concept Publishing Company, 1979.

Hader, J.J., *et al.*, *Dynamic Social Research*, London, Routledge Printers, 1933.

Hall, C., Margaret, *Women and Empowerment : Strategies for Increasing Autonomy*, Washington, Hemisphere, 1992.

Haksar, Urmila, *Minority Protection and International Bill of Human Rights*, Bombay, Allied Publications, 1974.

Harris, David, *et al.*, *The International Covenant on Civil and Political Rights and United Kingdom Law*, New Delhi, Oxford University Press, 1995.

Hassan, Shariful, *Supreme Court : Fundamental Rights and Directive Principles*, New Delhi, Deep & Deep Publications, 1981.

Hibbert, C., *A Great Mutiny : (India 1857)*, New York, Penguin Books, 1980.

Honfeld, W.N., *Fundamental Legal Conceptions*, New Haven, Yale University Press, 1964.

Hook, Sidney, *Political Power and Personal Freedom : Critical Studies in Democracy, Communism and Civil Rights*, New York, Collier Books, 1962.

Hunt, G., *Power and the Police Chief : An Institutional and Organisational Analysis*, New Delhi, Sage Publications, 1993.

Hussain, Shaikh Shaukat, *Human Rights in Islam*, New Delhi, Kitab Bhavan, 1990.

Hyman, *et al.*, *Interviewing in Social Research*, Chicago, Chicago University Press, 1954.

Immanuel, Kant, *et al.*, *Doctrine of Freedom*, Melbourne, Robertson & Company, 1913.

Inbau, *et al.*, *Scientific Police Investigation*, Philaldelphia, Chilton Publications, 1972.

International Bill of Human Rights, Colombo, Amnesty International, 1978.

Iyer, Krishna, *Human Rights and Inhuman Wrong*, New Delhi, B.R. Publishing Corporation, 1990.

—., *Of Law and Life*, Uttar Pradesh, Vikas Publications, Ghaziabad, 1979.

Jaeger, M., *Liberty* Vs. *Equality*, New York, Thomas Melson Sons Publishers, 1943.

Jha, R.C., *Resurrecting Human Rights in India*, New Delhi, Sheridea, 1995.

Jois, R.M., *Human Rights and Indian Values*, New Delhi, National Council for Teacher Education, 1997.

Jones, E.T., *Conducting Political Research*, New York, Harper & Row, 1971.

Kakonis, *et al.*, *A Practical Guide to Police Report Writing*, America, McGraw Hill Book Company, 1978.

Kalaiah, A.B., *Human Rights in International Law*, New Delhi, Deep & Deep Publications, 1986.

Kamenka, *et al.*, (ed). *Human Rights*, London, Edward Arnold, 1978.

Kapoor, H.L., *Police Administration*, New Delhi, Ess Ess Publications, 1989.

Karnataka Civil Service Rules with Revised Pay Scale 1982, Dharward, Ramashrya Book, 1982.

Kashyap, S.C., *Human Rights and Parliament*, New Delhi, Metropolitan Book Company, 1977.

Kasture, G.K., *Thoughts on Police Reform*, Mt. Abu, National Police Academy, 1966.

Katta, Kaya, *et al.*, *Crime and Society : Current Issues and Trends*, New Delhi, APH Publishing Corporation, 1999.

Kaul, J.L., (ed.), *Human Rights : Issues and Perspectives*, New Delhi, Regency Publications, 1995.

Kalkar, R.V., *Lectures on Criminal Procedure*, Lucknow, Eastern Book Company, 1989, 2nd ed.

Khan, S.A., Power, Police and Public, *Kurukshetra*, Vishan Publishers, 1983.

Khanna, S., *Civil Administration in India*, New Delhi, Uppal Publications, 1983.

Khare, Subhas Chandra, *Human Rights and United Nations*, New Delhi, Metropolitan Book Company, 1977.

Konvitz, M.R., *Expanding Liberties Freedom's Gain in Postwar America*, New York, The Riking Press, 1966.

Kosla, A.N., *Civil Services Rules*, Bombay, Compiler Press, 1955.

Krishna Rao, *Growth of Indian Liberalism in the Nineteenth Century*, Mysore, Venkataramaiah, 1951.

Krishnamurthy, S., *Human Rights and the Indian Police*, Bangalore, R.R. Publishers, 1994.

Kunzru, H., *Public Services in India*, Allahabad, Servants of India Society, Allahabad, 1917.

Laski, H.J., *Rise of European Liberalism*, London, Allen and Unwin, 1947.

Leahy, *et al.*, (eds.), *The Liberalisation Debate : Rights at Issue*, London Routledge, 1996.

Levin, *Elementary Statistics in Social Research*, New York, Harper & Row, 1973.

Locke, J., *Two Treatise on Civil Government*, London, Dent, 1953, London, Routledge, 1959.

Longaskar, R.P., *Presidency and Individual Liberties*, Ithana, Cornell University Press, 1962.

Marshall, E.D., *Administrative Vitality : Conflict with Bureaucracy*, London, Routledge, 1959.

Madan, J.C., *Indian Police : Its Development up to 1905 — Historical Analysis*, New Delhi, Uppal Publications, 1980.

Madariaga, S.D., *Democracy* Vs. *Liberty?* London, Pall Mall Press, 1958.

Mahajan Amarjit, *Indian Policeman,* New Delhi, Deep & Deep Publications, 1982.

Mallick, R., *Development, Ethnicity and Human Rights in South Asia,* New Delhi, Sage Publications, 1998.

Maritian, J., *The Rights of Man and National Law,* New York, Charter Scribner's Sons, 1951.

Marshall, B., (ed.), *The Supreme Court and Human Rights,* America, Washington D.C., VOA, 1982.

Marx, F.M., *Political Theory of Possessive Individualism : Hobbes to Locke,* London, Oxford University Press, 1970.

....., *Administrative State : Introduction to Bureaucracy,* Chicago, Chicago University Press, 1957.

Mathew, K.K., *Hundred and Thirteenth Report : Injuries in Police Custody,* New Delhi, Govrenment. of India, Law Commission of India, 1985.

Mathur Krishna Mohan, *Police in India : Problems and Perspectives,* New Delhi, Gian Publishing House, 1991.

Melnicoe, *et al. Elements of Police Supervision,* Calcutta, Berely Hills, Glenlcoe Press, 1969.

Meltsner, A.J., *Policy Analysis in the Bureaucracy,* Berkeley, University of California, 1976.

Mernissi, Fatima, *The Veil and the Male Elite : A Feminist Interpretation of Women's Rights in Islam,* New York : Addison-Wesley Publishers, 1991.

Mill, J.S., *On Liberty,* London, Watts, 1903.

Mill, J.S., *Utilitarianism, Liberty and Representation Government,* London, J.M., Dent, 1962.

Milne, A.M., *Freedom and Rights,* London, George Allen and Unwin, 1968.

Ministry of Home Affairs, *History of Services : Indian Administrative Service and Indian Police Service,* New Delhi, Manager of Publications, 1958.

Mishra, K.K., *Police Administration in Ancient India,* New Delhi, Mittal Publications, 1987.

Misra, B.B., *Bureaucracy in India : Historical Analysis of Development upto 1947,* Delhi, 1977.

Misra, S.C., *Police Administration in India,* Mt. Abu, National Police Academy, 1970.

Mohanty, M., *et al.,* (eds.), *People's Rights,* New Delhi, Sage Publications, 1998.

Mohanan, V.K., *Crime Community and Police,* New Delhi, Gian Publishing House, 1987.

Molley, O., *Indian Civil Sevices (1601-1930),* London, Frank Cass Publications, 1965.

Moreis, R., *Logic of Survey Analysis,* New York, Basic Books, 1968.

Morgan, C., *Liberties of the Mind,* London, Macmillan, 1951.

Moskowitz, M., *Human Rights and World Order,* New Delhi, Ocean Publishing Inc., 1958.

Muhammad, M.B., *A New Image for Indian Police,* New Delhi, Anmol Publishers, 1998.

Mullerson, R., *Human Rights Diplomacy,* London, Routledge, 1997.

Nandy Raj, *Perceptions or Reality : A Study of Job Attitudes of Delhi Traffic Police,* New Delhi, Indian Institute of Public Administration, 1982.

Nizami, *et al.,* (eds.), *Human Rights in Third World Countries,* New Delhi, KIRS Publications, 1994.

Nozick, R., *Anarchy, State and Utopia,* New York, Basic Books, 1974.

Odegaro, *et al., American Government : Theory, Politics and Constitutional Foundation,* New York, Halt Publications, 1961.

Paine Thomas, *Rights of Man,* London, Johnson's Court, 1929.

Palmier, L., *Control of Bureaucratic Corruption : A Case Study in Asia,* New Delhi, Allied Publishers, 1985.

Pandey, Ram Darshan, *Fundamental Rights and Constitutional Amendments,* Delhi, Capital Publishing House, 1985.

Parekh, B., (ed.), *A Critical Examination of the Declaration of Rights, in Bentham's Political Thought,* New York, Barnes and Noble, 1973.

Parmar, L., *Human Rights,* New Delhi, Anmol Publishers, 1998.

Paul, E.F., *et al.*, (eds.), *Human Rights*, England, Bail Blackwell Publishers, 1984.

Penniggton, Kenneth, *The Practice of the Law 1200-1600 : Sovereignty and Rights in the Western Legal Tradition*, Berkeley, California University Press, Publishers, 1987.

Perry, Michael J., *The Constitution, the Court and the Human Rights*, New Delhi, Wiley Eastern, 1982.

Ponda, B., *Indian Bureaucracy : Inside Story*, New Delhi, Uppal Publications, 1978.

Powis, D., *Signs of Crime : Field Manual for Police*, London, McGraw-Hill, 1977.

Prasher, R., *Police Administration and Structure, Recruitment and Training Unionism and Public Relations*, New Delhi, Deep & Deep Publications, 1986.

Puliani Sathpal, (ed.) *The Guide to Police Laws in Karnataka*, Bangalore, Karnataka Law Journal Publications, 1999.

Radha Kumar, *The History of Doing : An Illustrated Account of Movements for Women's Rights and Feminism in India 1800-1990*, New Delhi, Kali for Women, 1993.

Raghavan, R.K., *Indian Police : Problems, Planning and Perspectives*, Delhi, Standard Company, 1989.

Raj, Janak, *Bail Law and Procedure with Tips to Avoid Police Harassment*, Delhi, Universal Law Publishing, Co., 1998.

Ramsbotham, *et al.*, *Humanitarian Intervention in Contemporary Conflict : A Reconceptualisation*, Cambridge Polity Press, 1966.

Rao, Venugopal, *Police Administration*, New Delhi, Institute of Public Administration, 1982.

Raphael, D.D., (ed.), *Political Theory and the Rights*, London, Macmillan, 1960.

—., ed., *Political Theory and the Rights of Man*, London, Macmillan, 1967.

Rattan, R., *Gandhi's Concept of Political Obligation*, Calcutta, Minerva Associates, 1972.

Ray, Shaymal Kumar, *Indian Bureaucracy at the Crossroads*, New Delhi, Sterling Publication, 1979.

Reddy, P., *Judicial Review of Fundamental Rights*, New Delhi, National Publishing House, 1976.

Reiner, R., *The Politics of the Police*, Sussex, Harvard Press Microform Publications, 1998.

Rosenthan, Jean-Laurent, *The Fruits of Revolution : Property Rights, Litigation and French Agriculture, 1700-1860*, Cambridge, Cambridge University Press, 1992.

Rupesinghe, Kumar, (ed.), *Ethnic Conflict and Human Rights*, Tokyo, United Nations University Press, 1988.

Ruphel, C.D., *Political Theory and the Rights of Man*, London, Macmillan, 1967.

Rutland, Robert Allen, *The Birth of the Bill of Rights 1776-1791*, New York, Collier Books, 1962.

Saha, B.P., *Indian Police : Legacy and Quest for Formative Role*, New Delhi, Konark Publishers Pvt. Ltd., 1990.

Saksena, K.P., (ed.), *Human Rights : Perspectives and Challenges in 1990 and Beyond*, New Delhi, Lancer Books, 1994.

Saksena, K.P., *Human Rights : Fifty Years of India's Independence*, New Delhi, Lancer Books, 1999.

Saksena, N.S., "Police Introspection of 50 Years," *Indian Police Journal*, October. - December. 1998.

Santayana, G., *Dominations and Power : Reflections on Liberty, Society and Government*, New York, Scribner's, 1951.

Saxena, Anil, K., *Professionalism in Indian Police*, New Delhi, APH Publishing Corporation, 1997.

Schultz, (ed.), *Modern Police Administration*, Houston, Gulf Publishing Company, 1979.

Schwartz, Bernard, *The Great Rights of Mankind : A History of the American Bills of Rights*, New York, Oxford University Press, 1977.

Seliger, M., *Liberal Politics of John Locke*, London, Allen and Unwin, 1968.

Sens, Shankar, et. al., *Police Training : Problems and Prespectives*, New Delhi, Asish Publishing House, 1994.

Sen, Shankar, *Police Today*, New Delhi, Ashish Publishing House, 1986.

Sengupta, S.S., *Work Culture in Police Administration,* New Delhi, Ashish Publishing House, 1995.

Sethi, R.B., *Police Acts,* (Central and States), Allahabad, The Law Book Company, 1983.

Shamasastry, R., (ed.), *Kautilya,* Mysore, Raghavies Printers, 1956.

Shapiro, Ian, *The Evolution of Rights in Liberal Theory,* Cambridge, Cambridge University Press, 1986.

Shankardas, R.D., (ed.) *Punishment and the Prison : Indian and International Perspectives,* New Delhi, Sage Publications, 2000.

Sharma, L.N., *et al., Human Rights,* Patna, Patna Research Publications, 1999.

Sharma, P.D., *Police and Criminal Justice Administration in India,* New Delhi, Uppal Publications, 1985.

Shekhar, R., *Not a Licence to Kill : Police Needs Paradigm-Shift,* Delhi, Konark Publications, 1999.

Shukla, S.B., *Hayek on Liberty,* Allahabad, Vohra Publications, 1991.

Shute, *et al.,* (ed.), *On Human Rights : The Oxford Amnesty Lectures 1993,* New York, Basic Books, 1993.

Simpson, Antony, E., *The Literature of Police Corruption,* London, McGraw Hill Book Company Ltd., 1997.

Singh, Nagendra, *Human Rights and the Future of Mankind,* Delhi, Vanity Books, 1981.

Singh, M.P., *Police Problems and Dilemma in India,* New Delhi, Mittal Publications, 1989.

Singhri, L.M., (ed.), *Fundamental Rights and Constitutional Amendment,* Delhi, National Publications, 1971.

Sinha, P.C., *et al.,* (eds.), *International Encyclopedia of Peace, Security, Social Justice and Human Rights,* New Delhi, Anmol Publications, 1996, 6 Vols.

Smigel, *et al., Crimes against Bureaucracy,* New York, Van Nostrand, Beinhold Publishers, 1970.

Srinivas Sastri, V.S., *The Rights and Duties of the Indian Citizen,* Calcutta, Calcutta University Press, 1927.

Srivastav, V.P., (ed.), *Indian Police : Law and Reality*, New York, Manas Publications, 1997.

Stavenhagen, Rodolfo, *Ethnic Question : Conflicts, Developments and Human Rights*, Tokyo, United Nations University Press, 1990.

Strauss, E., *Ruling Servants : Bureaucracy in Russia, France and Britain*, London, Allen and Unwin, 1961.

Strauss, Leo, *Natural Rights and History*, Chicago, Chicago University, 1953.

Subramaniam, S., *Human Rights and Police*, Hyderabad, Association for Advancement of Police and Security Sciences, 1992.

Sunder, R., *Fundamental Rights and the 42nd Constitutional Amendment*, Calcutta, Minerva Associates, 1977.

Szymanski, Al, *Human Rights in the Soviet Union*, London, Stevens, 1984.

Tank, T.H., *Human Rights and International Relations in the Asia-Pacific Region*, London, Printer, 1995.

Taub, R.P., *Bureaucrats under Stress — Administrators and Administration in an Indian State*, Berkeley, University of California, 1969.

Taulor, H.O., *Thought and Expression in the 16th Century*, New York, Collier Publishers, 1962.

Thakar, L.K., *Comparative and International Human Rights*, Delhi, Authors Press, 2000.

Thomson, Jarvis, *Rights, Restitution and Risk : Essays in Moral Theory*, Cambridge, Harvard University Press, 1986.

Triloknath, *Indian Police in Action*, New Delhi, Sapra Publications, 1948.

....., *The Indian Police*, New Delhi, Sterling Publishers, 1978.

....., *Indian Police : Case for a New Image*, New Delhi, Sterling Publications, 1984.

Tyagi, A.R., *Rights and Obligations of Civil Servant in India*, New Delhi, Educational Publishers, 1961.

United Nations Educational, Scientific and Cultural Organisation, Cultural Rights as Human Rights, Paris, UNESCO, 1970.

Uvalic Milica, *Investment and Property Rights in Yugoslavia : The Long Transition to a Market Economy*, Cambridge, Cambridge University Press, 1992.

Vadackumchery, J., *The Police, The People and Criminal Justice*, New Delhi, APH Publishing Corporation, 1997.

—., Indian Police - 2001 : *What Went Wrong Here?*, Delhi, APH Publishing Corporation, 1998.

—., *Management Thoughts on Police Administrations*, New Delhi, APH Publishing Corporation, 1998.

—., *The Police, The Accused and Criminal Injustice*, New Delhi, APH Publishing Corporation, 1997.

Vanloon, H.W., *Liberation of Mankind : Story of Man's Struggle for the Right to Think*, London, Harrap Publishers, 1945.

Varma, R.S., *Bureaucracy in India*, Bhopal Progress Publications, 1973.

Varwell, *Police and the Public*, Plymouth, MacDonald and Crans, 1978.

Vijapur, A.P., *United Nations at Fifty : Studies in Human Rights*, New Delhi, South Asian Publications, 1996.

Vijay, C., *et al.*, *Human Rights and The Law : National and Global Perspectives*, Mumbai, Snow White Publishers, 1997.

Wade, H.W.R., *Government and Citizen's Rights : New Problems, New Constitutions*, Delhi, National Publications, 1974.

Waldron, Jermey, (ed.), *Nonsense upon Stilts : Bentham, Burke and Maex on the Rights of Man London, Methuen*, 1987.

Wallstobecraft Mary, *The Rights of Woman : The Subjection of Women*, London, J.M. Dent, 1970.

Weeramantry, C. G., (ed.), *Human Rights and Scientific and Technological Development* Tokyo, United Nations University Press, 1990.

Wegg-Prosser, Charles, (ed.), *The Police and Law*, London, Oyez Publishing Ltd., 1979.

Weiss, H., *et al.*, *Making Bureaucracies Work*, Beverly Hills, Sage Publications, 1979.

Westley, W.A., *Violence and the Police : Sociological Study of Law, Custom and Morality*, Cambridge, Mit Printers, 1970.

Wilson, O.W., *Police Administration*, New York, McGraw Hill, 1950.

Wilson, J.Q., *Varieties of Police Behaviour : Management of Law and Order in Eight Communities*, Cambridge, HUP, 1978.

Writ, *et al.*, *Introductory Problem in Political Research*, New Jersey, Englewood Cliff, Prentice Hall, 1970.

Year Book on Human Rights for 1973-1974, New York, United Nations, 1977.

Year Book on Human Rights for 1973, New York, UNO, 1977.

Year Book of the European Convention on Human Rights, The Hague, Martiaus Nijhoff, 1979.

Young, P.V., *Scientific Social Surveys and Research*, New Jersey, Englewood Cliffs, Prentice Hall, 1966.

Reports :

Government Press, *Karnataka Police Act, 1983 and Karnataka State Police Disciplinary Proceedings Rules*, 1965, 2nd Ed., Bangalore, 1997.

Karnataka Vigilance Commission, *Annual Report*, 1973-74, Bangalore, 1975.

Mysore, Police Department, *Report on the Administration for the Year 1956 Annual Report – 1969-70*, Bangalore, Government Press, Bangalore, 1958.

National Human Rights Commission Report, 1993-1997, New Delhi.

National Police Commission Report, Ministry of Home Affairs, Government. of India, August, 1979, March, 1981.

Report on Police Firing on Workers at Abhampur, Raipur, Madhya Pradesh, Peoples Union for Civil Liberties, 1990.

Index